NO LO
SEAT

RADICALS CHASING UTOPIA

NO LONGER PROPERTY OF
SEATTLE PUBLIC LIBRARY

RADICALS CHASING UTOPIA

INSIDE THE ROGUE MOVEMENTS
TRYING TO CHANGE THE WORLD

JAMIE BARTLETT

NATION
BOOKS
New York

Copyright © 2017 by Jamie Bartlett.
Published in the United States by Nation Books, an imprint of Perseus
Books, a division of PBG Publishing, LLC, a subsidiary of Hachette Book
Group, Inc.
116 East 16th Street, 8th Floor
New York, NY 10003

Nation Books is a co-publishing venture of the Nation Institute and the
Perseus Books Group

All rights reserved. Printed in the United States of America. No part of this
book may be reproduced in any manner whatsoever without written permission except in the case of brief quotations embodied in critical articles and
reviews. For information, address the Perseus Books Group, 1290 Avenue of
the Americas, New York, NY 10104.

The Hachette Speakers Bureau provides a wide range of authors for speaking events. To find out more, go to hachettespeakersbureau.com or call
866-376-6591.

Designed by Jack Lenzo

A CIP catalog record for this book is available from the Library of Congress.
ISBN: 978-1-56858-986-2 (PB)
ISBN: 978-1-56858-987-9 (EB)

LSC-C
10 9 8 7 6 5 4 3 2 1

To the best imaginable critic,
supporter, reviewer and believer.
She knows who she is.

Contents

Prologue

It's the hubris of every generation to think that they have arrived at the best way of living. That their laws, norms and conventions are natural, inevitable, even obvious.

But all the things we now take for granted, all the modern wisdoms we hold to be self-evident, were once derided as dangerous or foolish radical thinking. When the liberal philosopher and Member of Parliament John Stuart Mill sought to amend a clause in the 1867 Representation of the People Act from 'men' to 'persons', it sparked a furious and mocking response. English masculinity would be threatened, said opponents. His proposed amendment would debase women. Mill was roundly defeated. 'Mr Mill might import a little more common sense into his arguments', said one member of parliament at the time.

Sixty years later, and thanks to the efforts of another group of radical campaigners—the Suffrage movement—the 1928 Representation of the People Act finally granted women equal voting rights to men in the United Kingdom. Anything else now seems as ridiculous and dangerous as Mill's proposed amendment had appeared in 1867.

We live in an age of unprecedented progress and achievement. We have on average never been richer, healthier or lived longer. Yet we are simultaneously faced with a daunting series of problems. Nation states' ability to raise money and deliver services, enforce law and maintain a border is facing unprecedented strain. Globalisation—essentially the free mobility of goods, services and labour around the world—has created winners, but plenty of losers too. Settled communities have been transformed, and in some places limited public services have struggled to keep up. Income inequality has risen markedly in every liberal democracy for the last thirty years, and many people are no better off than their parents.[1] The environment is being trashed. Levels of depression, anxiety and unhappiness are at all-time highs.[2] That's not to mention the thousand smaller problems all bubbling under these megatrends: struggling public services, ageing populations, housing shortages, misogyny, racism, religious fundamentalism and on and on.

Then there is the internet, cheerleader and amplifier of disruption. It has made production of, and access to, new ideas and movements (both good and bad) easier than ever. It has created new, difficult to control sources of information and brand new centres of power. Representative democracy—slow, unresponsive, full of compromise—suddenly feels absurdly sluggish in a world of instant gratification. The flood of digital information—data and facts and charts and memes and hashtags and think pieces and infographics and retweets—is not making us more informed and thoughtful. It's making us more susceptible to nonsense, more emotional, more irrational and more mobbish. And although we have more information, fast computers and clever analysts to understand these problems, we seem less and less capable of predicting or affecting any of them.

In most Western democracies there's a broad consensus about the best way to order social, economic and political life. A set of received wisdoms about how to deal with the challenges we face. There are disagreements on the details and implementation of course, but since the Second World War the main questions have been practically settled: A nation state with a single legal system, managed by officials and professional political parties elected through representative democracy, who determine what its citizens can see, do, buy and put in their bodies; an economy based on private ownership and free (but controlled) markets and public services; welfare funded by forced general taxation; and human rights protect citizens, who are free to practice whatever religious belief they wish as long as those beliefs and practices do not harm others.

This set of ideas is sometimes called the 'Overton window', or the broad ideas that the majority of the public accept as respectable and normal. It was named after the American political scientist Joseph Overton, who described the range of policies that both left- and right-wing politicians needed to support if they wanted to get elected. Superficial deviations are fine, but anything outside of that window is too unusual, unworkable, unrealistic to be accepted by the public. Too radical.

The Overton window has barely moved for years. But when I started this book in late 2014 there were signs it was beginning to widen. Fewer people were voting, and those who did bother were drifting away from the centre-right and (especially) centre-left parties towards the edges.[3]

There is even a word for this collapse of the centre: 'Pasoki-fication', after the once-dominant Greek social democratic party Pasok, whose public support fell from 45 per cent to 4 per cent in 2015, a pattern mirrored in several other countries.[4] According to various surveys, citizens' trust in elected officials, parliament, the justice system and even democracy itself had been falling steadily for years and was at record lows. People born in 1980 were far less likely than those born in 1960 to think that living in a democracy is 'essential'.

It appeared that a new political space was beginning to open up. People were starting to look for change. They were beginning to listen to the people who did not agree with the accepted consensus. They were beginning to listen to radicals.[5]

'Radicals' is a term used to describe people who advocate fundamental social or political reform. The origin of the word is the Latin *radix*, meaning root. It describes those people who think that something is desperately wrong at the core of modern society, and believe that they have something better to offer. Today, radical ideas and movements are on rise. In streets, halls, fields, chat rooms and even parliaments, more and more people are trying to change the world. And for the last two years, I've tried to find them.

I've been across California campaigning with a trans-humanist running for president, invaded and shut down the United Kingdom's largest coal mine, been attacked by Danish anarchists, marched the streets and pubs with anti-immigration activists on a Europe-wide jaunt, joined the Psychedelic Society in a search for 'oneness', sat in mosques and listened to imams rail against Islamic State and got within a few watery metres of stepping foot on the world's newest and freest country, before the Croatian police attempted to capsize my boat. I've discovered why free love is the route to world peace, tackled the absurdities of setting up a new political party and learned how likely it is that I will live to be 150. I now know the exact difference between 'aggravated trespass' and 'trespass', between psilocybin and LSD and between anarchists, anarcho-capitalists and crypto-anarchists.

Radicals Chasing Utopia is an examination of the ideas and the people on the political and social fringes. It's an effort to explore how and why new groups and ideas emerge and gain currency. Of course, the distinction between radical ideas and mainstream ones is not always clear. Received wisdoms always change over time, and what passes for political consensus exists in a mild state of flux and change. But that process is quickening. Centre-right and centre-left parties across Western democracies are watching helplessly as their long-assumed monopoly on power slips away, and candidates spouting ideas once considered the lunacy of the tin-hat fringe-types—Marine Le Pen in France, Podemos in Spain—are surging in opinion polls. Against the wishes of the majority of political and business leaders, the United Kingdom voted to leave the European Union. In the United States the voters chose billionaire, ur-populist Donald Trump as president, and the Democrat Party almost selected a lifelong socialist (a label that not long ago essentially barred anyone from public office) as their candidate to run against him. In Italy an online movement set up by a foul-mouthed comedian and blogger in 2009 vied to become the leading party in both houses of parliament. In truth, by the time I finished this book in early 2017, the difference between 'radical' and 'mainstream' was less clear.

There are hundreds of movements that merit inclusion in this book. I couldn't follow them all, but some groups were omitted through choice. I've limited myself to movements in Western liberal democracies because radicalism has a very different meaning depending on the context (and especially in places where there is no freedom of speech or assembly. A liberal democrat in Saudi Arabia is certainly a radical there). Anti-capitalist movements like Occupy are only mentioned in passing because there are plenty of books written about them, and although important, they don't have a monopoly on the channels of frustration.* Other significant movements are absent because I wasn't sure I could do them justice, such as those that mobilise on identity markers—sexuality, race, gender— for example, Black Lives Matter. But I've tried to follow a wide variety of contemporary radical thinking I think is both interesting and important.

I approached each group with the intention of assessing them as honestly and objectively as I could. To listen to their ideas and immerse myself in their worlds in order to tell their stories as faithfully as possible. But I also tried to retain a

---

* For further reading on the anti-capitalist movements and their prospects, see, for example, Sarah Jaffe's *Necessary Trouble*, Paul Mason's *Why It's Kicking Off Everywhere* and Chris Hedges' *Wages of Rebellion*. Manuel Castells and Clay Shirkey are two examples of the optimistic social media school. Authors who write about anti-capitalism movements too often assume the future inevitably belongs to heroic anti-capitalist protestors who'll rise up and use technology—especially social media networks—to overthrow the system. Perhaps that's because people who write books tend to come from a similar—university educated, technologically literate, socially liberal and economically well-off—milieu as the people usually involved in anti-capitalist movements.

degree of scepticism. Extraordinary claims require extraordinary evidence.

This book is not an effort to carefully critique every idea, nor an argument either for or against certain political ideas. Do not expect dense political theory or a carefully worded manifesto for the future. Politics is an unpredictable, chaotic system: How precisely ideas shift from the fringe to the mainstream is an inexact science. More modestly, this is an attempt to understand why and how politics is changing: not from the viewpoint of the nervous mainstream, but from the heady perspective of those trying to change it. A combination of technological, economic and social changes are putting the Overton window under unprecedented strain, and Western democracies are entering an age of radicalism. The election of Donald Trump or the United Kingdom leaving the European Union are just early skirmishes in a more significant realignment, in which assumptions about what is 'normal' will change. This book, although certainly not a comprehensive guide to the political norms of tomorrow, is at least an introduction to some of the ideas and trends that may shape these changes. As far as possible, I leave it to you to draw your own conclusions. If this book loosens even slightly the grip of prevailing thought on what you think is possible in politics, then it will have succeeded.

Radical ideas are a powerful force: They can stir millions to action. But where they lead can't be predicted. Because radicalism demands fundamental, disruptive change, it can be as destructive as it is productive. The same year that Mill proposed his amendment to the Representation of the People Act, Karl Marx published *Das Kapital*. It too presented a radical and bold idea: that capitalism would inevitably and inexorably strangle and enslave the workers. It predicted a violent class struggle. The book's ideas spread across the world. In Russia worried censors decided against banning it on the grounds that no one would read it. But thousands did, and an underground movement moved by his theories began to grow.

Today's radicals are not all pioneers, idealists, brave heroes and not all (if any) will one day be seen in the same light as John Stuart Mill, or Marx. Yet neither are they all fundamentalists or fools. Because they reject common wisdoms, radicals are routinely misrepresented or ignored by media, and their ideas are dismissed. But, for better or for worse, the lesson of history is that today's radicals often become tomorrow's mainstream.

Whether you agree with them or not, radical ideas change society. Even when they fail, or are destructive, they force us to think—and to think again.

Our present way of organizing society is neither inevitable nor permanent. The world of tomorrow will certainly be very different from today. This book is a journey to discover what that might be.

1

The Transhumanist's Wager

There are thirty-eight numbers on an American roulette wheel: eighteen black, eighteen red and two green. To play, you place bets on which number, or colour or range of numbers the small white ball will land on when the wheel is spun. That's the decision facing Zoltan, Jeremiah, Dylan and me as we stand around a wheel in Harrah's Casino on Las Vegas Boulevard. Although it's approaching midnight in early September, it's incredibly hot outside. Not that you'd know it, because Harrah's and every other casino here is blasted with oxygenated air conditioning designed to keep us all awake. Like hundreds of other hopeful gamblers in Harrah's, we're losing.[1] For one last spin of the wheel, the four of us agree to put all our remaining chips, which is about $250, on black. If the ball lands on a black number, we double our money and walk out even. But because of those two green numbers, the odds aren't 50–50, but 45–55 against us. That 'house edge' means that, although you can win for a while, the longer you play the greater the likelihood you'll lose. If you play long enough, the probability you'll lose approaches certainty. The casinos obscure this unpalatable truth with free drinks, music, oxygenated air con and 'change your life' posters. In the end the house always wins.

'Are we going out on a loss?' says Dylan, as the croupier shouts 'No more bets.'

'We always go out on a loss,' replies Zoltan.

The four of us had arrived in Las Vegas the day before on a forty-foot-long bus redesigned to look like a giant coffin on wheels. Its nickname is 'the Immortality Bus'. Zoltan is a transhumanist, and he's running for president.

Transhumanism is a growing community of thousands of people who believe that technology can make us physically, intellectually, even morally better; that we can and should use technology to overcome the limits imposed by our biological and genetic heritage—especially mortality—and thereby exceed the constraints of the human condition. Like most transhumanists, Zoltan believes that death is a biological quirk of nature, something we should not accept as inevitable.

Transhumanists work on a dazzling array of cutting-edge technologies to that end, everything from life extension, anti-ageing genetic research, robotics, artificial intelligence, cybernetics, space colonisation, virtual reality and cryonics. For the transhumanists, there is no 'natural' state of man. We're always changing and adapting, and embracing technology is simply the next step along the evolutionary cycle. In the end, that might mean humans transforming themselves into something not really human, but rather *post*-human.

For transhumanists, not to pursue every techno-avenue available to improve the human condition is both irrational and immoral because, if we can relieve suffering and improve well-being with technology, then we must.

Although the quest for immortality arguably starts with the very first recorded piece of literature, *The Epic of Gilgamesh*, a 4,000-year-old poem about Gilgamesh's quest for the secret of eternal life, transhumanism's modern roots are found in the ideas of early twentieth-century science-fiction writers such as Isaac Asimov and the biologist Julian Huxley (brother of Aldous), who coined the term 'transhuman' to mean 'beyond human' in his 1951 book *Knowledge, Morality and Destiny*.[2] Huxley, an agnostic on religious matters, thought that man's natural evolution was of ever higher degrees of complexity, towards the 'fullest realisation of his own inherent possibilities', even if that meant transcending humanity. As science and technology started to have a profound effect on society in the 1960s and 1970s, those 'inherent possibilities' started to stretch. Organisations—often inspired by Huxley's or Asimov's writing—were founded to promote life extension and various types of radical futurist thinking. By the mid-1980s small groups of self-described transhumanists started meeting formally in California to discuss if and how technology might change human existence. In 1990— the year of the first gene-therapy trials, the first designer babies, and the World Wide Web—Max More set out a coherent philosophy of the movement in an influential paper called 'Transhumanism: towards a futurist philosophy'. 'Transhumanism shares many elements of humanism including a respect for reason and science' wrote More, but it is different from humanism 'in recognizing and anticipating the radical alterations in the nature and possibilities of our lives resulting from various sciences and technologies'.* This collection of academics, scientists and sci-fi nerds slowly grew into a movement that spanned the world. In 1998 Nick Bostrom and David Pearce founded the World Transhumanist Association, with the hope of having transhumanism recognised as a legitimate area of scientific research and public policy.

Over the last decade, technology has opened up transhuman possibilities that were once just science fiction. Life extension is now seriously studied in leading universities, while robotics and artificial intelligence receive millions of dollars of investment. There are now tens of thousands of self-declared transhumanists based all over the world, including influential people at the heart of the world's tech scene. Ray Kurzweil, a firm believer in the 'singularity moment' (the point at which artificial intelligence becomes so advanced that it begins to produce new and ever more advanced versions of itself), is a senior engineer at Google. Billionaire Peter Thiel—co-founder of PayPal, influential Silicon Valley investor and a member of President Donald Trump's transition team—is also a self-declared transhumanist and has invested millions of dollars into life extension and artificial-intelligence projects. Transhumanism is fast becoming the meeting point between science and science fiction.

---

* Transhumanists all agree that technology can and should be used to greatly advance our physical and mental capabilities, leading to something that is more than human. Different transhumanists have different specific interests. Some are primarily interested in artificial intelligence or robotics; others in the gradual evolution of the species. For Zoltan it is immortality.

Zoltan is obsessed with odds. And one wager in particular dominates his life: the transhumanist's wager. Derived from Pascal's more famous version (which argues that any rational person should believe in God because if he exists the gain is infinity in paradise; and if he does not, then the loss is only a few inconveniences here on earth for a limited number of years), the transhumanist's wager states that any rational person should spend their every waking moment on a quest to stay alive:

> The wager and quintessential motto of the transhumanist movement states that if you love life, you will safeguard that life, and strive to extend and improve it for as long as possible. Anything else you do while alive, any other opinion you have, any other choice you make to not safeguard, extend, and improve that life, is a betrayal of that life . . . This is a historic choice that each man and woman on the planet must make.[3]

Zoltan lives his life by this severe doctrine. His 'historic choice' is to spend 2015 and 2016 making an obviously hopeless effort to get elected for president of the United States. When Zoltan first telephoned me in mid-2015 to invite me to join the campaign, he explained that this would be no ordinary presidential tour. He knew he needed a weird campaign to make people listen to his message, so he planned a four-month road trip on a 1978 Wanderlodge bus redesigned to look like a coffin. He would visit evangelical churches and instruct the congregation to give up on heaven and live forever here on earth. He would hold rallies and marches with robots. He would visit a bio-hacking lab to get a chip implanted in his hand, and check out a cryonic freezing centre in Arizona. He would generally make trouble and probably get arrested. And for the big finale, emulating the Reformation radical Martin Luther, Zoltan would nail a Transhumanist Bill of Rights to the Capitol Building in Washington DC, which would proclaim that robots and artificial intelligence should have the same rights as humans. And he would bring as many journalists along as he possibly could to cover this madcap adventure, and would put no restrictions on what we could write or film.

Zoltan's wager is that this expensive, exhausting and risky stunt will generate positive publicity for the fledgling movement, maybe even propel transhumanism into a serious political force.

That's why I'm here, in Las Vegas, standing around a roulette wheel, throwing away my money. To see if he can pull this wager off.

The Immortality Bus

Zoltan Istvan Gyurko was born in Los Angeles in 1973. His uncle, a political dissident, had fled the Communist regime in Hungary in 1966, and his father followed suit two years later and claimed asylum. Zoltan had a conventional upbringing, and excelled at school, where he became a national-level swimmer. While other children played, Zoltan was usually in the pool training. This love of water continued throughout his life. At age twenty-one he abandoned a degree in philosophy to circumnavigate the world by boat equipped with 500 works of literature. During the trip, which took seven years in total, he became a war correspondent for *National Geographic* and a director of a non-profit wildlife group, WildAid, where he used militia tactics in South East Asia to protect endangered wildlife. While covering a story for *National Geographic* in Vietnam's demilitarised zone in 2003, Zoltan almost stepped on a landmine. His guide pushed him out of the way of the mostly buried device at the last second. The near-death experience made him acutely aware of his mortality, and terrified by the prospect of death. He remembered having read an article about transhumanism a few years earlier and went online to learn more. He was hooked by the idea that, with the aid of modern science, he might avoid death altogether. 'From that point on, I decided to dedicate my life to the transhumanist cause,' Zoltan says.

On returning to California in the mid-2000s Zoltan set up a small real-estate company, renovating houses and selling them on. As the Silicon Valley property market exploded in the wake of the tech boom, he made enough money to retire and focus on transhumanism full-time. He moved to Marin County, just north of San Francisco, where he settled with his wife, Lisa, and had two young daughters, Ava and Isla. He began dedicating between twelve and fourteen hours a day to transhumanist-related work: attending conferences, writing articles, recruiting friends and writing a work of fiction-cum-philosophy, *The Transhumanist Wager*. But after it was published, to some minor acclaim in transhumanist circles, he began to think the movement's appeal was limited because it was too academic, too obsessed with science.

If transhumanism was going to reach the masses, Zoltan thought, it needed a PR overhaul. It needed to become less about the science, and more about the big ideas. It needed to become more accessible to ordinary folk. And the quickest way to do that, he thought, was to pull off a big media stunt. In October 2014 Zoltan announced in a blog post on the *Huffington Post* that he'd be running for president with the newly founded Transhumanist Party.[4]

He created a board of influential transhumanist advisers and, following several meetings and discussions with them, sketched out an eye-grabbing transhumanist manifesto to take to the American people. This included a Transhumanist Bill of Rights advocating government support of longer lifespans via science and technology, rights for robots and cyborgs, phasing out of all individual taxes (because Zoltan believes robots will be taking most human jobs in the next twenty years), morphological freedom (the right to do anything with your body as long as it doesn't harm other people), replacing prisons with small squadrons of drones that will follow convicted criminals around, legalising recreational drugs (he wants to be the first president to smoke weed in the White House[*]) and eliminating all physical disabilities. But his main policy, his big-ticket pitch, is to create 'a scientific- and educational-industrial complex' that would replace the military-industrial complex and end ageing and death within a generation.

Zoltan found a classified ad for a 1978 Blue Bird Wanderlodge RV in nearby Sacramento, which he bought for $10,000, drove home and parked in his driveway. He then

---

[*] By the 1980s, Timothy Leary, the poster boy for LSD, had given up psychedelics and gone on to other things. He endorsed SMILE (Space Migration, Intelligence Increase and Life Extension), which he thought were the technologies needed to be advanced for humans to continue to evolve. He increasingly saw technology, rather than drugs, as the way to expand human consciousness.

set up a page on the crowdfunding website Indiegogo asking for $25,000 to fund the 'Immortality Bus with Presidential Candidate Zoltan' (including '$15,000 for making the bus; $5,000 for a full size interactive robot and other tech; $5,000 for gas, food etc"*).

By August 2015, 135 separate funders had helped him reach his target. As summer approached Zoltan and a couple of volunteers worked in his driveway from morning until night trying to make the bus look like a coffin: fitting new tyres and a wooden lid, and painting it brown.

He isn't quite finished when, on a gloriously hot and sunny afternoon in September 2015, I turn up to find him kneeling and hammering on the roof of a bus that vaguely resembles a coffin, with 'Immortality Bus' painted on the side in enormous silver letters. Zoltan is physically very fit and, although forty-two, still looks like a Californian surfer. 'Welcome to the Immortality Bus!' he says, simultaneously grinning and wiping sweat from his brow. 'We're almost finished. I need another couple of hours.' I'm the last to arrive. Dylan, twenty-five, is a super-smart

---

* Funders could donate $5 'thank you very much for supporting the cause . . . we will tag you and thank you among all our supporters in our social media channels' (twenty-one people); $20 'get a bumper sticker and e-book of the Immortality Bus adventure, written and photographed by Zoltan Istvan' (thirty-three people); $35 'Immortality Bus t-shirt . . . we will also thank you in our social media and spread the word about how awesome you are' (eleven people); $50 'get a signed first edition paperback copy of Zoltan Istvan's novel "The Transhumanist Wager." Called a masterpiece and futurist classic by some' (eleven claimed); $100 'Hop on the Immortality Bus, take a tour inside and chat with volunteers' (five claimed). For a whopping $1,000 you can ride on the bus itself. 'That's right! Take a ride on the Immortality Bus and be part of the action.' Three people have paid for that.

and slightly nerdy journalist from Washington DC who writes for the online magazine vox.com. He's doing daily dispatches. There's a Polish journalist in her late thirties called Magda, who's based in California as a foreign correspondent, and she's planning to join periodically. Jeremiah Hammerling, thirty-one, is a lone documentary maker and is already hard at work, zipping around the bus as he films Zoltan's every move from experimental angles. They are here for the same reason I am: the irresistible draw of writing about a man running for president promising immortality in a 1978 Wanderlodge designed to look like a coffin on wheels. Naturally there is a robot on board too: a $400, three-foot-tall robot made by Meccano, which Zoltan names Jethro, after the chief protagonist in his book.

Finally, there is Roen (pronounced 'Rowan'), who is one of Zoltan's volunteers and a 'true devotee', as he describes himself. Roen's job is to assist Zoltan and to document the experience and share it on Zoltan's many social media accounts.[5] Roen is twenty-eight, thin and tall, with long greasy hair and a wispy beard—and terrified of death. He has, he says, been obsessed with mortality since the age of nine, when he fell off his bike and ruptured his spleen. He lives at home with his parents, and doesn't work, which means he can spend all his time on his social media page, Eternal Life Fan Club, or researching nutrition and health. Roen first met Zoltan at a transhumanist conference in California in 2013 and they struck up an online correspondence. When Zoltan decided he needed an assistant for the campaign, he asked Roen if he'd be interested. 'It was the greatest honour of my life,' recalls Roen. He accepted immediately.

The campaign, explains Zoltan as we load our bags into the back end of the coffin, will comprise a dozen or so stages, each lasting a few days, as he winds his way from the west coast towards Washington DC. On this first stage we'll be on the road for five days, driving to a bio-hacking lab in Central California for Zoltan to have a chip implanted, and then on to Las Vegas for a technology exhibition and a set-piece speech. Most of the time, Zoltan says, will be spent inside the bus. Fortunately for us the Immortality Bus is reasonably comfortable. Two rows of seating line the front half, followed by a tightly fitted kitchenette and then two more rows of seating/beds. The bus, which is almost entirely brown or beige, can make 55 mph on the flat, but develops a noticeable rattle at anything over 40 mph. The only slight worry is the heat: Zoltan has unfortunately covered the air-conditioning vent with the wooden casket he's nailed to the roof. 'Guys, do not turn the air-con on,' Zoltan warns us as we climb aboard. 'Or there is a strong possibility we'll all die.'

Striking Oil

Five hours later than planned, Zoltan declares the presidential campaign is ready to begin. He hops into the driver's seat, carrying a bulletproof vest. 'This is important,' he says. 'We're taking this. Just in case.' A small crowd, including Lisa, Ava and Isla, have gathered on the street to see us off. Zoltan, sitting behind a hula-hoop-sized steering wheel, mutters under his breath, 'Let's hope this thing works,' as he starts the bus. And it does. 'The Immortality

Bus is on its way,' Roen says excitedly into his camera as
Zoltan slowly navigates the RV out of his narrow driveway. 'Let's try to live forever everyone! This is the moment
I've been waiting for. I'm not talking about a hundred
years or 300 years. That's for amateurs. I'm talking about
im-mor-tal-ity.'

The bus slowly bundles its way from the expensively
quaint Marin County into San Francisco, the heart of the
world's tech scene, and then joins California State Route 1,
which snakes along the Pacific coast. We have about four
hours of driving to reach our first stop, a bio-hacking lab in
the Mojave Desert in Central California. Zoltan is in front
driving, with Jethro riding shotgun. The rest of us are in
the back, getting acquainted, as Zoltan tries without success to get the cassette player to work.

Two hours in we stop for coffee at a roadside Starbucks. Zoltan, inspecting the vehicle in the car park, suddenly looks distraught. 'Oh man,' he says. 'We have got a
problem. A *big* problem.' Oil is leaking everywhere. Zoltan opens up the engine and starts peering about with his
flashlight.

'Either it's a blown gasket or any one of a dozen small
leaks,' says Zoltan. If it's the former, he says, the trip is
over, because finding gaskets for a 1978 Wanderlodge is
as difficult as it sounds. As we wait, Zoltan runs in and
out of the bus, pressing buttons and inspecting the engine
and then the oil pool that is forming on the road. 'Our
hope is that things go forward eventually,' Dylan says to
me clutching his notepad, 'following repeated snags and
catastrophes.'

After lengthy discussions over the phone with his father, Zoltan decides that we can probably continue after

all, but we'll have to add oil to the engine every hour. By now it's very late and there are no motels to be found. So we park in a McDonald's drive-thru car park and decide to sleep on the bus. Everyone is hungry, but the RV Wanderlodge won't fit through the drive-thru lane, so Zoltan stands in line behind three cars, and walks-thru. But when he gets to the front of the line the cash attendant tells him they can only serve cars. To cheer us up, Zoltan opens a bottle of bourbon and pours us each a cup.

He toasts that we'd made it this far (which, given we're travelling about 40 mph, isn't very far), that he's glad to be here together and relieved the bus works. He says he knows he won't win the election and will probably concede and support Democrat Hillary Clinton in the end. We raise our cups and drain the bourbon. Zoltan pours us another.

Bio-Hackers

The early morning sun dawns bright and directly through the shallow curtains, revealing strewn bodies in various stages of alertness. Zoltan is already up, pacing up and down the car park as he talks on the phone to his dad about gaskets and oil levels. Despite some grumblings, the Immortality Bus has decided not to expire during the night, and four short hours after we'd gone to bed we are back on the road, driving towards Tehachapi, and the bio-hacking lab.

Tehachapi looks like a frontier town. It's up an enormous sandy hill, which the bus just about conquers. There are a dozen rows of prefabricated houses dotted across the dusty dunes. Around twenty-five 'grinders' have come from all over the country for Grindfest, a three-day meetup to discuss ideas, share tips and operate on each other.[6]

Bio-hacking, or DIY biology, refers to biological research or experiments outside formal academia or corporate settings. It's biology of the home-made, rough-and-ready variety, usually undertaken in basements or garages. One of the first bio-hackers was a man called Kevin Warwick who, in 1998, put a microchip in his own body to see what would happen.[7] Two years later he had cybernetic sensors implanted into the nerves of his arms, allowing him to roughly control a robotic arm.[8] The movement soon spread. DIYBio, an international umbrella group founded in 2008, advertises, at the time of writing, seventy-five bio-hacking organisations or events across the globe, from Tel Aviv, New York, Munich, London, São Paolo and Sydney.[9] Other examples include BioCurious, a lab in California; Genspace, a 'community biolab' in New York; and the London Biohackspace.

Grinders are a branch of this movement who specialise in body modification and 'self-focusing', meaning they operate on themselves. They read academic papers, discuss studies, formulate ideas, build stuff using supplies they've bought from hardware stores or the Net and try it on themselves. Advocates of 'open source' technology, they publish and share all the results of their endeavours.[10] Rich Lee—one of the organisers of Grindfest, and the Transhumanist Party's bio-hacking adviser—estimates that there are around 3,000 grinders in the United States, and many more bio-hackers.

Grinders usually meet on the Web forum www.bio hack.me. But this weekend was the chance to meet fellow grinders in person and conduct experiments. Several plan to insert microchips and magnets into their body. One has designed a nineteenth-century duelling scar he'd like to run down the front of his face. Zoltan has decided to get a Radio Frequency Identification (RFID) chip implant.[11] An RFID chip is smaller than a grain of rice, and stores small amounts of information that can be recognised by other compatible devices if they are programmed to do so.

As we park up and jump off the bus, Rich Lee welcomes us and takes us into the 'lab' where the experiments are taking place. But it isn't really much of a lab; it's just a large double garage of the house. There are sterilised needles, and a big workbench around which several grinders are huddled looking at small cultures of bacteria. Strewn across the lab are wires, tools, microchips and laptops. There's a big dentist's chair in a separate, possibly mildly sterilised, room, which is where Zoltan will have his procedure.

Rich looks more like a rock star than a scientist, with a shaved head and long black beard. He works as a cardboard salesman during the day, he says, and grinds by night. In 2012 Rich was told by his doctor that he was slowly going blind. So he decided to learn to echo-navigate using sonar waves, a little like a bat. In 2013 he inserted two small magnets into his ears and then built himself a coil to put around his neck to create a magnetic field. The coil is picked up by the magnets and turned into sound. Although originally intended to pick up ultrasound, Rich quickly realised he could plug anything into it. He now uses it to 'hear' heat, take phone calls and listen to music. 'The sound quality is OK,' he says. 'Like a cheap set of headphones.' Rich is already working on his next project: a vibrating implant that he's going to embed under his pubic bone to make his penis vibrate during sex. He calls it the LoveTron9000. 'It's very difficult to get it right. But I think it's almost there.'

Grinders' approach to biology is 'try it and see what happens'. Steve is a twenty-year-old self-taught computer hacker who left school at sixteen. He's designed and made a gadget to translate signals into noise. It's about the size of a thick postage stamp. He's planning to insert it into the base of his skull so that his brain can hear these sounds directly.

'It's going to be awesome. I'll be able to connect my brain to the internet, I'll be able to *feel* sounds. And my brain will start to adapt. I'll be a node on the internet!' he says.

'What if someone hacks into your system and starts sending you horrible noises?' I ask.

'I think that would be awesome.'

'Why?'

'I'd love to know what they do, and how they do it.'

Nearly all the grinders have RFID chip implants. One has set up his phone so it unlocks when he holds it over his thumb. Another scans her chip to share contact information with me. Julius, a smart nineteen-year-old from Texas who works in software, walks me over to his car and unlocks it with his hand. He then starts it with his hand. Like every other grinder, he'd reprogrammed it all himself.

Zoltan doesn't have a chip yet, which is mildly embarrassing for a man hoping to become the country's first transhumanist president. After wandering around the lab and chatting to grinders, Zoltan sits down in the dentist's chair. He looks nervous.

'I'm not nervous. I'm excited!' he tells us.

'OK Zoltan,' says David, a red-headed grinder in his early thirties who is also a registered nurse. He will be performing the procedure. 'Good to have you here.' He's inserted two dozen RFID chips this weekend alone.

'I'm a little nervous now,' says Zoltan, as David pulls out a large needle. 'I told you I wasn't. I lied.'

'I've done much worse,' says David.

But the implant is very simple. Zoltan grits his teeth, looks away, looks back at his hand, and we all jostle to get a better view. Jeremiah works the angles with his lens fixed on Zoltan's worried face. 'Here goes,' says David, placing the needle between Zoltan's thumb and index finger. He pushes the syringe all the way down, which injects the tiny chip under the skin. It's over in thirty seconds.*

'Are you feeling more than human now?' I ask.

'I feel like I'm about to wake up in the Matrix,' laughs Zoltan, as he clenches and unclenches his fist. 'That wasn't too bad.'

There are millions of RFID chips in all sorts of daily devices already, such as fob keys and pets' collars. In 2015 the market in RFID chips was worth around $10 billion, and this is expected to almost double within ten years. But this RFID chip can't do much because it's not compatible with iPhones, which is what Zoltan has. So instead, his chip is programmed to say 'Win 2016' if someone else hovers their (Samsung) phone over it. Disappointment notwithstanding, he mentions his chip at every opportunity for the rest of the trip. He says he'll get it upgraded in six months: 'This is just the start.' (When I checked back in

---

* Dylan decided he'd get one too. Zoltan got his for free, but Dylan pays the standard fee: $40 for the chip, and $30 for the procedure. He says he's going to use it to swipe into his office because he always forgets his card. I decided not to get one. I asked David how to remove it and he said no one had ever asked before.

six months later, he hadn't upgraded but was still planning to.) In fact, he immediately declares he wants to have a cranium chip implanted, which could connect him to artificial intelligence, 'so I'd be one of the first to communicate with the machines'.

After the procedure, Zoltan does his best to persuade the grinders to get involved in the Transhumanist Party. Few have heard of him, and none of them say they will vote for him. It transpires that bio-hackers and transhumanists have recently fallen out. 'Transhumanists have been promising us jet packs and immortality,' Rich Lee tells me, as Zoltan woos the voters. 'And we've still not seen anything. I decided the only way anything would happen was if we just did it ourselves. We're sick of transhumanists' bullshit promises.' In early 2015 four grinders started a research group called Science for the Masses to test infrared sight. After reading some academic papers, one of them spent several months on a vitamin A–deficient diet and had chlorine e6 insulin and saline dropped into his eyes. He found he had improved vision in the dark for several hours, with no noticeable long-term effects. Some of the more traditional transhumanist scientists complained about the methods and ethics of the experiment, criticising this DIY approach to science. 'Everyone appreciated Zoltan coming,' says Rich, 'but opinion about transhumanism is still varied.'

Impressive as these relatively small advances are— especially given they are working out of garages— technology is moving fast. To get a sense of how fast, we leave Tehachapi and the grinders and head to Las Vegas for the CTIA Super Mobility 2015 conference. The conference brochure promises a huge exposition of the latest mobile technology. 'This is big' it reads. 'A trillion dollars worth of big. The entire-mobile-eco-system-in-one-place kind of big. Explore the game-changing emerging technologies that will power our wireless world of tomorrow.'

Zoltan is booked to deliver a keynote speech about transhumanism. Forty thousand people are expected at this conference, and Zoltan says he hopes a decent amount of them will be there to listen to what he has to say.

Starbucks Politics

The drive to Las Vegas will take several hours. The temperature rises steadily as we head inland and the coffin bus seems to slow. Thankfully we stop every couple of hours at roadside coffee shops so that Zoltan and Roen can access the free Wi-Fi to post and tweet stories from the road. (And top-up the leaking oil.)

'I need to get my message out in a busy information environment,' Zoltan tells me over the deafening engine as we drive through the desert. 'So I need to self-promote using every means available.' He has clocked an important new dynamic in modern politics: Social media gives new parties the opportunity to give the impression of substance and support. Roen's main job is to document the trip with his camera and video, and post it online. 'We are making history here,' shouts Zoltan to Roen periodically. 'Every time you post about the trip on social media, please add the link to the crowdfunding page! But not like a salesperson. Like an activist.'* At every spare moment, the two of

---

* There are few limits to what Zoltan will do to get his name out there. While researching him before the trip, I found a review of his

them are uploading pictures, blogs and videos of the day's adventures to Zoltan's social media accounts. We might be in a forty-year-old bus, but this is a very modern campaign.

To my surprise, all this frenetic activity was actually working. Zoltan was getting recognised. Dylan's first 'daily despatch' article for vox.com was picked up online and widely shared. En route to Las Vegas, a local journalist got in touch asking for an interview. And everywhere we go people stop and stare at the bus. The receptionist at our hotel near the bio-hacking lab had read about Zoltan on the website Reddit.

With wind in its sails the Immortality Bus arrives in Las Vegas. 'Jamie, wake up! Look at that!' Zoltan says as the skyscrapers come into view. 'That is *awesome*. Oh man, I love Vegas.'

The city is situated in the basin of the Mojave Desert surrounded by mountain ranges, and its subtropical climate generates just four inches of rain a year. It's a ludicrous location, yet it is one of the world's most popular tourist destinations. The 'Strip'—the long street of mega-casinos where we are heading—contains six of the ten largest hotels in the world. The Venetian hotel, where Zoltan is due to give his speech, has 7,117 rooms. Nothing would survive here without the electricity and irrigation

---

book on the website www.goodreads.com: 'I realize it's a bit strange for an author to comment or to review his own novel, however, since my fictional thriller involves a storyline that presents an original philosophy, I think a few comments are appropriate. The first is that I have been carefully thinking about this book for almost 20 years. The second is the amount of hours that went into the actual writing of *The Transhumanist Wager*: almost 7,000 hours.'

provided by the Hoover Dam. This mighty construction impounds a reservoir that holds 35,000 square kilometres of water, which is funnelled through tunnels blasted into the canyon walls to increase the pressure. Every year, the water relentlessly spins seventeen massive turbines, generating around 4.5 billion kilowatt hours, enough electricity for 8 million people. The overflow water irrigates 1 million acres.

Las Vegas is the closest thing there is to a transhumanist city, a story of humans using science to bend nature to their limitless whim. Its ridiculous skyscrapers spring out of the desert like out-of-place flowers that refuse to die. Hundreds of thousands of people from all over the world converge in the middle of a desert to spin a ball around a wheel in an oxygenated, air-conditioned room powered by a man-made river spinning a generator thirty-five miles away. It feels like the perfect setting.

We head straight to the Venetian to pick up press passes and name badges, and then on to the exposition itself, where over 1,000 exhibition stands display the latest in robots, drones and other devices. We test virtual-reality headsets and speed around on Segways. We meet Furo-I Series, a small robot on wheels that can complete simple household chores, including making small talk with the children, and even provides what the brochure calls 'emotional services'.

This display of technological prowess excites Zoltan, who nods approvingly at every cutting-edge device, turning to us periodically to say 'Awesome.' But it's nothing, he says over another coffee, compared to the transhumanist technologies he'll be telling everyone about later.

The Pitch

Zoltan's big speech is in a room that is tucked away through labyrinthine corridors on the third floor of the Venetian. It's a large, echoing room—big enough to hold 200 people—with ornate decor, a raised stage, podium and large projector screen. We arrive fifteen minutes early to take our seats but find only thirty people in attendance. Zoltan pokes his head around a door and walks over. 'I'm sorry you guys. I didn't realise the audience would be so small,' he says, apologetically. 'Let's make the atheist call—that usually works.'

He posts on Twitter:

#Aetheist [*sic*] Presidential candidate Zoltan Istvan speaking in 30 min . . . JOIN US.

He then follows with:

Strongly Pro #LGBT Presidential candidate Zoltan Istvan speaking in 15 min @ rm 3104 Lido @ The Venetian @CTIAShows #Supermobilty JOIN US!*

Before long another eighty or so people turn up to listen to the presidential candidate for the Transhumanist Party describe our wonderful and exciting technology-filled future. First Zoltan explains that very soon he won't be talking to the audience with a microphone, he will be

---

* Zoltan believes that the lesbian, gay, bisexual and transgender community is a natural supporter of transhumanism. He thinks that transhumanism's goal of total morphological freedom is an extension of sexual freedom.

communicating via a cranial chip in the brain ('I already have a chip in my hand,' he adds). Zoltan then says 'there is a very good chance' that within fifteen to twenty-five years we will overcome death. In fact, he goes on, within thirty-five years 'we're going to be able to rejuvenate ourselves to the age we want to be.' He tells the audience there is a 'very solid chance that within thirty to fifty years' we'll start trying to bring back dead bodies. There is nothing technology can't do, proclaims Zoltan, there are already robots with 'glimmers of consciousness'. And very soon we'll all have cooking robots and bionic arms.

Roen is nodding approvingly throughout, and Jeremiah is walking around the stage and among the crowd, filming. Dylan and I are sitting in the back row taking notes.

'Do you think anyone here believes any of this stuff?' I ask Dylan.

'I've no idea,' says Dylan. 'I doubt it.'

Vote for me, Zoltan tells the crowd, and we can make it happen. The science is almost there.

Here's the problem. Transhumanist science is undeniably exciting and fast-moving. And after all, technology has already transformed society in ways unimaginable only a few years ago. Why would that change now? Many of us—especially people like Zoltan—have longer, healthier, happier and easier lives thanks to technology we neither understand nor ever imagined. The proposition that we will someday use biotechnology to make ourselves stronger, smarter, less prone to violence and longer-living is not so outlandish. Already millions of people use mood-altering drugs, substances to boost muscle mass or selectively erase memory, prenatal genetic screening and gene therapy. These don't just ameliorate defects, but also enhance us. They were all viewed as unnatural, and immoral, not so long ago.

But the science is not almost there. Like every techno-utopian, Zoltan appears to flit with misleading ease between science and fiction, taking any promising piece of research as proof of victory. The three main transhumanist technologies that excite transhumanists like Zoltan are life extension, cryonic freezing and mind uploading. Each of them is advancing quickly. But they are also highly speculative.

Radical life extension seeks to use a variety of medical advances—tissue rejuvenation, regenerative medicine, gene therapy, molecular repair—to slow and eventually stop the process of ageing. Ageing, after all, is simply an accumulation of damage to cells, tissues and molecules, and so it stands to reason there are molecular and cellular solutions. Rather than seeing ageing as inevitable, Zoltan thinks it should be viewed like any other disease. A growing number of serious scientists seem to agree. There is already a broad scientific consensus in gerontology about things that go wrong with animal cells as they age, and that it can be slowed down with genetic manipulation. In 2013 David Sinclair, a decorated professor of genetics at Harvard Medical School, administered an enzyme called NAD^+ to mice. NAD^+ is active in cell reparation, and Sinclair found it reversed aging in mice by affecting how their mitochondrial DNA regulated ageing. So much so, in fact, that a similar result in humans would turn a sixty-year-old body into a twenty-year-old one.[12] Whether it would work on humans is a leap and the US Federal Drug Agency doesn't allow this kind of experimentation on humans, but several scientists think it could soon be possible to slow ageing by 10 per cent.[13] (One way around FDA regulations

is for volunteers to test experimental drugs on themselves—and some people have already tried, although it's
too early to present any results.)[14]

Far from being a marginal science, it's an increasingly
lucrative and well-funded area of research: billions of dollars are spent each year on regenerative science, a figure
that's grown dramatically over the last three years, partly
as a result of interest from Silicon Valley tycoons.[15] In 2013
Google launched Calico, an anti-ageing research centre,
with an initial investment of $750 million to 'harness ad-
vanced technologies to increase our understanding of the
biology that controls lifespan.'[16]

The second plank of research is cryonics. Alcor is the
largest cryonics centre in the world, based in Arizona. Its
1,000 or so members (who are rumoured to include Simon
Cowell) and 143 current 'patients' each pay $200,000 plus
yearly dues to be frozen in nitrogen when they die, in the
hope they will be unfrozen at some point in the future.[17]
Advocates believe freezing the body in this way gives the
best chance of preservation until a scientific breakthrough
arrives.[18] But there is no credible evidence that this would
work on humans, since no one has ever been defrosted.
The effects of freezing the body, and especially the brain,
are wildly uncertain and even the Cryonic Institute con-
cedes that it is 'unknown' whether future societies will
be able to revive cryonic subjects successfully.[19] But they
received a boost in 2015 when one test showed that the
roundworm *Caenorhabditis elegans* retains its memories
after being cryopreserved at liquid-nitrogen temperatures.

The final, and most speculative, of all the transhumanist technologies is called 'mind uploading'. Each person's
brain has a unique set of neurons and neural pathways,

shaped by all the things that person has seen, heard, felt and done. Whole-brain emulation involves creating a faithful 'map' of the brain using advanced scanning techniques. Advocates hope that an identical copy of a person's brain would be indistinguishable from the original, and so would replicate that person's mind, which could be stored on a (presumably very large) memory stick. If you die you can always re-upload a back-up file into a synthetic human body.[20] Several respected academic institutes are mapping the brain to better understand how it works, mainly to help combat various neurological diseases. Despite a lot of money and effort we still know remarkably little about how the brain actually functions.[21] So far, scientists have managed to map the connections between all 300 neurons of a worm's brain, while neuromorphic chips can now store over 1,000 synthetic neurons. The mapping of a worm's brain took a dozen years, though, and in size it is incomparable to the human brain and its 100 billion neurons.[22] Perhaps a wiring diagram of all the connections between a dead brain's neurons might be possible one day, but living brains constantly change and adapt to the information they receive.[23]

When Zoltan finishes his speech (by exhorting any rich people in the audience to invest in transhumanism technology), I look around the room. No one guffaws, heckles or leaves. In fact, quite a few seem taken in by it all. A disabled war veteran thanks Zoltan for the work he's doing raising awareness about these issues, because they might help him one day. 'What a presidential candidate that is,' says the emcee as Zoltan walks off the stage to applause. 'He's got my vote . . . as long as he's got weed!'

Clearly there is more to transhumanism's appeal than the science. According to Richard Jones, author of a critical review of transhumanism and professor at Sheffield University, its roots are not to be found in sci-fi literature or computer-science departments, but religious apocalyptic thinking of the Middle Ages and scientific Marxism, with its plans to mould and improve humankind.[24]

There is a strange religious undertone in transhumanists' belief that abundance and harmony is just about to arrive, that some kind of dramatic scientific leap forward can liberate us from the threats of death, of deterioration, of poverty, of suffering.[25] There is no doubt Zoltan has some kind of faith. It's not faith in a deity or a celestial spirit, but in the abstract idea of science and technology as a magical, mystical force, irrespective of the evidence. He thinks that, by combining or 'converging' nanotechnology, biotechnology, information technology and cognitive science, miracles of science will somehow emerge. It's not surprising many transhumanists are from California. It is home to the world's most advanced technology sector, and is also the capital of America's alternative religions.[26] It's this spiritual rather than scientific offer that explains transhumanism's popularity. In the United States, organised religion—which has long helped humans deal with the sorry fact of our mortality—is on the decline.[27] The proportion of Americans identifying as atheist or agnostic is growing, especially among the young.[28]

In many ways transhumanism feels like the perfect religion for a modern, selfish age; an extension of society's obsession with individualism, perfection and youth. I want to live forever—so why shouldn't I? And more profoundly, if there is no meaning after death without religion, rather than facing the possibility of the void, transhumanism offers the hope that it can be avoided altogether. Zoltan prefers to call himself an optimist. 'It's true, I'm not completely bound by science. I'm hopeful of something more.'

The Problem with Transhumanism

Perhaps immortality will always be a pipe dream. But there is little doubt that technology is developing at a terrifying rate, and will continue to shape our society in important ways.

Take artificial intelligence (AI), something which most politicians barely mention. The overwhelming majority of transhumanists think that AI is a positive development: it will help humans become more intelligent, help us make better decisions and will open up amazing new avenues of knowledge and understanding. Perhaps it will. But perhaps it won't. Elon Musk, the billionaire Silicon Valley entrepreneur, declared AI to be comparable to summoning the Devil and donated $10 million to research to make sure the super-machines of the future will be kind to us. Stephen Hawking said 'the development of artificial intelligence could spell the end of the human race.' Either way, and of more immediate concern, AI—or the ability of machines to replicate human decision-making—could leave millions without jobs.[29] Google's self-driving cars will replace drivers, drones will replace warehouse workers, machine-learning algorithms will undertake some (although not all) the work of lawyers and doctors. What will we do if half the population—especially the middle class tax payers—are laid off work? Of course, workforces change, and it's also possible that the gains of AI-produced wealth are distributed fairly amongst populations and free up people from repetitive tasks for more exciting and fulfilling roles. But it's far from certain. And despite its uncertainty, a growing number of serious scientists believe that at least some advance in life longevity is likely in the coming years. If people start living to 125, what does that mean for the retirement age, or criminal sentencing, or the education system or relationships? The truth is, no one knows. How we deal with these changes in the years ahead will depend as much on political choices as the technology itself. These issues will be, within a decade, major political questions as important as immigration or education are now. Zoltan is doing us all a favour by running his campaign. He's the only political candidate trying to imagine what politics and policies might be in a world of continued and accelerating technological advance.* He might force other politicians to start thinking about it.

But Zoltan's techno-utopianism comes at a cost. Transhumanists' exaggerated claims about the potential of technology to solve our most challenging tasks mean they ignore current problems and overlook the negative consequences of rapidly advancing technology. Politics involves trade-offs, difficult choices and compromises. Not for Zoltan, though, because there is no problem that technology can't fix. At various down moments on the bus, I quiz Zoltan on his policies. How to deal with crime, I ask. Simple, says Zoltan, we'll have pills that will make criminals

---

* With one exception: in 2012 the Italian MP Giuseppe Vatinno became the world's first transhumanist elected politician.

happier and less likely to commit crime, so all crime will eventually disappear. And racism? It's a mental illness, and some kind of pill or cranial implant can solve that as well. Poverty? AI will figure it out. Islamic State? Millions of miniature drones could follow militants everywhere. Will technology create greater inequality, making the powerful even more so? No. AI will make free versions of itself and there will be enough to go around.

For transhumanists, technology and science spells a world of happiness and plenty. But political scientist Francis Fukuyama, author of *Our Posthuman Future*, called transhumanism 'the world's most dangerous idea'. What if, wondered Fukuyama, some people can live much longer than others, or dramatically improve their memory, strength and so on, using aggressive technological fixes? (It is not helped that most transhumanists, including Zoltan, are well-off, highly educated men from California.[30]) Zoltan says he wants everyone to benefit from the transhumanist revolution. But a world in which rich people can afford to further improve their intelligence, looks and life expectancy would surely result in even greater inequality of every type. It could mean a dystopia like H. G. Wells's novel *The Time Machine*. Instead of happy ineffectual Eloi and underground devious Morlocks, a new divide could form between the wealthy and healthy immortalists and a hapless underclass of unemployed, digitally illiterate creatures with short lifespans and no hope of improvement. Some writers, such as George Annas and Lori Andrews, think rapid technology development could one day lead to genetic discrimination, and even human/post-human warfare.[31]

Immortality itself, which is Zoltan's main aim, throws up plenty of knotty problems too, sometimes at a very personal level. Once you start thinking that avoiding death is a genuine prospect, it can become a draining obsession. Zoltan's assistant Roen is fanatical about it. Avoiding death is all he ever thinks about, which makes the daily business of staying alive—something most of us manage without much thought—a very deliberate and carefully planned enterprise. He crosses the road with great caution. He doesn't fly. He avoids strenuous exercise. He doesn't drink, smoke or take drugs. We seriously discussed the possibility of wearing a bicycle helmet 24/7, in case of falling over. He is neurotic over what he eats (he used to eat only fruit until his teeth starting rotting from excessive sugar content). By the time we broke down in the Starbucks car park on day one, he'd already eaten seven vacuum-packed beetroots that he'd brought with him. At dinner on the second night he had steamed vegetables and three pints of water, into each of which he squeezed two whole limes. He scolded the waitress at Peggy Sue's 50's Diner en route to Mojave, saying it might as well be called 'heart-attack diner' and refused to eat. For dinner at the casino he ordered a side of carrots, a side of broccoli, a side of salsa and two sides of avocado.[32]

None of this makes life particularly enjoyable. Actually, it makes it very stressful. During a quiet moment on the bus, I ask Roen how he sees time. 'I think about it a lot. Literally I feel like I'm on death row *right now*. All I'm working on is how I can best ensure the maximum amount of future. Unless it's eternal it all seems pointless—because at one point it will be gone. All those memories, experiences, gone. Gone for-ev-er! Vaporised into nothing! It's just a big joke. An absurdity!' If death is all that one ever thinks about, it can sap all joy from life. Zoltan has

an innate love of life. He is one of the most energetic, enthusiastic people I've ever met. But all this fretting about
death surely limits his ability to enjoy the present. When
his family arrived, the night before his talk in Las Vegas,
he became noticeably more uptight, as if every moment
not spent on the mission is a moment wasted, rather than
a moment lived. He has seventeen fire alarms in his house,
at least three per room—and he checked them all before
leaving the house.

In fact, it's difficult to see how humanity could survive without death.[33] Even though Zoltan is radical, a world
of always-the-same people would make for the exact opposite. What could be worse than an entire world of old
people thinking the same thoughts forever? Immortality
would mean social and political revolutions grinding to a
halt, as dictators could live and rule for hundreds of years.
Death is often the spark for social change (and, ironically,
scientific advances). Transhumanism, far from being radical, could end up being the most conservative philosophy
the world has ever seen.

The Wager

The rules for forming a political party in the United States
are incredibly complicated, and the party donation system
is opaque for anyone but specialist lawyers. Just getting
your name on the ballot requires thousands of citizens to
register their support for you, which demands a lot of campaigning.[34] Getting on the Californian ballot as an independent presidential candidate requires 178,000 signatures
from state citizens. Even in smaller states such as Utah

and Hawaii, getting on the ballot requires 1,000 and 4,357 signatures respectively.[35]

This has created an effective bar to anyone outside the main two parties at almost every level of American politics. There are currently no members of the House of Representatives from third parties. Only one current incumbent, Gregorio Sablan of the Commonwealth of the Northern Mariana Islands, is an independent. There have only been eight in total since the Second World War.[36]

As we leave Las Vegas and head to Los Angeles— where I would leave the campaign—Zoltan tells me that the closed nature of American politics is the real reason he has put this whole tour on. 'I ran a whacky campaign because I needed something crazy. I know I'm not going to win. I know it could damage my reputation. But this is the only way to cause a stir and get my name out there,' he says, exasperated. 'Third parties are jokes and it pisses me off! The country can only move forward if it has new ideas, and those new ideas have to come from new parties.'

Without us journalists, he admits, there probably would not have been a tour at all. That created a mutual dependency between us: we journalists wanted interesting scenes and events to write about, and Zoltan would go to unusual lengths to provide them.

On the final evening, as we head towards Los Angeles (Dylan flew back home to Washington DC from Las Vegas), it approaches what film-makers call the 'magic hour'. This is the short period of time after the sun sets, but there's still light. It creates a beautiful glow, which makes the desert backdrop look more cinematic than normal. Zoltan convinces Jeremiah we should stop to film it and Jeremiah reluctantly agrees. So we park up in the middle of nowhere, get off the bus and make fake small talk. Zoltan keeps making us move—asking Lisa to stand here or there, to ensure we have the bus behind us, etc. 'Sweetheart,' says Zoltan to an increasingly frustrated Lisa, 'Jeremiah's camera has a range limiting what he can shoot, and it's best if we get everyone in one circle. Ava! Come here! We have just a few moments to give him exactly the kind of light that he needs. Be careful of rattlesnakes, Ava. Let's make sure we all walk into the Immortality Bus together.'

So brazenly trying to manufacture a scene in front of a journalist and a documentary maker is peculiar. And it happened more than once. On one occasion, he spoke with an interested member of the public, and then admitted to me straight afterwards that it was useful having his daughter with him, because it gave him an air of credibility even though his policies are ridiculous. On another, just before we reached Las Vegas, he said he'd broken campaign election laws, and didn't care because if he got caught it would be a good chance to write some articles about it.*

Yet even when he was trying to stage-manage events (and most politicians do), he didn't seem to care that we journalists were watching him do it. To me, this seemed

---

* 'I would be happy to break various laws, I *am* breaking various laws with campaign financing, I'm happy to admit that [referring to the bus] . . . I'm willing to take that burden myself because honestly it's just not . . . [S]omeone needs to stand up and say the FEC laws on campaign financing are absurd. An independent person can't afford to go through a 134-page legal document and work out how to do it. It's just another showing of how a two-party system is rigged to keep the little people out. My reaction is screw you, I'm going to have this campaign bus, it's going all over media and when you come to arrest me or do whatever, I'll stand my ground.'

like a dangerous thing to do, since it was possible that one of us might write about it. But Zoltan was more concerned about generating media and getting his name out there. What that media actually said was secondary. Running on such an outlandish platform, and as a rank outsider, he wagered that getting seen was more important than getting taken seriously.

But that tactic turned out to be riskier than he thought.

When we were drinking bourbon in the bus in the McDonald's car park, Dylan thought Zoltan's admission that he would probably endorse Hillary Clinton if he didn't get elected was an interesting aside. He included that in his first daily despatch for vox.com. It turned out that this was the first time Zoltan had mentioned it. People in the transhumanist community read Dylan's article, including members of the Transhumanist Party. As I flew back to London from Los Angeles, a civil war was breaking out among transhumanists over this throwaway statement, which threatened to derail Zoltan's entire campaign.

A few days after I arrived back home in London, I was contacted by a group of disgruntled transhumanists who'd spotted I was with Zoltan on his bus tour. They directed me to an article written by a man called Hank Pelliser, who was the secretary of the board of directors of the Transhumanist Party. When Hank read Dylan's article, he flipped out. Why had he, the *secretary of the party*, only found out about this vital decision via an article? Hank resigned and wrote an article entitled 'I Quit the US Transhumanist Party. Why? Zoltan's Non-Inclusive Leadership'. It castigated the party's lack of internal democracy: 'I realized that he seemed to make all the decisions, entirely on his own, apparently. There's an entity called "The

Transhumanist Party" but there weren't any strategy meetings involving me as an officer, or any group meetings, except one he hastily organized because a TV crew thought it would be interesting.'

Plenty of other transhumanists were also getting frustrated with all the media coverage Zoltan was receiving, because he was becoming the public face of the movement. They found some of his policies peculiar (such as prison drones) and thought he was making the whole movement—which prides itself on its serious, scientific claims—lose credibility. More than anything, something about the name of the party irked them. It suggested Zoltan represented the entire transhumanist movement. (And Zoltan was behaving as if he did.) This anti-Zoltan group started a petition titled 'Transhumanists Disavow Zoltan Istvan Candidacy for US Presidency'.[37] They started to dig into the Transhumanist Party paperwork, which, being a political party, must be publicly filed.

But they couldn't find anything. Because the Transhumanist Party didn't officially exist.

Before he declared he was running for president Zoltan tried to register the Transhumanist Party as a national political party, but he'd been unable to because he didn't meet the arduous Federal Electoral Commission (FEC) criteria. Not willing to give up, Zoltan registered a Political Action Committee (PAC) instead. A PAC is not a political party, but rather a simple vehicle that allows people to donate money to political campaigns. He cunningly called his PAC 'the Transhumanist Party'. He then registered himself as an independent candidate, running without a party. In short: Zoltan was running for president, but in the same way any lone individual can. But he could not do it as a candidate of the Transhumanist Party. This distinction is extremely important. Under electoral law, it is forbidden to claim to have a political party if you do not or to receive donations as a representative of a political party that does not exist. Zoltan had been doing both.

I Skyped Zoltan shortly after and asked him whether there was such a thing as the Transhumanist Party. Barely missing a beat, Zoltan fired back. 'My critics may have a *technical* point. But they are forgetting that everything that succeeds is a revolutionary party. So is the Transhumanist Party!'[38] Yes, he admitted, he'd been breaking the FEC laws all this time. 'But I'm trying to set myself up as someone who has broken laws for the benefit of Americans. I want to openly break them. I'm ready to be arrested. It's good press.'

President for Life

After I left the bus in Los Angeles, and despite the fact the Transhumanist Party didn't technically exist, Zoltan and Roen carried on. First to Arizona, where Zoltan fixed the oil leak (it was two small screws he hadn't spotted), to visit Alcor, where Max More is now the director. He went to Texas for a debate with Alex Jones, a high-profile conspiracy theorist and shock-jock who would go on to become a favorite of Donald Trump. He visited Alabama's largest megachurch (with a *Der Spiegel* journalist), where they discussed with the pastor the possibility of artificial intelligence being taken into God's grace and if bionic limbs might help disabled people get to church. In Charlotte, North Carolina, he met with John McAfee—the computer security genius who was also running for election with his newly formed Cyber Party. ('This is a historic meeting of minds of people involved in technology,' Zoltan told MSN for a short film they made on the subject.) In Florida he gave a speech at the Church of Perpetual Life, where people try to will themselves to immortality. He was pulled over three times by confused police officers, who always let him go on questioning.

As promised, in early December 2015 the bus rolled into Washington DC. He posted his Transhumanist Bill of Rights on the Capitol Building, after ignoring police instructions not to. Unfortunately it was a windy day, and the tape wouldn't keep it up. But, for a moment at least, it was there. Zoltan then took his bill of rights and delivered it to California senator Barbara Boxer's office. 'Anyway, the journey was the real purpose of the trip,' he told me, once he'd returned home. 'And the real posting is when it's posted on the Web,' which he did a few days later.

Zoltan became a smash media hit. Journalists *loved* the story. John Hendrickson covered the trip for *Esquire* in May 2015 ('Can this man and his massive robot network save America?'), as did Shane Madej for Buzzfeed ('Meet the anti-death presidential candidate'). The BBC and Vox covered it in September ('Forget Donald Trump. Meet Zoltan Istvan, the only presidential candidate promising eternal life.'); the Verge in October ('President for life: Can Zoltan Istvan beat Hillary, Trump, and death itself?'); then CNET, *Der Spiegel*, the Daily Dot, *Huffington Post*, ExtremeTech, BBC Future, IB Times, the *Daily Mail*, Salon and dozens more from all over the world. None thought to check whether the Transhumanist Party actually existed. The story of a presidential candidate driving across America in a 1978 RV Wanderlodge promising immortality was far too interesting for that. He outsmarted us all.

When the election finally came around in November 2016, a total of 1,762 individuals, including Zoltan, registered as a candidate running for president. But only thirty-one made it on official state ballot papers in at least one state, and Zoltan was not among them. People could vote for him, but only by manually writing his name on the ballot themselves. It's impossible to know how many people did: Although in Florida and New York he was one of a small number of independent candidates whose write-in votes were counted. Eighty-four people in those two states voted for Zoltan Istvan.

He might not have won the election, but he did win his wager. Aside from the Libertarian and Green Party candidates, Zoltan was probably the most visible third-party candidate in the whole election. His campaign generated more media, and reached more people, in four months than transhumanism had in the preceding decade. All it needed was a forty-foot-long coffin, a fabricated political party, breaking FEC law, a series of staged events, alienating a large chunk of his former colleagues, overly keen journalists desperate for unusual stories and, above all, a man willing to do almost anything to live forever.

Fortress Europe

Every Monday evening, thousands of men, women and children make their way through Dresden's narrow streets to its central square, the Theaterplatz. At 7 p.m., after listening to a short speech, the crowd sets off on a forty-five-minute silent march through the city. Returning to the square, they listen to more speeches and sing the German national anthem, before peacefully dispersing. The demonstrators are all supporters of Pegida—Patriotic Europeans against the Islamisation of the Occident—a nationalist, anti-Islam political movement.[1] A political group that President Angela Merkel said has 'hatred in their hearts'.

On one freezing Monday in January 2016, I was standing on the small stage, looking out at 10,000 peaceful Pegida supporters. Standing next to me were the leaders of the newly formed franchise Pegida-UK: Anne Marie Waters, Paul Weston and Tommy Robinson, the founder of the English Defence League.

It's a time of great change in nationalist circles. Faced with what they view as a common enemy—Islam—and growing levels of immigration from Muslim-majority countries, once-fractured anti-Islam and nationalist groups across the continent are beginning to get along. That morning Lutz Bachmann, the leader of Pegida, had driven from Prague, where he'd met with the heads of similar groups from Bulgaria, the Czech Republic, Estonia, Holland, Italy and Poland. Together they had written and signed what Lutz named 'the Prague Declaration', in which they all pledged to defend 'Fortress Europe' from Islam, from 'liberal elites' afraid to speak up for ordinary people and from the European Union, which is eroding national sovereignty.[2] It was a call to arms for all patriotic Europeans to put differences aside and stand together:

> Being aware of the fact that the thousand-year history of Western civilisation could soon come to an end through Islam conquering Europe, and the fact that the political elites have betrayed us, we, the representatives of different European nations, declare the following:
>
> We will not surrender Europe to our enemies. We are prepared to stand up and oppose political Islam, extreme Islamic regimes and their European collaborators.
>
> We are prepared to risk our freedoms, properties, jobs and careers and maybe even to put our lives at stake as was done by the generations before us. It is our duty to future generations . . . We refer to our common European roots and traditional values as well as historic alliances of our nations. We are determined to

protect Europe, the freedom of speech and other civic freedoms as well as our way of life together.

Paul, Anne Marie and Tommy took turns signing the declaration on the raised platform, to deafening cheers. Flags reading 'Rape-ugees not welcome' and *'Auf Deutschem boden'* fluttered and waved in the wind. Paul walked over to the microphone. 'As our numbers build our politicians will have to start taking notice,' he said angrily. 'We are not going to stand by and watch our countries slowly turn into Islamic countries. We are not going to stand by and watch our culture, history and heritage smashed before our very eyes!'

As his words were translated, a mighty roar erupted from the assembled audience. Then slowly a chant flowed through the crowd and echoed off the imposing Gothic architecture: *'Widerstand! Widerstand! Widerstand!'*

Resistance! Resistance! Resistance!

Tommy and Anne Marie joined Paul on stage and sang—or at least tried to sing—the German national anthem. The crowd applauded and began to leave. Ten thousand people efficiently disappeared into Dresden's streets, leaving an empty, perfectly clean square. It was as if no one had been here at all.

As I stood and watched Lutz pack up the small stage and sound system, Tommy said to me, 'It's not like the English Defence League, is it? I'm actually *embarrassed* when I think back to how we used to behave.'

Pegida is the face of the new far right. They aren't the jack-booted skinheads or pseudo-intellectual, race-obsessed white supremacists of the past. They are a mixed demographic, they are polite, they are orderly. They claim to be non-racist, support free speech and progressive social policies. On economic policy, they are often critical of globalisation and the effects of international capitalism on workers' rights. They claim to represent 'the people' against elites who've lost touch with ordinary citizens' hopes and fears. They want to protect national and European culture from large-scale immigration and above all from what they see as the existential threat of Islam.

Anti-Islam and anti-immigrant movements and parties like Pegida have been growing (albeit unevenly) across Europe for the best part of two decades.[3] In some countries, they are the second- or third-largest party and have even been members of or supported some conservative-led coalition governments, notably in Demark, Austria and the Netherlands.[4] Germany, perhaps because of its past, had been relatively sheltered from these trends until October 2014, when Lutz, then a forty-one-year-old nightclub publicist and owner of an advertising business, founded Pegida to protect the 'European way of life' from what he saw as the growing influence of Islam in Germany.[5] Lutz had the idea to hold a peaceful walk around the city centre every week at the same time and place. Early demonstrations were small but quickly swelled to as many as 30,000 people, with branches of the organisation founded in cities across Germany.

In August 2015 President Angela Merkel announced that Germany would accept all asylum claims from Syrians fleeing the civil war, around 1 million people entering Europe by the end of the year, most travelling to Germany. It was projected that 3 million refugees and immigrants would arrive in Europe by the end of 2017, overwhelmingly from Muslim-majority countries.[6] Pegida's numbers swelled too, but so did the number of its critics, who saw it as a dangerous strand of xenophobic nationalism and Islamophobia. Large counter-demonstrations were organised and started taking place alongside every Pegida march.[7] But Pegida continued to grow and to confound its critics. Because for every right-wing extremist and hooligan who attends the marches, there are several ordinary, middle-class, peaceful citizens.[8] Opinion in Germany is mixed: most people are opposed, but a significant minority confess to sympathising with at least some of Pegida's aims.[9]

Just after Angela Merkel's August 2015 announcement—and six months before I was in Dresden on that stage with Tommy, Paul and Anne Marie, Tommy phoned me up out of the blue. He told me Merkel would spark an 'invasion' of Muslims that would destroy European civilisation. And that he had a plan to try to stop it.

I was sceptical. I've been following Tommy Robinson ever since he co-founded the English Defence League (EDL) in 2009, when the radical Islamist group Ahlus Sunnah wal Jamaah organised a demonstration in the south-east city of Luton to protest the homecoming parade of members of the British Army. Tommy, twenty-six at the time and a successful plumber, organised a counter-demonstration, pulling together people he knew from the football-hooligan scene. He called his group the United People of Luton.[10] This quickly grew into the EDL, which became a street-based anti-Islam group that held regular demonstrations in front of hundreds of supporters. Those demonstrations often turned nasty, characterised by excessive drinking, fighting and offensive football-terrace-style chanting ('Allah, Allah, who the fuck is Allah?'). Tommy quit in 2013, as the group was riven by infighting and infiltrated by neo-Nazis, and he contemplated giving up his activism all together.

This time will be different, he insisted. He wasn't setting up another EDL-style group with its football fans and drunkenness: rather he was going to found a UK branch of Pegida. He'd been reading up on what was happening in Dresden under Lutz, and how they'd become a respectable, organised and resolute movement. He wanted to try the same thing in the United Kingdom. If politicians are to listen, he told me, we need doctors, civil servants, parents and even children to feel Pegida-UK is for them too. And to kick it all off, he said, he was planning to bring anti-Islam groups from across the continent to hold a single unity demonstration in early 2016.

It sounded very ambitious. I asked if I could follow him, and he agreed. Our first stop would be Prague, in November 2015. He was going there to meet with leaders of a large Czech anti-Islam group and Siegfried Däbritz ('Siggy'), the deputy leader of Pegida, to sell his idea to them.

That's Our President!

17 November is the most important day in Czech history, the anniversary of the Velvet Revolution. On that day in 1989 peaceful student protesters in Prague were attacked by riot police, sparking a week of mass protest that eventually led to the downfall of the Soviet-backed Communist government. The first free elections occurred in June the

following year. 17 November is a public holiday—'Struggle for Freedom and Democracy Day'—and political movements of all shades demonstrate in celebration, and wrestle over its legacy.

The most famous anti-Islam campaigner in the Czech Republic is Martin Konvička, a quiet-spoken biologist who lectures at the University of South Bohemia. In 2009 Martin had set up a popular Facebook page, 'We Do Not Want Islam in the Czech Republic', which was little known until 2015, when the migrant crisis propelled him into the spotlight. (Martin also occasionally translates books from English into Czech, including David Irving's discredited *Destruction of Dresden*.) Martin thinks Islam is a hostile, anti-human ideology, on a par with Nazism. He thinks it should be a criminal offence to publicly practise the religion. (At the time of writing he is being charged for inciting hate against Muslims, based on five status updates he posted on semi-open Facebook groups between 2011 and 2014. The legal process appears to be ongoing and he has not been convicted.*[11])

In mid-2015 he set up Bloc Against Islam (Blok proti islámu) as an umbrella group to bring together activists from any Czech political parties opposed to Islam. The right-wing populist party Úsvit joined them.† Bloc had

---

* These include calling for gas chambers to be set up for Muslims in the event of Islamic State invading Europe, saying if his movement is elected into Parliament they will 'grind Muslims down into bone meal', and calling for the 'removal of the civil rights of the 12–16 per cent of the population that sympathises with Islam'.

† According to Jan Culik, a specialist in Czech Studies at the University of Glasgow, Martin's popularity reached its climax during

teamed up with Úsvit to organise a large demonstration on 17 November to make these points, and Siggy and a handful of Pegida supporters had driven three hours from Dresden in a show of solidarity.

Milan Rohic, one of Martin's deputies, came to meet me, Tommy and Tommy's friend Deano at our hotel and escort us to the demo. Milan is a paunchy man in his early thirties, has longish hair and a wispy teenager's moustache. He's an IT specialist during the day and by night and weekends an activist for Bloc. Milan was also slightly comedic, because he laughed at the end of almost every sentence and was slightly star-struck by Tommy. 'He's the guy who started it all off!' he told me excitedly as we waited for Tommy and Deano to come down from their hotel rooms.*

The Bloc/Úsvit demonstration was technically a rally to praise the current president of the Czech Republic, Miloš Zeman. (Its official title translated roughly as: 'We support you, President Zeman.') Since being elected by direct public vote in 2013, Zeman has been outspoken against the EU, the refugee/immigrant crisis, and has likened those who believe in the Qu'ran to anti-Semites and Nazis.† Liberals in the Czech Republic say Zeman is

---

2015. But since the influx of Muslims into the Czech Republic hasn't taken place, the group has diminished, although general fear of Muslims remains. Úsvit was founded in 2013 by Japanese immigrant Tomio Okamura, and received 7 per cent of the vote in the 2013 parliamentary election and currently holds fourteen of the 200 seats in the Czech Parliament. They were allied with Bloc at the time of writing but fell out in 2016. By May 2016 Martin set up a new group called the Martin Konvička Initiative.

* I counted five people asking to take selfies with Tommy while in Prague, including Milan.

† Like many populist leaders, Zeman has a sardonic sense of humour.

a dangerous populist demagogue, but Milan thinks he's a plain-speaking hero who sticks it to the 'Prague Coffee House' set. 'Nationalism in central and Eastern Europe is different,' Milan told me as we walked toward the demonstration, carrying flags, banners and stickers. 'We have been victims of both fascism and Communism. We know what it is, totalitarian ideology. You in Western Europe don't. *You don't!* Our President Zeman knows Islam is a totalitarian ideology. That's why we've put on this demonstration, to say we support him.'

Even though the Czech Republic has very little immigration, it is one of the most sceptical countries in the EU when it comes to the subject.[12] The Czech 'national psyche' is influenced by a defensive nationalism, partly because the Czechs have historically needed to defend their relatively small community against larger foreign influences. That was visible when we arrived at the demonstration just after lunchtime. Tommy's old group, the EDL, even at its most popular, used to draw in crowds of between 250 and 3,000. Yet here, in a country of just 10 million, the scale of the demo was something else: 7,000 men and women, working class, middle class, young and old (and nearly all white). A succession of speakers—including Martin— proudly explained how the country fought off Communism and fascism—and that the EU and Islamism are the

---

On 26 May 2014 he quoted a section of the Qu'ran that says: 'A tree says, there is a Jew behind me, come and kill him. A stone says, there is a Jew behind me, come and kill him.' When criticised and called upon by the Organisation of Islamic Cooperation to apologise, his office replied 'President Zeman definitely does not intend to apologise. For the president would consider it blasphemy to apologise for the quotation of a sacred Islamic text.'

latest threats to Czech identity, outsiders trying to crush
this small but proud country's independence.

A strange rumble, a rumour, started spreading through
the dense crowd. I could feel something was happening—
the noise volume went up, people started waving their 'Fuck
Islam' flags—but not speaking Czech, we were the last to
know. Milan, once he'd calmed down, translated it to us.
President Zeman himself had decided to come and say a
few words to the crowd! Suddenly, a huge motorcade arrived from nowhere, and a frail-looking seventy-one-year-
old President Zeman climbed the steps to the podium,
tailed respectfully by a long and deferent entourage. Following one minute's silence for the victims of the Islamist
terrorist attack in Paris, Zeman took the microphone.

'Brainwashing is harder now that it used to be, but that
doesn't mean it doesn't exist,' Zeman said, in steady tones.
'We must not be silenced with insults like "Islamophobic"
or "xenophobic" or "fascist." An insult isn't an argument! It
just shows lack of thought!'

'Ha!' said Milan proudly, in between translating the
speech for me. 'This is our president!'

'And I must now turn to the immigration crisis,' said
Zeman. ('Yes!' exclaimed Milan.) 'We have no problems
with foreigners: there are half a million in the Czech Republic. But this culture is not compatible with ours. Ours
is not a culture of murder or religious hatred!' ('Ha!' said
Milan, 'that's perfect.')

'The immigrants are young men. Why are these men
not fighting for the freedom of their country against Islamic State!?' (Cheers) 'Why do they come to Europe?'
(Cheers) 'Why don't they stay to make their own countries

better?' (*More cheers*)

After a rapturous applause, it was time for the national anthem. After a jostle that resembled grown adults politely playing musical chairs Martin Konvička managed to manoeuvre himself next to the president when the music started. Milan frantically took photos, so he could post them on the Bloc's Facebook page. 'The president of the republic is standing on stage with Martin!' he said. 'Singing *"Kde domov můj"* together. Unbelievable! Haha!'*

This is what liberals fear most about groups like Bloc or Pegida. That their ideas drift into the mainstream, and in the process become somehow normal. And here was an elected head of state, a man who won 55 per cent of the popular vote, speaking at a rally partially organised by Martin Konvička, a man who once said Muslims should be ground 'into bone meal'.†

'This is mad isn't it?' said Tommy. 'Can you imagine me on a stage with the queen?'

No, I told him. I can't imagine that. But I also couldn't have imagined Zeman and Martin together, either.

Zeman's motorcade sped away, and the huge crowd dispersed. Milan took us to a nearby pub, which Bloc and

---

* This translates to 'Where is my home?'

† The following day Czech prime minister Bohuslav Sobotka and Human Rights Minister Jiri Dienstbier accused Zeman of encouraging xenophobia by attending the event. Andrew Stroehlein, European media director of Human Rights Watch, tweeted a photo of Martin and Zeman singing together. 'What would you say if your head of state shared a stage with an advocate of concentration camps and gas chambers?' (Zeman later said he didn't know these were Martin's views. Given how widely this was reported at the time, this seems unlikely to me.)

Úsvit supporters had hired for the evening, full of delighted activists. Tommy gathered Siggy from Pegida, Martin Konvička and Milan Rohic to a quiet corner in order to pitch his idea. Martin is a very slight man. Siggy is huge. The rumour is that he was once a notorious Hell's Angel, and he looks it.

Thanks to all those years of EDL activity, Tommy is still one of the best-known anti-Islam campaigners in Europe. If not a hero exactly, then definitely someone who can make things happen.

'Listen. We need to coordinate our efforts,' said Tommy to Martin, Siggy and Milan, all hunched around a small table. 'We'll be stronger if we work together. We need to show how big we are. We need one demonstration. All of us marching across Europe under the same banner: "Save our Culture. Save our Country. Save our Future." We can get the anti-Islam groups across Europe to do it with us. Will Bloc and Pegida take part?'

'Of course,' said Martin, quietly.

'This is an absolute *must*,' boomed Siggy, as if he'd never heard anything in his life so obvious. 'When?'

'Mid-February?' said Tommy. 'At the earliest. After Christmas everyone in the UK is skint for a month.'

'We can't wait that long!' replied Siggy, exasperated. 'Every single day that passes another 5,000 immigrants arrive into Germany.[13] Time is slipping through our fingers like sand, Tommy!'

They settled on Saturday 6 February. Just under three months from now. Everyone agreed that would be just enough time to coordinate it all, and make sure the Brits weren't still skint.

'But what about the UK?' asked Siggy. 'Who's going to demonstrate there?'

'We're going to set up a new group. Pegida-UK,' said Tommy. 'It's going to be respectable, like Pegida in Dresden.'*

'Great,' said Siggy. 'So you will be the leader, yes?'

'No. My wife will leave me if I become leader. I'm going to be facilitator.'

'Who's the leader then?'

'I have someone lined up,' said Tommy. 'And she's *respectable*.'

'Great,' said Siggy, who seemed satisfied.

'Right. I can have a drink now,' said Tommy, who walked to the bar and ordered himself a double vodka and lemonade.

Leadership

Now a date was settled—only twelve weeks off—everything had to move at breakneck speed. Tommy told me on the way back to London that he wanted at least twenty countries to take part. But first he needed to announce Pegida-UK to the world. The week after returning from Prague, Tommy invited me to a pub near his home in Luton, where he'd decided to record a short video formally launching the new movement, and unveiling its new leader.

It wasn't only threats from his wife that stopped Tommy taking the job on himself. He also knew that he could undermine the pretension to respectability. Tommy's violent past hangs around his neck. In 2003 he was

---

* Technically there was already a Pegida-UK, which had been founded a year earlier, although with no formal ties to the German group. Tommy told Siggy it was just a small far-right splinter group.

convicted for the drunken assault of a police officer. In 2004 he joined the British National Party, but quit soon afterwards, claiming he didn't know non-whites couldn't join. By 2005 he ran Luton FC's hooligan firm the Men In Gear, although never says much about the details. In 2011 he was convicted of 'threatening, abusive or insulting behaviour' during a mass football brawl, which he allegedly led. Several of his friends and associates have served time for possessing firearms, GBH or drug dealing. Tommy is not exactly respectable.

Soon after I arrived, I was introduced to someone who was: Anne Marie Waters, a former Labour and UKIP activist in her late thirties. She calls herself an old-school feminist who, as a lesbian in a civil partnership, claims she has much to fear personally from Islam, which she considers misogynistic.* Anne Marie writes for (and founded) Sharia Watch, a website dedicated to writing about the threats of Islam.[14]

Tommy, Anne Marie and I talked while we waited for the cameraman to arrive. Both stressed that Pegida-UK was a new departure, a decent movement of ordinary people dedicated to defending freedom from Islamism, not

---

* There is an interesting divide in feminism over the subject. Anne Marie thinks that modern feminists who ally themselves with other oppressed minority groups like Muslims are foolish, because they are promoting what she considers a misogynist religion that treats women as second-class citizens. Other feminists counter that oppressions are connected, and oppressed groups should stick together. In a peculiar example, in 2015 Goldsmith University Feminist Society declared it 'stood in solidarity' with the University Islamic Society in its efforts to silence feminist campaigner Maryam Namazie. It was later revealed that the head of the Islamic Society had posted a series of homophobic tweets.

advocating racism or violence. 'There will be no drinking at demonstrations,' said Tommy, 'that's what often leads to problems. We need to appeal to the middle classes: that's what makes politicians listen.'

'Do you think immigration is sometimes confused with Islam?' I asked Anne Marie.

'The immigration is from Muslim-majority countries!' she charged back. 'There was a 2012 worldwide poll of Muslims: 84 per cent of Pakistanis agreed with death by stoning for adultery. We can't have a society like that. We won't have it! . . . Why the hell should German women be raped by these men?! If you can't accept a German woman in a bikini then you can get the fuck out . . . I will fight every ounce if we have a war of civilisations. We should be trying to prevent it.'

Before I could reply, Anne Marie started shaking her head knowingly. 'Oh, this is the shit you lefty liberal journalists want to write about! That we're all violent racists. Well we're not,' she said.

'How do you know what I think?' I said.

'You lot are all the same.'

The cameraman, Mike, who'd been following Tommy for months for a documentary he's making, finally arrived over an hour late, and set up his kit. Anne Marie and Tommy—both respectably dressed, Tommy in his suit— sat at a table in the corner of the pub, facing the camera.

'OK, I'm filming,' said Mike.

Tommy opened: 'The reason why we're here is to discuss the launch of Pegida-UK. I'm here to introduce Anne Marie who will be leading it.'

Anne Marie turned to the camera: 'To be quite honest with you, I think it's time we *grew up*. We have got to face the reality of what is up against us. There are various different groups across Europe, but as far as I can see the only one that has clout is Pegida. There is no one better to bring Pegida to the UK than Tommy Robinson.'

Mike and I glanced at each other, both a little confused. Wasn't Anne Marie the new leader? Mike shrugged his shoulders and carried on filming. Anne Marie and Tommy took turns speaking, reiterating the threat from Islam and the need for a new respectable type of movement, where racists are not welcome and drinking is banned. Tommy was quick and to the point, but there were long pauses in Anne Marie's sections. She failed to remember the date of the demo. Her head lolled, her words were slurred and she appeared to almost fall asleep while Tommy was speaking. After ten minutes it all ground to an uneasy halt. Anne Marie was drunk.

Mike politely suggested re-filming in a day or two. Anne Marie and Tommy agreed, and Anne Marie slinked off to the toilet.

'You can't have a leader of a new party where there's no drink being drunk, Tommy,' said Mike.

'Oh fuck me. What a disaster,' said Tommy. 'You can't say stuff like that when there's a journalist around!'*

A few days later, Tommy called me to say that, unsurprisingly, the footage wouldn't be released. He had spoken to Anne Marie, who had apologised. They had agreed she would be deputy leader instead. He quickly found a new

---

* I took this section out and put it back several times while writing this chapter. Apart from this incident, I didn't see Anne Marie drunk again. Alcohol, and the role it plays in groups like Pegida is an important, but rarely discussed, aspect of how they operate. On that basis I have included it.

candidate: a former British soldier called Tim who fought in Afghanistan, and then against Islamic State alongside Kurdish militia. On 3 December 2015—two months from the big demo—Tommy unveiled Pegida-UK and Tim to the world in an exclusive interview for *Channel 4 News*. On camera Tim refused to give his surname, and then admitted it was 'Scott'. He attempted to explain exactly what Pegida-UK was trying to do: expose 'the truth of what was happening'. 'And what is the truth?' the interviewer asked. 'All that stuff to do with radical Islam.' Tommy phoned me the next day. 'Did you see that? What a car crash. Poor bloke.' Tim resigned a couple of days later.

I had no idea it would be this difficult to find someone. Finally, with time running out, Paul Weston, a former businessman in his early fifties, and leader of a small radical right-wing party called Liberty GB, agreed to take on the job. Paul left school without qualifications, but made money in property development before losing it all when the Allied Irish Bank called in its loans during the 2008 financial crisis. Aged forty-six, and penniless, Paul decided to get involved in politics because it was the thing he was truly interested in. He currently lives 'hand to mouth' in Cornwall, he told me, on donations he receives from 'American donors'.

Tommy and Paul couldn't be more different. Tommy speaks with a rough accent, wears football gear and talks breezily about 'filling in' this prick or that prick. Paul wears suits and speaks clipped RP. Tommy said Paul would lend a degree of respectability to the movement. But Paul is every bit as radical as Tommy. In the 2010 general election he was UKIP candidate for Westminster, although left the party to set up Liberty GB, campaigning on an explicitly

anti-Islam platform. (Policies include preventing any further mosques being built, and banning the Muslim call to
prayer and halal practices.¹⁵) In 2013 he released a YouTube
video entitled 'My name is Paul Weston and I am a racist', designed to illustrate, he said, the absurdity of being
called a racist for loving one's country. (His critics, such as
the anti-fascist group Hope Not Hate, argue he is indeed a
racist, and so the irony doesn't really work.¹⁶)

On 5 January 2016—now just one month before the
demo—Tommy, Paul and Anne Marie held a small press
conference in Luton to relaunch Pegida-UK (again) and
announce the 6 February demonstration. This time it
passed off without a problem.¹⁷

Copenhagen

With the date finally public, Tommy needed to start drum-
ming up media interest and introduce Paul and Anne
Marie to the ins and outs of protest politics. Both are blog-
gers and political activists, but neither had any experience
with street demonstrations. So Tommy organised a four-
day roadshow for the leadership team: first to Copenhagen
to speak at a For Frihed ('For Freedom') demonstration and
meet some anti-Islam bigwigs from neighbouring Sweden,
and then on to Dresden to sign the Fortress Europe declaration and witness a Pegida-Germany rally first-hand.

'It's a chance for Anne Marie and Paul to get a feel for
the movement,' Tommy told me at the airport on our way
to Copenhagen. In addition to the three of them, Mike
the cameraman joined us, along with journalist Tom Swar-
brick from the radio station LBC.

For Frihed (formerly called Pegida-Denmark) is run by a woman called Tania Groth.[18] Raised in Canada, she returned to her native Denmark in 2001, and became increasingly alarmed at what she thought was the slow Islamisation of the country. Tania came to meet us at our hotel, and accompanied us to the demonstration. She had arranged a two-mile silent march through the centre of Copenhagen starting from Axeltorv square and following the wide Vesterbrogade street in a long loop back to the square. There, Paul and Anne Marie would address the crowd. Not Tommy, though, because he was trying to remain in the background.

Around a hundred For Frihed supporters had braved the sub-zero temperatures. I joined their ranks, pressed up against a line of seventy or so absolutely enormous Nordic anti-riot police officers. On the other side of the police, only feet away, 200 anti-fascist protesters jostled angrily, shouting at us.

Anti-fascists are a loose collection of activists who try to disrupt, expose and counter-demonstrate against the far right. Many are peaceful, preferring non-violent demonstration and solidarity marches. But some have a reputation of attacking far-right demonstrations. Tommy Robinson is notorious among anti-fascist groups all across Europe thanks to his role in the EDL, and Tania warned us that she'd heard rumours that members of Antifascistisk Aktion, a militant Danish anti-fascist group, were planning to attack the march.[19] (I didn't know at the time, but later learned that members of AFA from all across Europe had travelled to Denmark to disrupt this demonstration.)

UK police have learned over many years of hard experience that the key to peaceful demonstrations is keeping protesters and counter-protesters apart. They do this by designating permitted 'rally' points where each side is allowed, usually at some distance from each other. I didn't realise how smart this tactic is until the Danish police opted not to use it. As our march began, around half the riot police formed a large ring around us to protect us from the anti-fascists who were walking alongside us on the other side of the ring, just feet away, screaming abuse in our direction. The street was of course shut to traffic, and shopkeepers, tourists, office workers and confused children had lined the streets to watch this spectacle. Tania told everyone not to retaliate. 'We have to remain respectable,' she said. 'All these citizens need to see who the good guys are here.'

Tommy, Anne Marie, Paul and Tania walked at the front, holding a banner which said 'Freedom'.

'You fucking Nazis!' chanted the counter-demonstrators, as they shadowed our slow progression up Vesterbrogade street.

'Say it loud, say it clear, refugees are welcome here!'

Paul and Anne Marie looked miserable. Both had determined looks on their faces, but clearly were not used to having high-grade abuse hurled at them from close range. Meanwhile Tommy, the demo-pro and expert provocateur of anti-fascists, appeared to be having an absolute blast. 'If they wanted to have a fight, they would have done something already,' he told me, cheerfully. 'This bunch are cowards!' He handed his side of the banner over and broke outside the police ring, waving and swearing at the anti-fascists, filming it all on the app Periscope.*

---

* Periscope is an app that allows for real-time video streaming that your followers can watch. It has revolutionised Tommy's life. He frequently videos people without telling them.

'Tommy are you wearing your bulletproof vest?' shouted one AFA.

'Fuck you!' Tommy shouted back, giving him the finger.

'Tommy you're a dickhead' shouted another. 'And we're going to get you.'

'Come here and say that!' shouted Tommy.

And he did, rushing at Tommy and readying himself to throw a punch. Before he could, Tommy punched him with the sort of punch that only people that have thrown a lot of punches are capable of: very precise and very hard. The AFA member listed around dazed, and the police quickly intervened, ejecting him with the help of their batons.

'Mike!' shouted Tommy, laughing. 'Mike! Mike, did you get that on camera? Hahaha. Brilliant. Fucking *bri-lli-ant.*'

Brilliant? I was standing right next to him, and at any point a big punch-up was going to erupt with me, Tommy and Mike at its epicentre. These AFA types looked angry, and so did For Frihed. If this had been the EDL, this was the cue—the welcome cue, perhaps—for inebriated demonstrators to charge the AFA, swinging punches. I was doing my best to look very visibly like a journalist, theatrically scribbling notes, taking pictures, trying to *look* neutral. But over the very tense hour it took to complete the march, Tommy's punch was the only moment of violence from the For Frihed crowd (and that was self-defence). There were repeated clashes with the police, but to my surprise it was all anti-fascists who kept trying to break the police lines and attack us. It's not always this one-sided of course.[*][20] In January 2016, for example, over 200 Legida

---

* According to one unpublished doctorate thesis (submitted in late 2016), over the years of EDL demonstrations, between the EDL

supporters (a local branch of Pegida) were arrested after they went on a rampage in Leipzig.[21] But I hadn't realised that anti-fascists—or at least groups like AFA—are often at least as violent and aggressive as the people they are opposing. They took a real beating from the giant Nordic police that day, though, who looked like they might have even enjoyed it slightly.

'Fascism' and 'Anti-Fascism'

When we arrived back at Axeltorv square, Tania grabbed the microphone and got on the steps (unlike in Prague where there was no stage, so the speakers climbed a couple of steps that led up to a shopping-centre entrance) and said she wanted to defend 'equality, liberty, democracy, security and freedom for women'.

As she said this, anti-fascists chanted 'Fascist!' at her. 'We're living in strange times,' said Paul, shaking his head.

Paul was right: This *was* strange. Tania was saying things that, on the face of it, were explicitly anti-fascist.[22] Although definitions are varied and argued over, generally speaking, fascists believe liberal democracy and free expression are decadent. Fascists are typically ultra-nationalist, believing in racial superiority and embracing violence to achieve a 'rebirth' of a mystical, racially pure, past society. These groups do exist of course, like the Aryan Strike Force, Combat 18 and the National Front. And some of them are growing. In Greece's 2015 general election, the

---

being founded and Tommy's departure, there were a total of 1,551 arrests made, of which around 400 were counter-demonstrators.

quite openly fascist party Golden Dawn finished third, with a respectable 7 per cent of the vote.[23]

But this is not the ideology of groups like Pegida. Yes, racists and fascists do sometimes turn up to their marches—sympathisers of the defunct German far-right terrorist group National Socialist Underground have been seen at Pegida demonstrations in the past—but Pegida is not a fascist movement.[24] Even calling it 'far right' is too simplistic.[25] In fact, most Pegida supporters see themselves as *anti*-fascists standing up to Islamist totalitarianism. The speeches I heard, whether here in Prague or later in Dresden, usually contained the antithesis of fascism: support for free speech, liberty, democracy and gay rights.* Pegida supporters believe they are engaged in a historic struggle over Western culture, identity and values that they believe are under serious and real threat from Islam. Pegida supporters see themselves as 'realists', as people who have the courage and integrity to ignore politically correct elites who are afraid of speaking up about Islam.

Try telling a Pegida supporter that he's 'Islamophobic', exaggerating fears and unfairly demonising a whole religion. You'll always get the same answer. They always reply that their fears are not *phobic*, but a perfectly rational response to events they are seeing. And they are armed with statistics to prove it. I put it to them that a 2015 ComRes poll found 90 per cent of British Muslims approved of the British way of life and 95 per cent were loyal to the country.

---

* Consider the names of many of the groups that share Pegida's ideology. 'For Frihed' translates to 'For Freedom', as does Geert Wilders' anti-Islam party, the PVV. The Swedish Democrats, the Danish People's Party, even Pegida itself: they are names that progressive, moderate liberals would be proud of.

They replied that the same poll said 27 per cent had 'some sympathy for the motives' of the people who attacked the *Charlie Hebdo* office.[26] I cited a 2016 poll which found that 86 per cent of British Muslims felt a strong sense of belonging to Britain, which is more than the national average of 83 per cent. But it also found that over half believed that homosexuality should be illegal.[27]

The internet provides Pegida with an endless supply of stories to bolster their canon—a bottomless treasure chest of stories that portray Muslims in a negative light. Tommy is information-sharer-in-chief, a reservoir of tales, a digitally networked millennial.[28] Whenever I was with him, he'd regularly scan Twitter for stories that he could share with the over 100,000 people who follow him. On Tommy's Twitter feed on 21 May 2016, a day I picked at random, he shared stories about: a doctor who had written prescriptions telling patients to follow Islam (from the *Metro*), a church minister who had been investigated for tweeting about Pegida (Breitbart), the European Court of Human Rights ordering the UK Home Office to pay £14,000 compensation to an Iranian sex offender because it took too long to deport him (the *Sun*), a Swedish journalist who had told the press that he wasn't allowed to write anything negative about immigration (Spesia), three imams in High Wycombe accused of preaching hate (bucksfreepress.co.uk), French terror suspect Abdeslam refusing to speak to judges (the *Daily Mail*), fifty-seven workers with access to runways and airports being on a watch list as potential extremists (*Evening Standard*).

It's like this, all day every day. And these stories aren't made up, nor do they come from fanatical underground blogs or rabbit-hole forums. A decent number come from respectable, mainstream news outlets, and are reporting things that really are happening. According to Joel Busher, an academic embedded with the EDL for sixteen months, supporters use certain 'frames' to make sense of all this, tagging particular phrases onto each anecdote: the 'incompatibility of West and Islam', 'cultural Marxism' controlling public life, a 'two-tiered' system set against the white British. That transforms one-off stories into explanations of the perceived injustices they face and are used to unlock meaning and stimulate emotional responses.[29]

Any positive stories about Islam, those that can balance or lend perspective to isolated incidents, are simply washed away in a sea of negativity, or framed as propaganda or liberal journalists refusing to accept the truth.[30] Academics call the tendency to find or interpret information that confirms our existing beliefs 'confirmation bias', and it is hardly new. But the Net magnifies this effect, since it's now far easier to find anything you already believe, and surround yourself with it 24/7.[31] What I didn't hear from Pegida supporters were the following stories, the stories that I see regularly: that it was a British Muslim, Nazir Afzal, who, as chief crown prosecutor for the Crown Prosecution Service in North-West England, pursued grooming gangs, honour killings and female genital mutilation more vigorously than anyone else; that British Muslims give the most to charity of any group in the United Kingdom; that British Muslims overwhelmingly work with the authorities to stop Islamist terrorists; or that it was Muslims Women's Network UK who have been calling out the 'systematic misogyny' of Muslim men in the British Labour Party, and on and on.[32] Or the fact that, far from being silenced, Tommy himself has been on almost every single television and radio programme of any note. It doesn't matter. Pegida supporters are able to find enough credible information to construct and sustain an intelligible and coherent world view that mixes genuine facts and anecdotes with frames, narratives and emotion to paper over any inconsistencies or tensions.

It's lazy and simplistic to call Pegida supporters racist, ill-informed bigots. The people who do so not only misunderstand them; they risk making the problem worse, because it provides Pegida supporters with the ammunition that the liberal elite are trying to silence them. The problem with groups like Pegida is more subtle. They have a tendency to tar all Muslims with the same unfair stereotypes, often in an intentionally inflammatory way, and do not apply their 'defending Western values' message consistently.

Tommy wasn't meant to speak at the Copenhagen rally. But after Tania had finished her speech he climbed up onto the little steps in front of the shopping centre, took the microphone and pledged to defend freedom, to defend Europe from people who 'refuse to integrate' and complained about the AFA.

But he couldn't stop there. He would also defend Europe from 'the visual scars of minarets', from the 'sounds of call to prayer' and from 'halal food'.

Things get said in the heat of the moment. But the generalisations made by Pegida supporters, and often leaders, and the way they are expressed turn Muslims into 'the other', the 'not-like-us'. (In 2016 Lutz Bachmann— the Pegida boss from Dresden—was found guilty of inciting racial hatred in Facebook posts, in which he called refugees 'cattle', 'scumbags' and 'filth'.[33]) They lump in millions of ordinary, law-abiding, decent Muslims—surely natural allies in fighting the extremism they claim to fear—with terrorists, disloyal crypto-extremists and sex offenders. When the Labour politician Sadiq Khan—a Muslim—was elected London mayor with a strong majority in May 2016 Tommy said he 'found it very hard to trust' him.[34] Khan is a respected human rights lawyer by training with years of experience in front-line politics as a Labour politician. But Tommy tweeted 'what comes first to Sadiq Khan, the interests of Islam or London? We all know the answer to that.' Tommy then mistook Sarah Joseph (who wears a hijab) for Khan's wife (who doesn't) and suggested Khan had forced her to adopt it.[35] This was, I think, definitely an irrational fear of Islam.

In the end most Pegida supporters feel, deep down, that Islam is not compatible *in any form* with Western values. That is at odds with the anti-fascist principle of religious liberty, freedom of conscience and the overarching belief that people should be judged based on what they think and do, not what religious group they belong to. Paul Weston told me he doesn't think Muslims should run for political office because their allegiance will always be to Islam rather than the country.[36] British Protestants used to make this argument about Catholics. In fact, Paul openly admits that discriminating against the majority of innocent Muslims because the minority are extremists 'is a price worth paying'.[37] No anti-fascist would say any of this. In addition to being extremely unfair and illiberal, this also stokes up general anti-Islam feelings, and perhaps (it's impossible to know for sure) even Islamophobic crime, which is increasing.[38] Anders Breivik had 'liked' the EDL on Facebook back in 2010 and praised the group in his 'Manifesto' (but he said they were insufficiently hard-line). In 2014 EDL supporter Ryan McGee was jailed for two years for making a nail bomb and promising to 'drag every last immigrant into the fires of hell'.[39]

Tommy, Lutz, Tania and others told me that they can't control everyone who might turn up to demonstrations or follow the group online, and that they make efforts to re-move actual Nazis when they do turn up (which is usually true).* We can't be held responsible when a couple of ex-tremists turn up, they said, or if people commit violence and claim to do it in our name. That's true, although when I spoke to them, they never seemed to accept the same line of argument when Muslims said the same about the terrorists.

These F***ing People!

The last few pages probably won't win me many friends. Suggesting these people are not all racist scumbags, that they understand themselves to be anti-fascists, that their information world is different to mine and that they some-times have a point does not go down well in polite soci-ety. The correct description of Tommy Robinson and those like him is ignorant, fear-filled racists who hate people who don't look like them. Strangely, this is usually most forcefully expressed by people who pride themselves on their tolerance, openness and moral rectitude.

---

* Nazis turned up at the first EDL demo, and although Tommy forced them to leave and even released a video burning a Swastika, they kept coming back. Tommy has probably had more fights with neo-Nazis than most anti-fascist supporters.

Most, although not all, supporters of groups like Pegida-UK (and the EDL) are drawn from the white working class. Fifty years of peace, wealth and mobility have allowed a greater diversity in lifestyles and values in the United Kingdom. Large-scale immigration, including from Muslim-majority countries, has enriched many communities, powered the economy and made Britain a far more interesting and open place to be. But its positive effects haven't been felt evenly. The communities where new immigrants live, the poorer parts of town, were typically the places where they would first arrive, which placed pressure on whatever limited public services or housing was available, along with creating, for some at least, a sense of bitterness and loss.[40] Gone are the settled communities and secure manufacturing jobs of the 1960s and 1970s. While many are better off, large lumps of the white working class are now a precariat class reliant on short-term, unreliable work, living in rented accommodation, without transferable skills, with low (and falling) wages and few prospects.[41] White men are also, by some margin, now the least likely to do well at school or go to university compared to other ethnic groups of similar economic background. They are looked down upon as a minority underclass.[42]

Tommy was born in 1982 and spent his young years in Farley Hill on the outskirts of Luton, which he remembers as a working-class neighbourhood with a strong sense of community. But things were changing quickly. By the 2011 census, Luton was one of only three towns in the United Kingdom that were white minority, and one in four residents declared themselves Muslim. Many people in Luton welcomed the growing diversity. But Tommy's memories are dominated by fights between British Asian youth and white youth in the town. ('British *Muslim* youth,' Tommy insisted. 'It was never the Sikhs or Hindus. Only the Muslim lads.') Serious and sustained racism in many UK towns was endemic in the 1970s and 1980s. When Tommy was growing up, young British Asians, unwilling to put up with the racist abuse their parents had received, started fighting back.[43] A flashpoint occurred in 1995, when a friend of Tommy's uncle, Mark Sharp, was murdered by a gang of British Asians who were given only four years in prison. It caused enormous tension at the time, and is still talked about by locals.[44] Tommy claims someone he knew well was the victim of grooming by a group of British-Pakistani men, which cemented his view—which hasn't really changed since—that in the end Muslims will always stick together against non-Muslims.

In the mid-2000s Tommy's home town of Luton had a reputation as a hotbed of Islamist radicalism. 'Magnificent 19' posters had been found across the town after the 9/11 attacks; and the extremist group al-Muhajiroon had set up base there, and would spend Saturday afternoons leafleting in the town centre. In 2004, shortly after the Beslan school massacre in Russia, Tommy organised a protest entitled 'Luton Taliban: No Thanks' and asked the police to close down al-Muhajiroon's Luton offices and stop their recruitment.[45] The EDL might have become a national movement, but its roots are the very real integration problems in Luton. A fast-changing town, and, on the streets, often quite a divided one.

There used to be political parties that would represent people like this, where these worries might have a respectable political outlet. But by the early 1990s the Labour Party had signed up to a 'progressive' consensus better suited to the swelling number of university graduates and metropolitan liberals who voted for it: pro-diversity, pro-immigration, pro-technological change, pro-globalisation. Its MPs increasingly shared this outlook too.[46] Over the last two decades the working class has abandoned the Labour Party. Perhaps that's why left-wing journalists and MPs—the people one might expect to want to help this underclass—treats them with such derision: it's a form of subconscious guilt.[47] If they didn't dismiss them as a bunch of stupid racists, they would be forced to feel some form of moral obligation towards them, which would be a nuisance. 'Try arguing with facts' wrote the perplexed *Guardian* journalist Polly Toynbee in June 2016, on meeting people planning to vote to leave the EU, 'and you get nowhere.' What *idiots* these people must be! Perhaps they deserve what's happening to them!

Journalists routinely adopt a sneering and patronising tone towards groups like Pegida, and sometimes they get caught out. Tommy and his followers are frequently told they are too hateful, confused and stupid to have learned the basic facts about the religion they supposedly fear so much. Nothing infuriates them more than being told Islam is a religion of peace, because, they are told, the Qu'ran says 'if you have taken the life of one person, it's as if you've taken the lives of all mankind' (verse 5:32). The Qu'ran does indeed say that, and it is a powerful verse. If I quoted that to Pegida supporters, they had the next verse (5:33) ready to fire back at me: 'Unless they have caused mischief in the land, then they can be executed, and have their hands and feet cut off, and exiled from the land.[48] In February 2016, an Al Jazeera presenter quoted violent parts of the Old Testament to Tommy, pretending they were

from the Qu'ran. 'When you hear those quotes,' he asked
Tommy, 'what do you think that speaks to?'

'I'd ask you why you're reading the Old Testament to
me,' replied Tommy immediately. 'I'm not stupid.' Pegida
supporters *loved* that.

The disconnection between left-wing politics and
white working-class attitudes, in particular on issues of
national sovereignty, social liberalism, immigration or economic openness, is producing new political alignments
across Western democracies.[49] When the United Kingdom
held a referendum about its continued membership of the
European Union in the summer of 2016, the Labour Party's official position was to remain. But huge swathes of
the white working class voted to leave. A similar dynamic
is taking place in the United States too, where large numbers of the white working class, traditionally Democrat
because of its pro-worker and pro-union stance, are drifting away from the party, feeling it has become culturally
distant from their lives and their concerns. As I discuss in
Chapter 5, with the story of Beppe Grillo, this is in part a
rebellion against a professional political class that speaks
its own PR-honed language. But it also reflects a fundamental rift within many left-wing parties that now seek to
represent both a socially and economically liberal graduate class and a less liberal blue-collar working class. The
two groups' interests don't always align, and most political
leaders—well-educated liberals themselves—are more at
ease with the language, politics, lobbying groups and ideas
of the progressive wing. As a result, billionaire right-wing
politicians with economic policies that won't help them,
like Donald Trump, can attract millions of working-class

voters who feel forgotten with the right language and identity-based promises. That a billionaire has been able to successfully position himself as a man of the people should shame liberals. It's an indictment of their stunning failure.

Left-wing Labour leader Jeremy Corbyn joined the anti-Pegida-UK demonstration on 6 February, marching under the banner 'We Chose Hope.' He was joined by local Labour MP Liam Byrne who said 'We don't want our [community] threatened by racists.'[50] Jess Phillips MP called Tommy's plans a 'costly hate rally'. Racists. Idiots. Not a frustrated group of people who find, in the flag-waving and chanting, some reclamation of power in a system that ignores them. Not a group of derided people for whom the bravado and aggressive patriotism is something they can feel some pride in. Not a set of citizens who have become politicised and are, even if I think they are misguided in their targets, getting involved in politics for the first time in their lives, and so should at least be given a hearing.[51] Heaven forbid it might be any of those things. They're just hate-filled racists. So it's a good job we abandoned them. Look at what these idiots think after all!

'Je M'Appelle Top Dog'

When Tommy got off the steps in Copenhagen the demo was over. Almost immediately the police started to leave, which left us surrounded by angry-looking AFAs. Tommy, Tanya, Mike the film-maker and I ran to the nearest taxi and asked the driver to take us to our hotel, via a detour, to avoid being followed. One AFA in his midtwenties rushed at our taxi and tried to get in. 'Lock your doors!' shouted the driver, and screeched off, leaving the AFA stumbling over as he tried to hold on to our door handle.

'You just saved that guy's life,' said Tommy.

'I'm a Muslim,' replied the taxi driver. 'I read about Pegida. Do you hate me?'

'Of course I don't,' said Tommy. 'I only have a problem with *radical* Islam. Are you a Salafi Muslim?'

'No, I'm just an ordinary Muslim.'

'Of course I don't hate you mate,' said Tommy, and shook his hand. The driver didn't seem convinced.

When we arrived back at the hotel, two police officers were guarding the hotel entrance, having been tipped off that AFA were now roaming the streets looking for us. The two officers were still there in the morning, and at Copenhagen airport when we left the following day.

Police at hotels? Charging demonstrators and screeching taxi wheels? Detours? Yes, these people are frustrated by how the world is changing, and they believe they need to defend Western culture. But there's something more. This trip was also a social occasion, and the adrenaline rushes were addictive. For a group of people who feel underrepresented and powerless as the world changes around them, Pegida offers the chance to be transformed from an insignificant nobody into a heroic warrior fighting a mortal enemy, a chance to put yourself into a historic struggle of Western civilisation against its foes. Just like the Christians had done in 1683 at the gates of Vienna when they pushed back against the Muslim Ottomans. There is a thrill that goes with being part of something bigger than yourself: a sense of purpose, of excitement, of belonging. This is an especially powerful draw if you feel, as many Pegida supporters do, otherwise helpless in a changing world.

You rarely read this in the accounts of anti-Islam protests, which are usually portrayed as mean-looking skinheads angrily pointing and shouting vitriol. (There are a small number of identical stock photographs that are used in the media when reporting on these groups, and they're always angry men.) Miserable affairs full of miserable people. But that's not the dominant feeling from the inside, where camaraderie, backslapping, excitement, shared stories and general messing around prevails. It's a given that Tommy is charismatic—you have to be to run groups like this—but he's also a prankster. He laughed and joked the whole trip, and constantly poked fun at everyone, especially Paul. Even when things were going disastrously wrong, he made light of it, and never once asked me not to include anything in this chapter. He found the debacle of Anne Marie's leadership announcement utterly hilarious. Whenever there was a story about him in the news, he read it to us on his phone, chuckling.*

Because these trips are social events, they usually involve alcohol. In that quest for respectability, booze is often banned during demos. (In Prague, Copenhagen and

---

* I'm a non-Muslim man, which of course helped a lot when researching this book. It's far easier for me to blend in, to feel part of this community. When the journalist Hsiao-Hung Pai—whom Tommy prank-called—spent time with the EDL, she said it was 'surprisingly easy' to get them to speak to her, but did sometimes feel they were trying to manage their image. I suspect that Paul would not have talked to me in the same way if I were a practising Muslim.

Dresden there was no alcohol. Tommy partly blames alcohol for having ruined the EDL.) Therefore drinking usually took place immediately after the marches. Everyone has their own drinking style, and Tommy's is enormous one-off benders. We all have at least one friend like him: fun for three drinks and on the fourth gets the glazed eye, on the fifth becomes belligerent, then refuses to stop drinking and refuses to go to bed.

The day after the Copenhagen demo Tommy, Paul, Anne Marie and Tania were due to meet with Lars Hedegaard and Ingrid Carlqvist—two veteran counter-jihadist journalists from Sweden—to discuss the possibility of starting a Pegida-type group there.[52] Film-maker Mike and I waited for Tommy in our hotel lobby to walk to the restaurant with him. Tommy wandered in, calm as you like, a full hour late, reeking of booze. He'd forgotten to put his clock forward, and was clearly still half-cut. The reception phone rang. The receptionist had stepped away so Tommy reached over and answered it: 'Bonjour! Je m'appelle Top Dog. J'ai quinze ans,' and hung up laughing.

When we arrived at the lunch following a meandering walk across town, Tommy was too distracted to speak about serious business. Lars Hedegaard, who lives under twenty-four-hour police protection after being attacked by an Islamist in 2013, said he expected to see the disintegration of nation states within five years and anti-Islam vigilante groups protecting secular enclaves of Western liberalism. This sounded interesting and I wanted to ask more questions, but Tommy kept referring to me as 'the left-wing journalist', ordered a flaming Sambuca, made a prank call on speakerphone, and repeatedly pretended to Periscope everything.

Anne Marie drank slowly, and in moderation. Paul was also drinking slowly, but steadily. He never appeared drunk, but he must have been since he drank with impressive regularity.

From Copenhagen, we all flew to Prague, and from there took a train to Dresden for the big Pegida rally, and where Paul, Anne Marie and Tommy all signed the Prague Declaration in front of thousands of cheering Germans. The following morning we did the reverse trip: taking the train from Dresden back to Prague so we could fly home. Paul cracked open a large can the moment we boarded the train. As we rolled into Prague two hours and four beers later, Paul mentioned this trip was the first time he'd been back to the Czech Republic since fleeing the country in 1999 after being arrested and imprisoned, having spent eight years working there as a property developer.

What were you doing, Paul?' I asked.

'I was caught drink-driving,' he said, 'after finishing a bottle of absinthe with one of those worms at the bottom.'

'Are you happy for me to print that?' I asked. Anne Marie was shaking her head. Tommy had his mouth open, gobsmacked.

'Of course I am! Any bloke who has a problem with that isn't ordinary,' said Paul. 'I just paid £50 to the police officers, who were always corrupt.'

'So how did you end up in prison then?' I asked.

'Oh that wasn't for drink-driving,' he replied, sipping on his beer. 'I was *ramming* into police cars. I broke out of prison by climbing out of my cell window. But then I remembered they still had my passport, so I had to break back in again.'

'Jeeeeeeesus Christ, Paul!' said Tommy. Everyone fell about laughing, even Anne Marie.

Birmingham

Only people who've been involved in organising demonstrations know how much time and planning is necessary to get even a few hundred people on the street at the same time. Behind every exhilarating public demo is an unseen desert of tedium: sorting security, police liaison, coordination meetings, making flyers and banners, preparing speeches. And although technically not the leader, Tommy was doing nearly all of it. As 6 February drew closer, and in between his new day job (fixing repossessed houses and selling them on) Tommy was phoning Paul, Anne Marie, Siggy, Milan and Tania frequently, making sure preparations were set. The trips to Prague, Copenhagen and Dresden were a success, and more anti-Islam groups from the Netherlands, France, Poland and elsewhere were signing up to take part in the demonstration. In late-January Tommy dashed over to Ireland and back to help launch Pegida-Ireland. On his Twitter feed and the new Pegida-UK website that message of respectability was repeated over and over: no drinking, no chanting, no violence. This is a movement for everyone.

Pegida-UK decided to hold its demo in Birmingham, hoping its central location could bring in people from all over the country. Tommy spoke with East Midlands police and agreed it should be held in a non-Muslim part of town to avoid trouble, at a business park near Birmingham International Airport. Pegida-UK supporters would meet outside Birmingham International train station and then walk to a rally point. The main anti-fascist counter-demo (entitled 'Never Again') was held ten miles away, near the city centre. The night before the demonstration Tommy stayed up until 2 a.m. making posters. He was nervous about whether it would be respectable, and whether enough people would turn up.

Having seen first-hand how much time and effort went in to pulling this off, I was almost nervous too. For all Tommy's many faults, it is hard not admire his indefatigability. Being a leader of a group like Pegida-UK is a lot harder than people think. It's not easy being called a racist, or being attacked by AFA activists. It's not easy dealing with the multiple death threats he's received (some of which led to a police Osman warning—meaning a credible threat to life, forcing him to move home), or having your children targeted by radical Islamists. The way Tommy has been treated by the police appears, on the face of it, outrageous. He's no angel, and during his time leading the EDL he broke the law repeatedly. So it's not surprising that many people—including the police—see him as a bit of a thuggish troublemaker, especially given his links to football hooliganism. But that doesn't mean Tommy shouldn't be granted the same civil rights as everyone else. He's been arrested and released a staggering number of times, and often when strangely close to marches he was planning. He's had all his bank accounts frozen and was sent to prison for mortgage fraud in 2013 based on a loan he made several years ago and from which no profit was made. He has been arrested and acquitted (or released without charge) for assaulting a police officer, for obstructing a police officer, criminal damage, burglary and for assaulting a prison inmate. It appears to me that there has been a sustained and deliberate effort by the police to use prosecutions and charges to cause the maximum amount of disruption to his life and activism.[53] Civil liberties groups don't seem to care about this, though, because no one wants to be associated with Tommy Robinson. But nothing seems to phase him.

When I arrived at Birmingham International train station early on Saturday 6 February, in the torrential rain, I carefully checked the crowd of about 300 that had gathered outside the train station ready for the march. Although there were some familiar faces from the EDL days, it was slightly different, somewhere between an EDL demo and the more respectable Dresden strolls.* 'Fewer than I'd hoped for,' said Paul Weston, a little disappointed. 'But it's a start. And it's *not* the EDL.'

The day of protest started in Australia, where 250 people attended a 'Reclaim Australia' event held in Canberra, outnumbering the forty or so counter-protesters. There were no arrests.[54] In Prague, Milan, Martin and 2,000 supporters of Bloc/Úsvit demonstrated and 'clashed' with pro-migrant groups. In Denmark around a hundred people marched with Tania. So did anti-fascists, but this time without trouble. Eight thousand turned out in Dresden, fewer than the 15,000 they'd hoped for.[55] (Siggy told the crowd Germany needed to take back control of its borders.) In Calais, a couple of hundred defied the ban on public demonstrations following the Paris terrorist attacks, leading to several arrests.[56] One hundred and fifty people demonstrated in Dublin but were outnumbered by counter-protesters, and they were attacked by anti-fascists,

---

* Steve 'Eddowes' ran Tommy's bodyguard team—as he did while Tommy ran the EDL, and other known 'faces' were there: Alf Polwin, Jeffaz Carr, Marty Bradley, David Coppin and others.

who hospitalised Identity Ireland leader Peter O'Lough-lin.[57] One hundred Pegida supporters showed up in Amsterdam (they'd hoped for 500) and around twenty were arrested, mostly anti-fascists.[58] The Pegida-Graz event in Austria managed about 500 people, but 5,000 turned out to counter-demo.[59] In Bratislava just over one hundred marched, a few hundred in Tallinn, Estonia, and about 150 in Helsinki.[60] Two thousand people attended a demonstration by the Ruch Narodowy ('National Movement') party in Warsaw, Poland, but the Pegida-Polska event in Wrocław was cancelled when the far-right Radical Nationalist Camp threatened to sabotage it, calling it a 'German import'.[61] The day of protest was certainly international, but attracted only 15,000 people in total.

'Oi everyone!' shouted Tommy from the front of the procession, where he held a home-made banner with Anne Marie and Paul. 'No talking on this walk until we get to the rally point.' We all trudged along one mile in the driving rain towards the business park: sober, peaceful and nearly silent, surrounded by at least two dozen journalists. We arrived at the rally point and there was a small raised platform for the speakers. Anne Marie, Paul and Tommy all gave speeches. There is a problem with Islam. It's a form of fascism, inimical to the West. We need to fight it, to stand up against it because the politicians don't listen to the people.

But even if politicians did listen, I'm still not quite sure what Pegida would actually tell them, apart from to stop immigration from Muslim-majority countries, and perhaps ban any new mosques being built. There is a vague desire to protect 'traditional culture', but what that actually is was never clear to me. They want Muslims to integrate more, but exactly how they're supposed to do that—especially when they are being singled out and shouted at—was never really explained. It's all emotion and indignation. Feelings rather than a set of demands, and feelings are almost impossible to satisfy.

The final speaker was Tommy, even though he wasn't technically the leader, who declared that Pegida-UK would be following Germany's example and demonstrating every first Saturday of the month. We will be the respectable face of the anti-Islam movement, he promised. 'We're planting the seed of something huge,' he said. 'Next time there will be twice as many.'

Tommy had succeeded: The demonstration *was* respectable. There was no chanting, no boozing and everyone behaved well. The only arrest of the day was from the anti-fascist demonstration. But it was too respectable. Compared to our adventures in Copenhagen and Prague, Birmingham felt a bit sullen. The media didn't really cover it, because nothing much happened. Tommy's old group, the EDL, was popular not in spite of the drinking, the swearing, the chanting and the ever-present possibility of a fight with anti-fascists, but *because* of those things. The EDL was a day out, a buzz, just like in Copenhagen. That was enough to persuade a few hundred people every other weekend to spend their own money and time travelling the country, braving the weather and marching. Scuffles and clashes may have undermined the movement, but it also guaranteed media coverage that drew in new recruits.

Caught between the desire for respectability and the need for people to turn up, Pegida-UK petered out. The next demo was early April and Lutz Bachmann himself flew in to address the crowd. But the crowd hadn't doubled, it had roughly stayed the same. The one after that—in Rotherham, the town notorious for child-abuse scandals involving men of Pakistani origin—only managed about 150. By the summer of 2016, Paul and Anne Marie began to focus their energies on other methods of fighting what they see as the Islamisation of Europe. Tommy also told me that he wasn't planning to spend much time on Pegida-UK either. Within six months of starting it was all over. Pegida-UK had failed.

But then everything seemed to change again. In June 2016 the United Kingdom voted to leave the European Union, laying bare the cultural gulf that had opened up between the white working class—people like Tommy— and the leaders of the left wing in the United Kingdom. For some voters at least it was a chance to register anger at politicians who had ignored or patronised them for years. It also resulted in a spike in anti-Islamic crime, and renewed fears that xenophobia was on the rise.

A few months later saw an even bigger victory: Donald Trump was elected as president of the United States. His unlikely win was helped along by a new and very disparate political movement loosely called the 'alt-right', which combined several of Pegida's ideas with internet trolling culture, libertarian attitudes on free speech and, for some supporters, white supremacy. During his campaign, Trump said things that would not have been out of place at Pegida rallies, including a pledge to stop all immigration from Muslim-majority countries, until elected officials can 'figure out what the hell is going on'. (In fact Pegida supporters often carried placards that read 'Donald Trump is right.') 'Thank you America, thank you Donald Trump,' Tommy said, the day after his election. 'You've given us all a fighting chance.' In August 2015, when this all started, the right-wing, Euro-sceptic German political party Alternative for Germany was polling around 5 per cent. By late 2016 it was 15 per cent.

Pegida-UK had gone, but many of its ideas—the belief that Islam is in some ways a threat to Western democracies, that liberal politicians and journalists are too ignorant or scared to speak up and say so—had become mainstream. Many things worked together to make that happen: significant levels of distrust towards what some perceived as 'establishment press'; the general popularity of outsider candidates; genuine concerns about levels of immigration and terrorism; years of real or perceived frustration about being 'silenced'; many years of unfairly negative stories about Islam in much of the mainstream media and a new outlet in social media that allowed for the creation of self-reinforcing bubbles of belief that could be quickly and easily shared. But it was also helped, in a small but definite way, by the restless activism, belief and energy of people like Tommy Robinson.

In January 2017 Donald Trump signed an executive order suspending the entire US refugee admission system for 120 days, and banning citizens from seven majority-Muslim countries—Iran, Iraq, Libya, Sudan, Syria, Somalia and Yemen—entry to the United States. At the time of this writing, it's difficult to predict where this will lead. Pegida might be misunderstood, patronized and lazily smeared as a bunch of ignorant fascists and racists, but that doesn't mean their ideas are harmless, or that their desire to defend Western values won't be twisted by others to promote illiberalism or xenophobia. Tommy celebrated the United Kingdom leaving the European Union and Donald

Trump's election, but so did David Duke, former Grand Wizard of the openly racist Ku Klux Klan, who said he has 'the same message' as Trump. 'We have the moral high ground, 100%,' tweeted Duke the day after Trump's win.

Are you happy with how this went? I asked Tommy as he walked off the stage in Birmingham. 'Yes!' he replied. 'This is just the start!' And although he didn't know it at the time, he was right.

The Trip Report

"If the doors of perception were cleansed every thing would appear to man as it is, infinite. For man has closed himself up, till he sees all things thro' narrow chinks of his cavern."

William Blake, *The Marriage of Heaven and Hell*

In the summer of 1960, Harvard psychology professor Timothy Leary was holidaying with a group of friends in the Mexican town of Cuernavaca, when a local acquaintance asked him if he'd like to try magic mushrooms. Leary was intrigued. A couple of years earlier he had read a 1957 article in *Life* magazine, which recounted the American banker Gordon Wasson taking 'sacred mushrooms' during a Mazatec ritual in a remote Mexican village and going on a mind-bending trip.

Sitting in his swimwear by the pool in the glorious sunshine, Leary ate five or six black mushrooms picked from the nearby mountainside, and sat back. One of his group, a man named Bruce, abstained in order to take notes. As the mushrooms kicked in, Leary observed time and space start to change, everything seemed connected and the world came alive with colour. Leary looked over at Bruce, diligently writing his observations, and burst out into hysterical laughter. The states of consciousness Leary was experiencing were so outside the norm, so ineffable: How could Bruce possibly describe them?[1]

Fifty-six years on, I am sitting in a circle with twenty-one other people, in a secluded wooden lodge just outside Apeldoorn in the Netherlands, with pen and paper at the ready.[2] The recently founded Psychedelic Society has rented the lodge and grounds for the weekend so no one will be disturbed. It's a very carefully picked location: peaceful, scenic and with lots to do. Its three buildings give on to a sizeable and tasteful patio, which merges into an enormous garden, complete with pond and hot tub, which in turn backs on to a forest. There is a 'chill out' room, a loud music area outside, a painting room, even a volunteer chef, ready to feed us anything we might like. Stephen Reid, the quiet-spoken and thoughtful founder of the Psychedelic Society, the brains behind this inaugural 'Psychedelic Weekend Experience', the convener of this 'opening circle', the Tim to my Bruce, is holding up two bags of what look like mouldy mushrooms. The reason we are here.

'This is fifteen grams of vacuum-packed truffles, which contain twenty-five milligrams of psilocybin,' he says, in a semi-reverent tone. 'And I have some good news!' he adds, smiling. 'Peter, who runs trufflemagic.com has given them to us for free, because he's very excited about our project.'

Tomorrow lunchtime each member of the circle will be given one bag of these Class A psychedelic drugs, which would normally cost about £15, and go on a mind-altering trip, just like Leary's. A handful of sober facilitators, including Stephen, will watch to ensure the trips are as safe and positive as possible. And I'll be sober too, a twenty-first-century Bruce.

Psychedelic drugs—such as psilocybin, mescaline, ayahuasca (which is a preparation of dimethyltryptamine, or DMT) and lysergic acid diethylamide (LSD)—induce altered mind states: mood changes, perturbations, visual hallucinations and changes in perception. They are frequently associated with the 1960s hippy counterculture, with 'turning on, tuning in and dropping out', with Jefferson Airplane and Deadheads, with New Agers feeling at one with the universe.

But Stephen believes they're much more than that. He thinks that when taken carefully, with what he calls 'intention', psychedelic trips provide life-changing spiritual experiences that can reveal an underlying truth about the nature of reality: 'It's something that you can't really describe, but only feel. It's a core realisation and experience of unity. The unity of all things,' he says. It can have a profound effect on how you see the world and your place within it. It can improve your well-being and help you deal with any difficulties in your life.

A growing number of people agree with him. Between 2013 and 2016, at least thirty psychedelic societies were set up in the United States, Mexico, Spain, Israel, the Netherlands and elsewhere. There is a small but fast-growing business in ayahuasca and peyote 'retreats' in Peru and Mexico.

Approximately 3 million Brits have tried psychedelics at least once in their lives, and the number is increasing. This includes celebrities, who credit the drugs with all sorts of personal benefits. According to the US National Survey on Drug Use and Health, psychedelics are as common now as they were in the 1960s: approximately 17 per cent of all American adults admit having used them once, and there was little difference between the baby boomers and those currently aged between twenty-one and twenty-five.[*3]

One of the little bags travels around the circle. Each person cautiously feels it, and as they do, they explain what they hope to get from the weekend. Paolo, a youthful sixty-five-year-old yoga instructor and office worker from Birmingham, says his job has been getting him down—he's passing retirement age—and he's been worrying about what's to come. The trip, he hopes, will help him work this all out.

Sarah, a twenty-one-year-old student from London has been struggling with her family relationships. 'I'm hoping this experience will help me resolve some of these issues,' she says.

Jake, an artist in his midthirties, says he takes psychedelics to help him deal with anxiety and depression. Three years ago he was addicted to psychiatric medication. He credits psychedelics with helping him to stop. 'Psychedelics quite literally saved my life,' he says. He doesn't see the weekend as fun; he sees it as work. 'They're

---

* Not just predictable celebrities like Sting, either. Others include: Angelina Jolie, Steve Jobs, *South Park* creators Trey Parker and Matt Stone, Shia LaBeouf, Susan Sarandon, Lindsay Lohan, Frances McDormand and Tim Ferriss.

a tool for growth. This weekend is a means of personal development.'

The bag finds itself in the hands of a bearded greying Swedish man in his fifties called Alexander Bard, who calls himself a philosopher. Alexander is also currently a judge on the Swedish version of *Pop Idol*, where he is known for his harsh criticism. He's taking the truffles as a creative aid (he's writing a new book).

Floppy-haired London consultant Jon says the drugs made him a nicer person. 'I used to be a Tory before I took LSD,' he says, to laughter. Most are in their twenties, are all healthy, and all but one have taken psychedelics before.

A correspondent from a major UK newspaper says he wants to write about psychedelics, and has convinced his editor that he needs to take a trip in order to write about it properly, and that the major UK newspaper should pay for it, which it did. When the bag reaches me, I say I'm also here on a research trip but won't be taking the drugs.

Stephen suggests that everyone should take one bag, which equates to a trip of about six hours. This Weekend Experience isn't about getting high, he tells us. It's a very deliberate and thoughtful exploration of inner space. 'It will be insightful and profound. But don't expect it to be pleasurable in the conventional sense. Expect to learn something. It's often enjoyable, but there are sometimes difficulties.'

Most drugs—legal or banned—have a set of understood and fairly predictable effects. But psychedelics aren't like other drugs. They depend to a large degree on what's called the 'set' (the psychological 'mindset' that a user has) and the 'setting' (the surroundings in which they are taken), which means their effects can vary wildly from one individual to the next, even from one trip to the next. Although psychedelics aren't addictive or toxic to the body, and there is little evidence of serious long-term effects on users, around 20 per cent of UK adults who've taken them say they've had periods of prolonged anxiety and fear.[4] If people feel uncomfortable, unhappy or suffer from serious mental health problems, psychedelics can be dangerous.[5] Three months before our Experience, a twenty-six-year-old British man, Unais Gomes, was killed at an ayahuasca ceremony not unlike ours.

That's why the Psychedelic Society have tried to create a welcoming, safe and positive atmosphere for our experience. Everyone filled in a consent form before coming.[*] And to get us in the right mindset, in the days leading up to the trip we all met in a secret Facebook group, where Stephen posted some recommended reading: *The Book* by Alan Watts ('explaining man's role in the universe as a unique expression of the total universe', says the blurb) and Tao-te-Ching, the foundational text of Taoism, an ancient Chinese philosophy that emphasises naturalness, simplicity, spontaneity and 'non-action'.

This is the first Weekend Experience. We are Stephen's guinea pigs. If it goes well, he tells the circle, he'll put them on regularly. Perhaps every two weeks. Four hundred people have already expressed an interest, and that's just from the Psychedelic Society's sizeable mailing list.

---

* 'I am taking these psilocybin-containing truffles of my own volition. I acknowledge that no substance is entirely risk-free, and that I am familiar and comfortable with the risks of psilocybin truffles.'

He hopes that one day thousands of people every week will experience 'a sense of the profound, the mystical', and perhaps even change their lives with drugs.

Leary

The word psychedelic comes from the Greek *psyche* (mind) and *delos* (to make visible). Naturally occurring plants or mushrooms with these characteristics have long been used in traditional communities, usually for religious ceremonies or medicinal purposes. Native American cultures have used San Pedro cactus (which produces mescaline) since as early as 8,000 BC; while rock paintings from 7,000 BC portray mushrooms as the 'flesh of God'. Some academics have even speculated that psychoactive fungi caused the emergence of religion in prehistory.

Despite their long history, psychedelics' introduction to Western culture is remarkably recent. Both LSD and psilocybin were first 'discovered' by Western scientists in the 1940s and 1950s. The Swiss chemist Albert Hoffman first synthesised LSD in a lab in 1938, thinking it might be a new type of stimulant. Five years later he accidentally ingested some while re-synthesising it, and went on a very powerful trip, which he later described as 'an uninterrupted stream of fantastic images of extraordinary plasticity and vividness and accompanied by an intense kaleidoscopic play of colours'. Soon after he also isolated the active ingredient in magic mushrooms, psilocybin.[6] Pharma companies hoped these strange, but perfectly legal, new substances might have some commercial uses and started producing the drugs and shipping them to academics, scientists and psychiatric hospitals keen to test their effects.

Investigator-in-chief was that highly respected psychologist from Harvard University, Timothy Leary, who'd won acclaim for his work on how to spot personality patterns. His experience in Mexico was a life-changing moment: He later said that single trip with Bruce taught him more about how the mind worked than his fifteen years of studying psychology. It seemed to Leary that by inducing hallucinations and emotions, psychedelics were the key to the human subconscious, far more powerful than slips of the tongue or dreams.[7]

Leary rushed back from Mexico to Harvard to study the drugs seriously. And so did dozens of other academics—especially psychiatrists—who began testing the effects of psychedelics under careful clinical and scientific settings. They gave psilocybin to people with obsessive-compulsive disorder, depression, autism, schizophrenia, alcoholism and terminal-cancer anxiety. They gave LSD to perfectly healthy artists and scientists to study creativity and spirituality. Although not rigorous by today's standards, these early studies showed incredible promise: alcoholics were miraculously cured, manic depressives showed drastic improvements, those with anxiety suddenly felt calm. In 1962 one of Leary's students, Walter Pahnke, gave twenty healthy volunteers who'd never taken psychedelics before a dose of psilocybin. Almost all of them reported having a 'spiritual experience'. Even twenty years later many said it was one of the most meaningful things they'd ever done, and had shaped their lives in profound ways.

Psychiatrists had never seen anything like it. The working theory was that psychedelics were some kind of change agents acting on the brain and the individual psyche. In a supportive psychotherapeutic setting, the drugs seemed to stimulate the development of insight into the mental and behavioural processes that contribute to conditions like anxiety, depression and alcoholism. Often accompanied with emotional catharsis, a clear mental space was then 'left', within which the patient could, with the guidance of the therapist, incorporate new and more adaptive ways of behaving and interacting with the world.[8] The strange changes in perception could also spur bouts of creativity and provide meaningful spiritual experiences. Such was the potential that the US government spent $4 million on 160 studies involving LSD between 1953 and 1973, while the UK government ran tests on soldiers to see what affect it might have on their ability to conduct military operations.[*]

What to do with these 'wonder drugs' divided expert opinion. Some, like Aldous Huxley—who had written *The Doors of Perception* about his own experience on mescaline, the active ingredient in peyote, which he took in 1953—thought it should be subject to very careful and rigorous academic examination.[9] Psychedelics, worried

---

[*] The US military had been researching the drug extensively as part of its unconventional warfare projects, including a programme code-named MK Ultra. For a while they thought it might be a 'truth drug'. The British Army also spent money trying to research LSD, under a secretive project called Operation Moneybags. It did not go very well. One solider gave up on his equipment and climbed a tree to try to feed a bird.

Huxley, give access to 'contemplation that is incompatible with action and even with the will to action, the very thought of action'.[10] If too many people took them, they would do nothing else but sit around doing nothing. Others, like the beat poet Allen Ginsberg, took a very different approach. Ginsberg had taken mushrooms with Leary in 1960 and had a profound experience: He declared it was time to start a 'peace and love' movement. He told Leary that these drugs shouldn't be the preserve of academics and intellectuals like Huxley. Psychedelics, he thought, could be the motor of a social revolution that would lead to a new era of peace and harmony.

After Huxley died in 1963, Leary—and his close colleague Richard Alpert (who later changed his name to Ram Dass)—drifted closer to Ginsberg's view of the world. Some of his experiments began to resemble recreational drug binges, for which he was eventually sacked from Harvard. Released from academia's shackles, Leary started to see himself as a spiritual prophet. He tried (and failed) to set up a psychedelic summer camp in Mexico, and in 1966 founded the League for Spiritual Discovery, to 'change and elevate the consciousness of every American within the next few years'.

Ginsberg's and Leary's ideas were taking root in fertile soil. Psychedelics were fast becoming the drug of choice for the counterculture movements sweeping America at the time. The Beatles, Bob Dylan, Ken Kesey and the Merry Pranksters, Jack Kerouac, the Doors (named after Huxley's book) were all getting high, and writing and singing about it. Civil rights activists were getting high. Anti-Vietnam protesters were getting high. Conservative America didn't like it. In 1966 California became the first

state to outlaw psychedelics, at which point Leary gave up
any remaining academic pretences and gave his famous
'Turn on, tune in, drop out' speech, urging people to join
the 'psychedelic revolution'.* Thousands of Americans followed the advice, but they weren't taking drugs in a careful clinical setting accompanied by seasoned guides: they
were dropping tabs at parties and festivals. Horror stories
of 'bad trips' started to appear in the media, and in 1968
the federal government outlawed psychedelics across the
whole country. President Nixon declared war on drugs.
Leary, he said, was 'the most dangerous man in America'.

In 1971, under pressure from the US government, the
UN categorised psychedelics as Class A drugs, meaning
the most dangerous to the user. And despite those promising academic studies, they were also placed in Schedule 1,
which meant they were deemed to have no medicinal uses,
so could not be prescribed or easily tested by researchers.
Much of the world followed suit, including the United
Kingdom. Interest in and money for psychedelic research
dried up, and was soon forgotten. With a few exceptions,
scientists working in this field grudgingly accepted the
new laws and ceased their experiments.†

It lay dormant until the mid-1990s, when a group of
'psychedelic elders' met at Esalen, a spiritual-retreat centre

---

* The meaning of this speech was slightly misunderstood. Leary was
  referring to the way in which the drugs should be taken. It was not
  a call to 'drop out' of society, although that is how it was seen (and
  what some people did). Tuning in was to pay attention to the set and
  setting, turning on was to take the drug and then drop out of negative behaviour patterns. This speech took place in San Francisco at
  what he called 'the gathering of the tribes for the first human be-in'.
† In the 1970s, Leo Zeff ran (illegal) group trips in Chesapeake Bay, of
  around ten to twelve people tripping and three 'gurus' staying sober.

in California. They were convened by a man called Bob Jesse, a senior vice president at the technology company Oracle, who had an interest in spirituality and wanted to reignite the academic study of psychedelics. After that meeting, Jesse was put in touch with Roland Griffiths, a respected professor of psychiatry and neuroscience who had an interest in consciousness, and Bill Richards, a psychologist known for guiding people through trips in the 1960s.[11] In 1999 the three of them secured academic approval to administer psilocybin to thirty healthy volunteers in a clinical setting for the first time in two decades, and see what affect it had on their attitudes and life. When the results came back, the slightly sceptical Griffiths was astonished. 'Almost unbelievable,' he told me over the phone from Johns Hopkins University, where he is still a professor. 'I'd never seen anything like this in other studies with other drugs.' A full year after the trial, 30 per cent said taking the psilocybin was the single most significant experience of their entire lives; 70 per cent said it was one of the five most meaningful things they'd ever done.

When they published this paper in the *Journal of Psychopharmacology* in 2006, a new generation of researchers started digging up the original studies, rerunning experiments and designing new ones to test what else these drugs might do. Over the last decade or so, there has been a steady increase of serious academic studies into psychedelics' effects. LSD has been shown to reduce anxiety levels, and also effectively treats addiction and depression. Ayahuasca has demonstrated significant reductions in depression symptoms: patients experienced—on average—a decline in depression symptoms of 62 per cent after just one dose. Ibogaine, another psychedelic compound drawn from the roots of an African shrub, has been found to help people overcome addiction. Richards', Griffiths' and their colleagues' latest work, published in 2015, found psilocybin to greatly reduce anxiety among people diagnosed with terminal cancer, and to be an effective aid to quitting smoking. (Their study of fifteen lifelong addicts found that one year later, eight had still given up.) Researchers at Imperial College London found equally impressive results using psilocybin on people with depression for whom other treatments hadn't worked. MDMA, which is considered by some a psychedelic at very high doses, has been found to reduce common post-traumatic stress disorder symptoms such as anxiety, paranoia, nightmares and depression by over 75 per cent, even three to five years after treatment. More studies—including phase-two clinical studies on the effect of MDMA on post-traumatic stress disorder—are underway.[12]

Remarkably some studies have even shown that psychedelics might change your personality, increasing your score on what psychologists call the 'openness' domain, which encompasses aesthetic appreciation, imagination and tolerance of others' viewpoints.[*][13] In short, more liberal. In Roland Griffiths' landmark 2006 paper—the study that reignited psychedelic science—participants who had the 'mystical experience' showed significant increases in

---

[*] Openness is also thought to be a good predictor of creativity, which is why LSD is so often associated with music. Steve Jobs said taking LSD was one of the two or three most important things he'd ever done. (The interesting overlaps between the early computer scene and psychedelics are brilliantly documented in John Markoff's 2005 book *What the Dormouse Said*.)

their openness scores. Another study, from 2011, found nearly 60 per cent of those who'd taken psilocybin just once reported an increased desire to travel, to listen to new music, to reconnect with family, to read new books, and not to shut themselves off from change.*[14]

Many of these studies are relatively small, sometimes involving just a dozen or so people. And there are lots of technical difficulties in doing good science. When academics like Roland Griffiths administer psychedelics in their lab, participants are put through a strenuous series of tests: they are carefully screened for any mental health problems, given professional psychiatry sessions before and after, and even receive a carefully curated music playlist (which includes songs by Brian Eno). During the trip itself, participants are always attended by two professional 'guides'.† Their 'best practice' guidelines for conducting this sort of research cautions against giving hallucinogens to people at risk of psychosis or certain other serious mental disorders. And their effects are so uniquely identifiable

---

* At the very least, there may be some kind of two-way relationship: People with higher levels of openness, or more open to the prospects of self-development, appear to get more out of their experience; and the more people get out of their experience, the more open they become. The way to really test this would be to give LSD to people who had very low openness scores, under a perfect double-blind randomised control trial. This would be exceptionally difficult to do for lots of reasons.

† At Johns Hopkins, one of them is often Bill Richards. He told me that 'Sometimes, some monster will appear in people's minds. I tell them to go toward that mental image. I tell them to say "Hello monster," you know? "Are you scary, what are you made of? Why are you here? What can I learn from you?"' Richards says that if people decide to run away from the monster they can develop paranoia. 'And they might well end up in a psychiatric emergency room.'

that finding a believable placebo is practically impossible. (Some have used Ritalin, but it's not ideal.) Nevertheless, what scientists call 'the effect size'—how much they seem to improve the condition—are unprecedented. A GP giving you LSD is still a very long way off, but this is one of the most exciting aspects of modern psychology and medicine.[15]

But just like in the 1960s, it is proving difficult to keep these drugs in the lab. They're too powerful.

Stephen

In the summer of 2011, when he was twenty-five years old, not long out of Oxford University, Stephen tried psychedelics for the first time. He was at the Shambhala music festival in the English countryside, and a friend gave him the drug 2-CB, which is like a mix between LSD and Ecstasy. Like so many before him, Stephen's trip experience was profound. He sat quietly on his own for hours with eyes closed, in 'a vast infinite world of colour and pattern', he recalls. 'Even though my eyes were shut I felt a sense of connection with the stars.'

The experience got him thinking. Nine months earlier he and a dozen others (including Danni Paffard, from Chapter 7) had set up the anti-austerity direct action group UK Uncut, in response to revelations that the telecommunications company Vodafone had paid very little corporation tax following an agreement with Revenue and Customs. Sixty people—including Stephen—occupied and shut down Vodafone's flagship store in central London later that month, followed by Boots in January 2011,

Fortnum & Mason (where Stephen was arrested for trespass, but later cleared) and several banks. Each demonstration was bigger than the last, and by mid-2011 it was the most visible campaign group in the country.

'I thought that drugs were my private life, and climate activism and anti-austerity was my political life,' Stephen says. But 2-CB had made him feel a strange new connection with other people and the environment. Over the next three years, Stephen started researching, and carefully taking, psychedelics.

He increasingly felt that a spiritual malaise was at the heart of many of the world's problems, a result of the alienation that comes from being what Alan Watts in our required reading *The Book* calls 'an ego in a bag of skin'. We feel separated from the earth, which is why we trash it. We feel separated from each other, which makes us miserable and competitive. Modern capitalism has atomised us, turned us against each other. In 2015 Stephen set up the Psychedelic Society, and slowly drifted away from his old activism. 'Sometimes people need join the barricades,' he told friends at the time. 'But there needs to be a spiritual dimension as well.'[16] More than just an addled change of perception or a warm feeling of unity, Stephen increasingly felt psychedelics could provide a route (just one of many; meditation is another) into what he called 'non-dualism'.

Dualism is the philosophy of seventeenth-century French thinker René Descartes, who argued that the mechanical body and the immaterial mind are fundamentally different, and made of different things, operating in different spheres. Non-dualism by contrast is an approach to understanding the world with roots in both Hinduism and Buddhism, which sees all things as connected, that 'the universe and all its multiplicity are ultimately expressions or appearances of one essential reality'.[17] Non-dualism is almost like the philosophy of the psychedelic state: an elusive idea that cannot be explained. It just *is*. The universe *is*. I asked Stephen to describe non-duality, and he replied that it is '*this*'. (Even more frustratingly elusive is the fact that non-dualists also reject a description of their own philosophy, because it would mean there would be a description and a not-the-description. 'It can't be truly described,' says Tony Parsons, a leading non-dualist thinker. 'You can't get it right or wrong. There simply is only what is and is not . . . that's it.'[18]) I've described it as best I can, and I still don't understand it. Maybe that means I do understand it. But the core of it seems fairly simple: There isn't really a 'me' and a set of things that are 'not me'. Rather, we are all part of a single consciousness. That consciousness is not something that is generated by the grey matter between your ears, but is everywhere. Psychedelics, thought Stephen, seem to dissolve the taker's perception of the primacy of the self. It not only improves their own well-being, but, through that strange feeling of unity and oneness, others' well-being too. 'Once you see that separation is an illusion,' he told me, 'then it often leads to people living more empathetic, more giving lives.'*[19]

Stephen started spending much of his time organising events, conducting research and lobbying for a change in drugs law. When the UK government announced its

---

* The writer Jonathan Rowson has recently set up a new research institute, Perspecteeva, suggesting a 'spiritual turn' is necessary in politics, one that appreciates relationships, experiences and time, rather than consumption. Although he hasn't mentioned psychedelics.

Psychoactive Substances Bill in summer 2015, which clamped down on a number of so-called 'legal highs' (drugs that mimic the effect of illegal narcotics), Stephen realised that his battle would not be won. What he really wanted, ultimately, was for people to experience what he felt at the Shambhala festival. So why not just head to a country where psychedelics were not banned?* Psilocybin has been illegal in the United Kingdom since 1971. Being found in possession can land you up to seven years in prison. But in the Netherlands the truffle form is still legal.[20]

The Trip

The morning after our opening circle, under bright winter sunshine, we all convened in the beautiful lodge garden in front of a twelve-foot-tall wooden door frame. 'That's meant to symbolise Huxley's door,' said a very relaxed-looking Stephen. 'It's an invitation to people to take the experience seriously. I think people can get more out of it that way.' Paolo—the yoga instructor—was wearing a poncho and was carrying a small frame drum. The artist Jake was holding the biggest wooden recorder I'd ever seen (technically a Native American flute, he later told me) and a Tibetan singing bowl, which is a metal bowl you chime

---

* The design of the Weekend Experience is remarkably similar to that described by Leo Zeff, who ran similar—illegal—experiences in the 1970s and 1980s. There were also around a dozen people, sober 'gurus', something close to an opening circle where intention was established (although Zeff did not like having 'circles' as he felt it put too much pressure on people). Stephen seems to have arrived at this model independently of Zeff.

with a stick to create a soothing ring. Jon, the London consultant, was wearing skin-tight leggings covered in pictures of cats. He said he was planning to spend most of the time in the hot tub, reflecting.

We gathered in another circle for some final words of advice from Stephen: drink some water and eat lots of fruit. You might feel nauseous for a while, he said, but that will quickly pass.

I was slightly nervous, because although the Psychedelic Society had gone to considerable effort to make this safe, there's no way to eliminate the risk that people might have very negative experiences.[21]

'If at any point you're feeling slightly weird or having a difficult moment,' Stephen reminded everyone, 'just let one of the facilitators know, and we'll help you through it.'

Stephen and the three other sober facilitators stood ceremoniously and solemnly by the gate, handing out the vacuum-packed bags of truffles along with the juice and some chewing gum, to help with the nausea. Each person took their supplies and walked through the door. Stephen bonged his bell, which was also Tibetan.

'Here goes,' said Paolo, looking a little nervous, chewing. 'No going back now!' Within five minutes, everyone was through the door of perception and standing around in small huddles, talking excitedly, swigging juice, and asking each other if it's 'kicked in' yet. (Are you feeling it yet, not yet, I'm not sure, are you feeling it, I think I'm feeling it, etc.)

They were lounging around in the sun when the drugs began to take hold. The trippers started to become acutely aware of textures and colours on previously unremarkable objects, which seemed to be invested with deep significance. The blades of grass, the patio wall, the hot tub, the lampshade in the kitchen area, the twelve-foot-tall wooden frame: what miracles of nature! How *meaningful* they all are! Time started to feel irrelevant, even non-existent. A moment that lasts a few seconds seemed to drag on for aeons.

Paolo was walking alone by the flowerbed next to the gravel patio, quietly beating his little shamanic drum. He was radiating joy, staring intently at everything, as if he was seeing for the first time.

It's hard to know what sort of questions to ask people when they're tripping. I was worried that saying the wrong word might send them spiralling into an internal hell. Keep it simple, I thought.

'Does everything look different?' I asked Paolo.

'Everything is moving. The colours are freshly painted,' he replied, pausing between words, grasping for an adequate superlative. 'The sky is the most beautiful blue you could . . . ahhh. It's just . . . wonderful. It's . . . beautiful.'

He was looking up, shaking his head in awe. As he lowered his gaze, he gasped: 'Those trees! Each of the leaves is taking on a life of its own. They're all waving at me. They're . . . they're *laughing* at me! They're saying to me: "You're not doing our beauty justice."'

Artist Jake was sitting on the lawn, clinging to his Tibetan bowl and wooden recorder, chanting 'ommmmm'. He was, he said, experiencing 'a union of the senses', 'seeing every blade of grass, pebble on the ground, cloud in the sky for the very first time'.

One hour in, we reached summit point. By now the trippers had dispersed. A handful headed for the hot tub

(Jon spent the entire day in there, emerging occasionally looking shrivelled). A group of three danced to music in the field. Paolo wandered off to the forest where for an hour 'I played my drum for God. Or God played the drum for me. And we met somewhere in the middle.' Stephen and the facilitators wandered around, handing out food, checking in on people.

Psychedelic hallucinations can either be simple or complex. At lower doses people see geometric patterns, colours, flashes of light. There is often distortion of the senses, and inanimate objects come alive. A wall looks like it's breathing or melting or flowing like a river. At higher doses, hallucinations can include landscapes, memories, dragons, plot lines, visions.*

For some still unknown reason, Fibonacci spirals and intricate geometric patterns are often visible on everyday objects. One tripper, a hippy-ish woman called Maura, slipped off to the bathroom where she stood motionless in front of a mirror staring at her face, which was covered in mathematical-looking geometric lines. 'It was quite amazing,' she said. 'Sacred geometry. Beautiful, amazing.'

But the most profound aspect of a trip, and the reason the trippers are all here, is that feeling of connection. The trippers started to tell me, independently, that boundaries between them and every other *not-them* thing was melting. Even the possibility of there being a difference between them and things that were not-them started to seem

---

* When Valentine Wasson, the wife of Gordon Wasson, who wrote the *Life* feature in 1957 that had inspired Timothy Leary, took part in a magic-mushrooms ceremony in Mexico in 1955, she claims to have witnessed a full Regency ball at the Palace of Versailles.

slightly absurd. Filters that condition how they saw the world in the sober state dropped away. Paolo was on his knees, caressing an exceptionally average-looking plant. 'I can see how it's connected, how it's part of nature, the mosaic of its structure is connected with me, my body, with everything. There is no matter, really. There is no difference between me and this plant. There is no "I." There is just oneness with the universe. It's amazing. It's really fucking great. It's hard to find the language.'

I am aware how ridiculous this all sounds. And as someone who'd never done psychedelics before, I was finding it difficult to describe an experience that everyone kept saying could not be put into words. But many trippers, over many years, and in different places, have described this sense of unity in surprisingly similar, if ungraspable, terms. A feeling of transcendence. An ineffable and yet overwhelming sense of connectedness and existence. A mystical experience. Huxley described it like a revelation: 'the glory, the infinite value and meaningfulness of naked existence . . . an obscure knowledge that All is in all—that All is actually each'. Neither agreeable nor disagreeable, he wrote. 'It just *is*. Is-ness.'[22] This sensation is seemingly so untranslatable that people are reduced to strange uses of nouns, pronouns and verbs: it's *being*, *be-in*, it's *it*, it's *this*, it's *is*, it's *is-ness*. Our words, they say, explain the 'normal' state of consciousness—there simply isn't the shared vocabulary to describe this new realm.[23] (Maybe that's why very few writers have been able to get close.) It was all too much for the correspondent from the well-known UK national newspaper. Instead of writing, he spent six hours alone in his room, where he learned, he later told us, that 'is *is*'.

Freed from the neurotic boundaries of thought, perhaps we are free to have the deeply personal experiences that some refer to as so beneficial, and perhaps the brain is free to rebuild the links between perceptions and conceptions in ways that are not so likely to lead to maladaptive patterns of behaviour (such as smoking cigarettes, or depressive ruminations).

In 2014 researchers at Imperial College London injected thirty volunteers with psilocybin and scanned their brains using magnetic resonance imaging (MRI). Rather than turning the brain on, psychedelics appear to switch important parts of it off, changing which bits of the brain talk to each other.

Our senses are overwhelmed with information from the external world. A part of the brain called the thalamus has the job of filtering it down to a more manageable amount—enough to help our distant ancestors stay alive. The thalamus acts like a relay control room in which messages come in and other messages go out. In the psychedelic state the thalamus more or less goes to sleep. This allows the brain to make all sorts of new connections and experience new perceptions.[24] What Huxley called 'the measly trickle of everyday consciousness' turns into a flood of images, sensations and hallucinations.

Another part of the brain, the default mode network, is also unusually calm in the psychedelic state. This is what's called a 'high level' realm of the brain, most active when we are engaged in meta activities such as self-reflection, planning or daydreaming. Neuroscientists suspect this is where our sense of self, Freud's ego, comes from.[25] The Imperial College MRI scans showed that, while tripping, this network also becomes very restful, like the thalamus. The ego, it seems, temporarily switches off. Scientists think that this might explain why the boundaries between the self and world, the subject and object, Paolo and those trees, all seem to dissolve. Without ego, there are no boundaries. That's the 'oneness' everyone was talking about.

That oneness is behind the miracle medical studies too. The positive results people report are not a result of the chemicals of the drug. When eaten, it takes about forty minutes for the psilocybin to enter the bloodstream at which point it turns into psilocin and then is thought— no one is sure exactly—to bind to the brain's serotonin receptors, mimicking serotonin's effects of well-being and happiness and disrupting the brain's visual processing system. But these effects wear off after a few hours, and the chemicals leave the body after twenty-four hours. The magic is in the trip itself. Experiencing a feeling of unity and oneness seems to make people view the world, and their place in it, differently.[26] 'There's something about the sense of the interconnectedness of all people and things, the sense of unity, sacredness, that gives people a renewed sense of perspective and, more importantly, self-efficacy,' Roland Griffiths told me, admitting that it doesn't sound very scientific. One theory is that conditions like depression trap people in a very rigid and sometimes cyclical frame of mind. When the ego switches off, these thought patterns can be reset, like shaking a kaleidoscope, which could then make it more sensitive to change, or at least some kind of other therapy. But no one is entirely sure. 'The truth is,' Griffiths explained, 'we don't really have a scientific explanation.'

The Other Side

Five or so hours after walking through the wooden door of perception, the trippers' thalamuses and default mode networks slowly got back to work, boundaries started to re-appear, the hallucinations became less intense and every-day objects started to lose their shine and wonder. People drifted indoors exhausted. Paolo went to bed. A handful listened to a lecture. Not all the boundaries returned. A couple of trippers stayed in the hot tub, getting frisky.

Huxley said in *The Doors of Perception* that the person who walks through the door never comes out quite the same. The next morning I asked everyone how 'profound' the trip had been for them. Three people said the trip was the most profound thing they'd ever done; seven said it was one of the most. Three people said it hadn't been—but all of them said other psychedelic experiences had been. The correspondent from the well-known UK newspaper said the trip was 'up there with the birth of my children as things that have changed my conscious-ness'. He had felt 'an absolute undeniable truth about the true underlying nature of the universe'. Paolo said it was incredible—those plants really had been communicating with him. Artist Jake said it felt like he'd had 1,000 hours of therapy. The Swedish philosopher and talent-show judge Alexander spent three hours under his duvet cover, con-fronting demons, which he said was 'fantastic' and that it had produced a 'creative surge' that will form the basis of his next book.

The weekend finished as it had started: the twenty-two of us in a circle, this time describing and discussing our experiences. Everyone seemed to have got a lot from it. I heard the same things repeated: that simply *being* was the truth. That *existence* was the glorious revelation. 'I've learned not having to do anything to validate *myself*,' said Maura. 'Not to anyone else, and not to *myself*. I just have to *be*.' We all murmured in satisfied agreement. Sarah said she'd learned love was everything. 'I feel so charmed, to feel love. What else is there?' she said. Everyone nodded sagely. In that secluded field in the Netherlands, it did all feel sort of true too.

But it was hard to work out how much was the drugs, and how much it was the people themselves. Everyone on the Weekend Experience appeared to share a very similar world view: socially liberal, environmentally conscious, anti-capitalist. The whole weekend, like so much of psychedelic culture, was steeped in Eastern philosophy (Tibetan singing bowls, yoga, meditation, enormous wooden recorders, etc.) rather than Abrahamic religions or Western scepticism. Did they take psychedelics because they were all like that, or had the drugs made them that way?

Whatever it was, the Weekend Experience had meant a lot to the people who were part of it. But it was a small, carefully selected group. And bringing psychedelics to the masses is not without its problems. Shortly after the Weekend Experience, Stephen posted on the Psychedelic Society Facebook page that he was now taking group applications.[27] At the time of writing, a hundred people had registered. Stephen hopes, one day, to see religious-medical psychedelic centres, retreats modelled loosely on the way American Indians use peyote: to help ill people get better and encourage healthy people to develop spiritually.[28] According to the Psychedelic Society's website, the aspiration is that by 2023 you could walk into a pharmacy and pick yourself up LSD, 2-CB or psilocybin with nothing more than the pharmacist asking some questions 'to ensure you understand how to take the substance safely'.[29]

As psychedelics become more popular, and I think they will, the harder it will be to maintain a safe and friendly setting. Stephen is aware of the risks and told me he will do whatever 'seems necessary and appropriate'. He also says repeatedly that psychedelics aren't for everyone. But taking psilocybin in a field with a group of people you don't know that well is probably not the best way to do it. And if use does become more widespread, as Stephen hopes, it is inevitable that people will take them, as they did in the 1960s, at festivals, at parties, mixed with alcohol, surrounded by strangers, by people in the wrong frame of mind. For some people, that would be catastrophic.*

Nevertheless, I left Apeldoorn with my own revelation: that the psychedelic experience, as felt by Albert Hoffman, by Huxley, by Leary, by Stephen and by everyone on the Weekend Experience, can clearly be profound and meaningful when it's done in a supportive, careful setting. Perhaps there's a scientific explanation, like the brain's information filter coming off, or our mind trying to find meaning in random visual stimuli. Stephen thinks

---

* Even though the scientists are a little worried, I think they are also quite sympathetic to what he's doing. Jay Stevens in *Storming Heaven* (p. 56) recounts that even the cautious Huxley was ambiguous about this. Although he thought psychedelics should be best treated as a scientific and academic endeavour, 'who, having once come to the realisation of the primordial fact of unity in love, would ever want to return to experimentation on the psychic level?' He thought there should be scientific tests, 'but it would be wrong if there were nothing else'.

it unlocks some far deeper and mysterious truths. (Some people are so taken in they speculate far less plausible and impossible-to-scrutinise theories about parallel universes, stoned apes and 'spirits of the plant'.[30]) Maybe it's something else entirely. Does it really matter? Psychedelics can help people with mental health conditions, and can provide an all too rare opportunity to expand mental horizons or simply touch the mystical in a world where growing numbers of people think life is 'meaningless', and stripped of its mystery.[31] The Psychedelic Society is the vanguard edge of a quest that many of us are on in one way or another, and have been for millennia: to find meaning in our lives and the world around us.* 'There is a very human desire [to] transcend every day consciousness' Stephen told me. 'For the last few hundred years, in much of Western society at least, that desire was met by organised religion. But nothing has replaced it.' Materialism and consumerism hasn't offered any long-term fixes—and the result is a spiritual gap in many people's lives. In a 2012 Pew Research Center survey, 19 per cent of Americans said they were not religiously affiliated, but of those, 58 per cent said they often feel a 'deep connection' with nature and the earth; and 30 per cent said they believe in spiritual energy.[32] One in five British adults say they have 'spiritual

---

* 'We have no evidence that Moses munched on magic mushrooms as he climbed Mount Horeb,' Bill Richards told me, 'though he may have. He certainly had a profound mystical experience.' (An experienced meditation teacher also familiar with psychedelic experiences told me that the mystical experience achieved through meditation was quite different from that obtained through psychedelics. The psychedelic experience is through one of the senses, often an inner sense, whereas the mystical experience achieved through meditation is through no sense or process.)

beliefs' although do not adhere to any specific religion.[33] It's the same reason Zoltan Istvan's promise of avoiding mortality altogether has attracted so many supporters. (It's no coincidence that by the 1990s Timothy Leary had more or less given up on psychedelics as a tool to enlightenment, preferring to focus instead on networked computing and transhumanism.) There's a spiritual hole in a lot of people's lives—and the Psychedelic Society is trying to fill it. It won't always work, but when it does, the results are quite remarkable.

I met up with some of the trippers three months later. Paolo credits the weekend with helping him make a big transition in his day job: it gave him belief that he could change roles to something more creative, a switch he'd wanted to do for a while but for which he could never summon up the courage. 'I couldn't see a way forward until then,' he told me. 'It's great, *really* great.'

Sarah, who'd spent much of the day in tears with a facilitator, went back home and found the weekend was a catalyst to have dinner with her mother, with whom she'd had a very difficult relationship.

For artist Jake it was an important part of his ongoing journey to stay free of addiction and depression. During the trip he'd thought about his dad who'd recently passed away. 'Not just thinking, but really *feeling* the way I felt about him. I could almost sense him. I felt an acceptance of the way our relationship had been.' He let a lot of things go and has felt better for it since. He's still depression- and medication-free.

The correspondent from the major UK newspaper never did publish his article. I suspect he may have freaked out his editor a little.

If you're going to take psychedelics, the safest place is in a laboratory. But Stephen's Weekend Experience must come a close second. The Psychedelic Society will help you realise that the world you see is not the only objective representation of matter, energy and colour. They will help you experience things you haven't before, and perhaps that will give you some insight into yourself and perspective on the world around you. They will awaken you to the possibility that our daily consciousness is not the only one there is. Many of us encounter development stages in our lives, characterised by a desire to better understand ourselves and develop our abilities, to grow into our potential. Much psychological therapy is about helping that process along, and psychedelics are potentially an aid to that end. You might experience some difficult moments, but if you're open to them, and in the right 'set' and 'setting', I reckon there's a decent chance you'll also experience something that feels transcendent, and even benefit enormously from it.

But I'm still not convinced you'll leave in possession of an underlying truth: that the world is merely a subjective reality constructed by our own consciousness, or that we live in a non-dual universe. Matter is nothing but energy, and solidity is merely an illusion. Consciousness is unfathomable. Our perceptions of colours are not objective, but simply the way our visual system interprets the way some photons of light are reflected. Though they may appear static, the plants and trees are alive with manic activity. We are a tiny insignificant part of a universe that we barely understand. We are all—humans, plants, every-thing—made of the same basic energy and matter. You don't need psychedelics to be initiated into these profound and important insights, although the drugs help. A science textbook might also do it.

Experience

Over the course of the weekend I noticed occasional looks being exchanged between the trippers that seemed to say: 'If only Jamie knew what we know. Then he'd understand.' My mind wasn't 'expanded', I was still listing around in normal everyday consciousness. In the early days of Leary's research programme at Harvard, psilocybin divided people into those who'd had the experience and those who hadn't, with the former 'displaying a superiority, or feeling of being above and beyond the normal world'.34 Cosmic consciousness can do that to you.

The more I read up on the science, and visited people like Jake and Paolo, the more questions kept nagging me. What if Stephen was right? What if there is something more to it? Can I really write about this without trying it myself?

A few months after the Weekend Trip, I returned to the Netherlands with a small group of friends, rented a large house in the countryside, and persuaded a psychedelic shaman-type called Robin to guide us, just as Stephen had done, through a psilocybin trip of roughly the same intensity.

Just like in Apeldoorn, Robin prepared it all for us, sourcing the goods and dosing it out to the group. He talked us through the risks, what to do if we felt uneasy, and checked carefully that everyone felt ready. There was no wooden door or Tibetan bell, but I ceremoniously ate the truffles—which took no more than a minute or two—and nervously waited.

I first felt the drug's effect in the legs and arms. My limbs felt incredibly heavy, and I felt quite dizzy. It wasn't particularly unpleasant, but certainly very strange.

A friend and I sat on a wooden bench in the garden, as we felt the drug starting to rise up in us both. He suddenly felt the plants and trees were out to get him. The moss on our bench offered no refuge, since that was teeming angrily too. He wasn't enjoying this at all. So we wandered indoors and sat in the more familiar surroundings of the front room.

Except the room suddenly felt alien, different in its proportions. I kept trying to describe why that was into my Dictaphone, but found that all my powers of attention had evaporated. Every time I started to speak I became immediately distracted by an inanimate everyday object. One small silver lamp in particular kept stopping me mid-sentence. This didn't trouble me, since I was perfectly happy to stare silently at this lamp, although I had no idea why it was of such immense fascination. In fact, everything in the room appeared new again. I became absolutely convinced that the music Robin put on in the background was somehow being played under water, and spent five minutes with my ear pressed up against the speaker saying repeatedly 'But how is this possible?' None of this was an uncomfortable sensation: in fact it was quite pleasant. 'This is interesting,' I kept saying, to no one in particular.

A Russian doll up on the top shelf above the fireplace started staring right back at me with a hint of menace. I tried to ignore her, but I found her glare difficult to shake.

'What are you looking at?' asked my friend, who was now periodically laughing hysterically.

'A Russian doll,' I said.

'Will you introduce me?'

'No way,' I replied. 'I don't think you're ready.'

I decided a cup of tea was in order. But I had very little conception of how precisely I'd go about getting one. Making a cup of tea felt like a colossal and complicated undertaking, something that would probably require Robin's assistance. But I was wary of approaching him, since he seemed to be emitting a different energy to me. It felt like he was floating around the house—suddenly here, then suddenly gone again—like a man with something to hide. I opened the cupboard to look for some sugar, but it was so full of items that I shut it immediately. Anyway, what the hell does he want, this Robin chap? I thought to myself, and ran upstairs with my precious tea to scribble down some notes: 'Robin scary! Nothing to say, staring at objects. Things seem new . . . although not. Were they always like that? What's the time? Feel like I'm more quiet than normal. I'm writing this. Remind myself to swallow.'

This is powerful stuff, I thought, reading it back. Not like other drugs. I can see why some people get a lot from it. I jotted down a note to self: 'Do not *under any circumstances* take psychedelics at a party surrounded by strangers and loud music.'

At about five o'clock I decided to go outside on my own for a while. The house was on top of a hill, and I found a nice spot from which I could gaze down at a nearby wood.

When I looked intently at the trees, they slowly started to change. They appeared to be pulsating, as if they were breathing. It was a far more harmonious movement than merely waving about haphazardly in the wind. In-out, in-out, they went, in a slow hypnotic rhythm. In-out. In-out. And the grass, although still green, looked a much greener green than I'd noticed before. It was in fact the *greenest* possible green. It was the definition of green. All other greens were watered down derivatives. It was the telos of green. And every blade of it seemed to be precisely where it was meant to be. What a divine arrangement of grass that is! I thought. How on earth did I not spot this before? Minutes or hours passed, as I stood slack-jawed—mouth literally hanging open—rooted to the spot, and wanted to do absolutely nothing else in the world except stare at those crazy breathing trees. I repeatedly tried to type on my phone why I wanted to stare at the breathing trees, but nothing came out. It was indescribable. Not because it was beyond words, but because there wasn't anything to describe. Only a content feeling of nothing, a joyful feeling of being empty of thoughts. Both aware of being devoid of thought, and also acutely conscious of that fact. I didn't quite feel like I was 'at one' with the trees in the way Stephen or the others described, or that I was connected to a universal consciousness. But I had somehow blended in. I was simultaneously there and not-there. For one brief moment I had to remind myself that I was not a fixture of the landscape I was looking at.

I had no idea how long I was there, rooted to the spot, open-mouthed, empty-headed, staring blissfully like a child. All I knew was that I had little interest in doing anything else. A bat flew past my head and broke the trance. It was pitch black: I couldn't even see the trees anymore. How long had I been standing here for? I turned around and walked back inside the house.

4

Interlude: Prevent

On the morning of Friday 29 May 2015, nineteen-year-old Rasheed Benyahia left home telling his parents he was off to college. Instead he made his way to Birmingham International Airport and took a flight to Turkey. From there, he crossed the border into Syria with the help of Islamic State–supporting smugglers, and was sent to a secretive military training and indoctrination camp.

Rasheed was born in Wales and grew up in Birmingham in a religious, but not particularly conservative, family. But as a teenager studying electrical engineering in college, he started to change. The war in Syria and the murderous Bashar al-Assad regime made him angry and desperate to do something. He started reading up about Islamic State online, and—the authorities now suspect—got involved with extreme Islamists who ran a stall in Birmingham city centre. He started becoming more religiously observant, and sometimes more confrontational. 'Something had been ignited in him,' his mother said later. Six months after leaving the United Kingdom, Rasheed was killed near Sinjar by shrapnel from a coalition drone strike.[1]

Rasheed was one of an estimated 800 UK nationals—and thousands of other Muslims living in Western democracies—who have been lured to Iraq or Syria by a very simple but powerful narrative: that the West hates you, and as a Muslim you have a religious duty to come to Syria and join Islamic State. His story is repeated by thousands of other young Muslims living in Western democracies. Around 6,000 have travelled from Europe, with most coming from Germany, France and the United Kingdom. Around 250 are thought to have travelled from the United States. And many more are believed to be active supporters of Islamic State, although have not taken the step of trying to join the group in person. Awaiting is the exciting prospect of building an Islamic utopia and heroically fighting the crusaders and infidels.[2] Violent Islamism has been one of the most consistent ideological threats to Western democracies for most of this century. And the response to it from liberal governments has resulted in illiberal policies and laws being approved. It's a creed that wants to introduce a regime based on Islamic religious law, largely or completely unchanged from its original seventh-century version. It's totalitarian, since it seeks to impose this on everyone else, including (perhaps especially) other Muslims. Its adherents consider 'the West', democracy and secularism to be enemies of this grand project, and will use violence to pursuit it. In 2016 alone, followers of this ideology have attacked several major Western and many other cities, notably in Muslim-majority countries like Turkey, Lebanon, Iraq and Pakistan. The US intelligence community considers the Islamic State the dominant global-terrorist threat, including 'home-grown' terrorists inspired by the Islamic State or al-Qaeda without necessarily even leaving the country.

How should a liberal democracy deal with the spread of radical ideas that directly seek to undermine or destroy it? Censorship, in addition to being illiberal, doesn't always work. It has a tendency to backfire, adding glamour and even vindication to ideas and movements that often don't merit it. And digital technology makes it exceptionally difficult to silence ideas, especially given that most radical groups are extremely skilful users of modern technology.[3] In an ideal liberal society, radical arguments—even dangerous ones—should be allowed to flourish and compete. The theory, at least the liberal's hopeful theory, is that the good will outcompete the bad in the marketplace of ideas. With debate and discussion the stronger, more rational arguments always win out.

But they don't always win out. Irrational, emotional, even violent ideas have a certain appeal too—and always have. How tolerant we should be of those ideas that seem to drive hatred or violence is a question that has plagued liberal society since Socrates was charged with teaching young men to disrespect the gods in 399 BC. This is a question that also plagues this book. So what role should a democratic government play in preventing the spread of violent or illiberal ideas when the marketplace doesn't appear to be up to the job? And what happens when it tries? Over the last decade, the UK government has embarked on a novel approach to this problem, by funding policies and projects designed to stop violent, extreme or illiberal ideas from gaining traction, called 'Prevent'. Other countries set up their own versions inspired by the United

Kingdom's example, including France and Denmark. The
United States model, although slightly different, is also
based on the UK's Prevent, and is called 'Countering Violent Extremism'. According to the Department of Homeland Security, it aims to 'build and sustain local prevention
efforts and promote the use of counter-narratives to con-
front violent extremist messaging online'.

Prevent

In late 2001 British security services were in turmoil. Having spent the previous decade worrying about the IRA, nationalism and Communism, the United Kingdom suddenly
found itself facing a violent ideology it didn't understand at
all. In 2003 the government produced an internal strategy
to respond to the threat of al-Qaeda, called CONTEST. It
was built around four Ps that aimed to lessen risk through
reducing the likelihood, vulnerability and impact of terrorist attacks: Pursue, Prevent, Protect and Prepare. Three
were well-established concepts in counter-terrorism work,
but 'Prevent' was completely novel. 'We'd never really done
anything like it before,' explained the former director of
Government Communications Headquarters (GCHQ) Sir
David Omand, who was responsible for creating CON-
TEST. But everyone felt it was necessary to do something,
because al-Qaeda seemed to be a new type of terrorist outfit. There was no possibility of negotiation, and it appeared
bent on causing maximum destruction. Omand drew in-
spiration from successful and popular community-led programmes that tried to stop young men from inner cities
joining criminal gangs, and recent experiences in Northern

Ireland: the Good Friday Agreement of 1998 had resulted
in the men of violence in the Provisional IRA decommis-
sioning their weapons, but not giving up on their ambition
of a united Ireland. 'The crude thinking of Prevent at the
time was that it would be difficult to change someone's
world view,' said Omand. 'But you could persuade them
that extreme violence didn't advance their goal.'

Between 2003–5 a few small Prevent projects were
rolled out, including one to encourage mosques to employ
imams who were used to life in the United Kingdom and
who spoke English. At the time, none of this was publi-
cised. Then on 7 July 2005 four British Muslims blew
themselves up on the London transportation network, killing fifty-two people. The attacks sparked a heated public
debate about 'home-grown' terror, Britishness and 'British
values'. Some commentators felt the root cause of these attacks was Muslims living separate lives to other groups in
society, and that enclaves of extremist thinking and ideas,
even if non-violent, were creating 'mood music' for terrorism.[*4] Prime Minister Tony Blair convened a large group
of influential Muslims to come up with a 'community-led'
response to make sure al-Qaeda's arguments wouldn't find
a responsive audience. Dilwar Hussain, who was working
at the research organisation the Islamic Foundation at the
time, was part of the group. 'The atmosphere was very

---

[*] In 2006 journalist Melanie Phillips published the bestselling *Londo-
nistan* which argued Britain was allowing enclaves of extremism to
exist unchallenged, which provided fertile recruiting ground for terrorists. Several shocking polls jacked up the sense of panic: a survey
of 1,003 adult British Muslims in late 2006 found 7 per cent admired
al-Qaeda, another found that 13 per cent believed the 7/7 bombers
should be regarded as martyrs.

positive and collaborative following the meeting,' he told
me recently. 'Doing something preventative was welcomed
as a way Muslim communities and public servants might
work together to try to stop this happening again. Most of
us thought it was an important and positive move.'[5]

The government concluded it was safe to make CON-
TEST and Prevent public, and put local councils in charge
of delivering it. With money and political support behind
it, Prevent quickly became a flourishing cottage industry. Think tanks and academic departments were set up
to study these issues and examine how to prevent violent
ideas from spreading.* New grass-roots initiatives appeared,
promising access to 'hard to reach' communities. Training-
course providers started offering courses about how to spot
terrorists in waiting. For a while in the 2000s, it was widely
known around Whitehall that if you could link your project idea to Prevent somehow—for example a housing initiative that would also help vulnerable people stay out of
trouble—there was a better chance of getting money for it.
(This created an incentive for industry experts, which still
exists today, to keep inflating the problem, since there were
contracts, jobs and careers tied up with Prevent money.[6])

But stopping people from buying into certain ideas was
more difficult than anyone expected. Although Prevent
was conceived by Omand to focus solely on preventing *violent* extremism, it was increasingly plain that an almost
infinite number of factors could contribute in some way
to a person becoming or supporting terrorists: economic
deprivation, perceived injustice, friendship groups, mental

---

* I include myself in that: the organisation I work for has delivered
  'Prevent' projects in the past.

health problems, and on and on and on. No one could agree on precisely what mattered most. Perhaps inevitably, the focus of Prevent became increasingly unclear. In some local areas projects encouraged Muslim communities to work with the police, in others it looked at integrating Muslims into the labour market.[7] Some programmes unfairly targeted perfectly law-abiding and peaceful Muslims, while other local authorities were handing out money to extremist groups or spending it on frivolous projects such as curry clubs or football training.[8] Intervening in the marketplace of ideas was proving to be very messy.

In 2011, and in response to growing criticism, the government revamped the programme, pledging a sharper focus on terrorism and extremism; more work to counter 'non-violent extremism' ideas the government felt 'inspired' the terrorists; and to look at all types of radicalisation, not just Islamist.[9] Partly in response to the arrival of Islamic State, the Counter-Terrorism and Security Act 2015 ramped Prevent up further, requiring public bodies to have 'due regard to the need to prevent people from being drawn into terrorism'.[10] Universities were told to monitor student groups and invited speakers, teachers were told to be alert to signs of radicalisation, doctors asked to be mindful of people expressing radical ideas.[*][11] By 2016 Prevent had

---

[*] This uncomfortably overlapped with a much wider debate about free speech in universities, about 'safe spaces'. The two things are remarkably similar. One comes from the authorities, the other from students; both are premised on the notion that ideas in themselves are dangerous and harmful and so should be prevented from being aired. The government agreed to a provision—section 31—stating that when carrying out its functions under the Counter Terrorism and Security Act 2015 a university must 'regard' their duty to ensure freedom of expression.

become an established part of the UK's counter-terrorism efforts. Its annual budget is approaching approximately £40 million per year, and in 2016 had funded 142 community-based projects that reached over 42,000 people.[12]

As Prevent has grown, so has concern about it. It has made a lot of Muslims feel somehow suspect, which has led to distrust of the whole programme, a significant problem given that it depends on the active involvement of Muslim communities. According to David Anderson QC, the independent reviewer of terrorism legislation, there is a 'very wide sense' among British Muslims that Prevent is part of a plan to threaten Islam. It's even been boycotted by several organisations, including the National Union of Students, and a recent report by the Open Society Foundation, based on an in-depth study of several Prevent projects, found that the programme is 'counterproductive' and damages the trust between the police and members of the Muslim community.[13]

Radicalisation

The underlying purpose of Prevent is to stop something academics call 'radicalisation'. This term—which didn't really exist before 2001—describes the process by which someone goes from being an ordinary law-abiding citizen to a terrorist. The problem is, human behaviour is rarely linear or predictable, and there are several competing models of why and how radicalisation occurs.

According to Rizwaan Sabir, a lecturer at John Moores University and a vocal critic of Prevent, the government follows a dubious model of radicalisation called the 'conveyor-belt' model. The model goes something like the following: someone starts off normal, picks up some extreme religious ideas, gets frustrated about something in their life, and then progresses linearly and predictably into becoming a terrorist.[*] Prevent is about intervening early in the process. 'Empirically it doesn't make sense,' Rizwaan told me. 'There is no evidence to prove that extremist views graduate into violence. Ideas may *justify* violence but do not cause them.' People who undertake violent acts hold radical views, but the overwhelming majority of radicals don't commit violence.

The inevitable result of using this model, say critics like Rizwaan, is that Muslims end up getting targeted for being radical, religiously conservative or just plain angry at the UK government because a tiny number might become terrorists. That's alienating, unfair and illiberal.

Such fears are not completely unfounded. The focus on Muslim communities is partly driven by an analysis of the current threat—mainly but not solely Islamist

---

[*] In May 2008 Rizwaan, then a twenty-two-year-old master's student at Nottingham University studying international relations, downloaded the al-Qaeda training manual from the US State Department. After an administrator discovered the document on a staff member's computer who was helping Rizwaan with his research, the university management contacted the police. Rizwaan was arrested and spent seven days in solitary confinement in a prison cell, before being released without charge. Even though it wasn't technically a Prevent programme, he thinks it reflected the general suspicion of the time. 'Universities do not exist in a vacuum,' Rizwaan told me. 'The government decided terrorism is about ideas, which means it made those ideas criminal.'

in nature—but there are several occasions when Muslim communities have good reason to feel unfairly targeted.[14] Like seventeen-year-old Rahmaan Mohammadi who was questioned by the police after distributing pro-Palestine leaflets. Or when the Safeguarding Children Board of the London borough of Camden, which published a pamphlet advising parents to look out for possible signs of radicalisation, included mistrust of mainstream media and appearing angry about government policies.[15] More broadly, said Rizwaan, there is always plenty of money made available to Muslim-related projects—jobs, integration, housing—but with the underlying aim to stop Muslims blowing people up, which is hardly a positive approach to engaging with people.[16]

After speaking to Rizwaan, I went to see Matt Collins, the director of Prevent at the Home Office. He strongly denied that the government used a conveyor-belt model and pointed out that there is no mention of it in any official Prevent documents (which is true, Prevent documents use terms like 'vulnerabilities' and 'safeguarding'). According to Matt, Prevent is built on a 'complex, multifaceted model' that suggests overlapping vulnerabilities—such as friendship networks, perceived injustices and so on—combine to make someone more susceptible to supporting terrorism. Prevent is about trying to target those vulnerabilities.

The fact that Prevent has stimulated argument over arcane academic theories on risk aversion illustrates just how divisive the program has become. Depending on who you speak to, it's either a terrible initiative that targets, alienates and stigmatises innocent people, or a vital and very sensible way to support people who might be targeted by recruiters or fall prey to terrorist propaganda.

Prevent is structured like a pyramid: At the bottom are broad-brush initiatives aimed at thousands of low-risk youngsters who might benefit from being more knowledgeable about how recruiters operate. The farther up you go, the more high risk the targets and the more focused the projects. In the West Midlands, not far from where Rasheed lived, Hifsa Haroon-Iqbal, a British Muslim originally from Leeds, is the local Prevent lead for further and higher education, which entails delivering low-level Prevent projects to schools and universities in the area. 'Most people don't fully understand what Prevent is about,' Hifsa told me when I went to watch her deliver lessons to several classes of sixteen- to eighteen-year-olds just outside Birmingham. 'For me, it is about helping young people develop better critical-thinking skills. There is so much propaganda and misinformation out there—especially online. Teenagers are getting recruited and travelling to Syria to become glorified prostitutes or die on a battlefield!' she said. 'Are we supposed to just do nothing about that?!'[17]

Although Prevent is usually attacked for stigmatising Muslims, Hifsa's class was the opposite. She started by asking pupils what a terrorist looks like. She showed photos of Islamic State fighters, but also Norwegian terrorist Anders Breivik and the IRA. 'They're terrorists too,' she said. 'People sometimes think this is just about Islam, it's not.' (Actually not one student said they thought terrorists were always Muslims, which sort of ruined Hifsa's set-up, but in the best possible way). We then watched a video showing how the neo-Nazis and Islamists use similar recruitment techniques, and Hifsa told the students they should speak to someone if they were worried about a friend who might be getting drawn in.

At the top of the pyramid is Prevent's most controversial and secretive component, called 'Channel'.[18] People who have been spotted by (usually) public servants as potentially at high risk of radicalisation, even though they have not broken the law, are referred to a local authority–run 'Channel Panel'. This is a multi-agency group who decide whether an individual requires tailored support or help to stop them from becoming extremists. Channel was first piloted in 2007 in a handful of areas, and it has grown every year since. In 2015 around 4,000 people were referred to a Channel Panel for consideration (80 per cent were deemed not to be a risk and no action was taken).[19] There are now Channel Panels in every single local authority, and most meet monthly.

Channel Panel

In December 2016 I was granted permission to sit in on one of these confidential Channel Panel meetings, at a London borough. I turned up to a very ordinary-looking room in an ordinary-looking council building to find half a dozen people sitting around a large table: an offender management officer, a couple of police officers, an NHS staff member, a local authority commissioner, a social worker and a Prevent officer. After everyone had signed a confidentiality agreement, the panel reviewed its portfolio of six open cases, and a new referral that had recently been sent over. The chair—a local authority commissioner—handed around notes on each, with information and updates.

The panel's job is to determine if an individual is 'vulnerable' to radicalisation, which is an exceptionally

difficult task. Every specialist now agrees there is no 'typical' terrorist profile.[20] And although the field is now more
empirically driven than a decade ago—for example, having friends support Islamic State is now understood to
be more important than how poor you are—prediction is
widely understood among Prevent practitioners as a fool's
errand.[21] Men, women, children, grandparents, angry teenagers, punk rockers, ex–medical students, scholars and former gangsters have all headed to Syria.[22] (Having followed
radicals of all different shades and ideologies for two years
I still cannot explain why some people become radicals
and others stay at home. It's some mysterious alchemy of
timing, networks, personality type and opportunity. People are simply motivated by different things.)

To help them judge, the panel tests vulnerability
against a list of twenty-two indicators, which include 'excitement, comradeship and adventure', 'family and/or
friends support extremism', 'us and them thinking' and a
history of criminality. (According to Matt Collins of the
Home Office, these are based on available evidence and
continually revised, but the studies behind the indicators
are not public.) If the panel deems that a person is vulnerable, an 'intervention' is designed to match their specific
case. It can vary from cognitive-behaviour therapy to simple mentoring to ideological training or even help getting
a job. Because the whole thing is voluntary—the person
involved has to agree to take part—the interventions need
to be designed with great care. Some refuse them.

Our cases varied greatly, although most were men in
their teens or twenties who'd been referred by worried
family members, teachers or social workers, who'd seen
them watching jihadi videos or talking suspiciously but

very vaguely about going to Syria.* One of the referrals had made comments about 'attacking the West' while drunk in custody at a local police station. At the last meeting the panel had looked at information gathered by the police, and requested an officer speak to him. 'We had a long, informal conversation,' said the officer, reporting back to the group, 'and on further questioning, we don't believe he's a realistic threat.' It was agreed by the panel that this was evidence enough, and the case was closed.

A second case involved someone who'd been expressing support for Islamic State online. He claimed little understanding of their ideology, having just heard a few things in passing. The panel offered him free classes in Islamic studies from a local scholar, which he accepted. The panel agreed to keep monitoring the case, and to have a chat with the scholar at some point in the future. A third had been involved with criminal gangs that were suspected of supporting Islamic State, and the panel—with input from a social worker—thought much of the problems was down to a chaotic family life and mental health problems. He was offered help from a social worker or mental health nurse.

The new referral was a particularly difficult case. It involved a man with a history of violence, who was of unknown address, and using several aliases. He had, the referral said, been talking about jihad to his friends, seriously enough that one of them approached the council asking for help. On this occasion the panel decided they

---

* The fact that all referrals here related to violent Islamism was a reflection of the local demographics. In some parts of the country, far-right referrals are the most common type.

needed to know more about the man before making any judgement—including finding his full address—and the police officer, scribbling in his notepad, said he'd try to find out more and report back next month with an update for everyone.

The most common type of intervention offered by these panels is a mentor who keeps an eye on the individual and meets them periodically to talk things out. Hanif Qadir, a former radical in his forties, has mentored several people as part of Channel, from several different local authorities. He reckons his outfit, the Active Change Foundation, a youth centre based in East London, stopped around ten people from going to Syria in the last couple of years. Hanif travelled to Afghanistan in his twenties to fight with al-Qaeda in 2002, thinking he could help Afghanis he had been told were under attack from the West. But when he got there he was disgusted by what he saw. He quickly returned home and the following year set up the foundation to stop other people falling into the same trap.[23] The foundation offers a gym, boxing ring, pool tables and a pet snake. Hundreds of young people come through his doors every month to use the facilities.

'What's amazing is how naïve and gullible they sometimes are,' he told me at his centre. The key to pulling them back in, reckons Hanif, is not to tell them they are wrong, since it won't work. But many have internal doubts and that's an opening. Even though Islamic State provides a lot of religious justifications for their actions, liberally quoting directly from the Qu'ran in most of their propaganda, Hanif has noticed that a lot of the people referred to him don't actually know much about Islam at all.[24] (Recent studies, including those by the UK government, have found most supporters of violent Islamism are religious novices.[25]) Over the course of hours of meetings at his centre, Hanif often tells the story of the Khawarij, a faction that rebelled against some of Muhammad's disciples in the time of the third and fourth caliphs, and who Muhammad said were 'the worst of both men and animals'. He sometimes reads lines from the Hadiths, the story of Muhammad's life, such as: 'Whoever does not show mercy to people, Allah does not show mercy to them.' He doesn't tell them they are wrong, he just asks them to think about it for themselves. (Other Channel mentors told me very similar things.) 'You can't just get people to change their minds overnight,' said Hanif. 'But sometimes just getting people to question recruiters' knowledge and loyalties is enough to stop them travelling.'

Unintentional Side Effects

Prevent has probably stopped people getting killed and diverted young people from being recruited. It's unfairly maligned, often with little regard for the good it's done. Matt Collins told me Prevent alone has stopped 150 people from travelling to Syria.[26] But it's impossible to know if that's true, since the Home Office has never published any of its internal evaluations. And evaluating things that didn't happen is notoriously difficult. And perhaps some people have been in Prevent projects and still ended up supporting terrorist groups.[27] 'We haven't done a good enough job of showing people what we do,' admitted Matt. 'We need to be more transparent about what we [are] doing and why we are doing it.' In the United States meanwhile, where the experience with prevention work is more recent, there remains a lack of empirical evaluation of its success. Data would help, although it pays to be suspicious of unpublished evaluations that apparently—*if only you saw it*—show wonderful results.

But methodological and measurement problems are minor quibbles. The bigger issue is what happens when governments enter the marketplace of ideas. Prevent is a lesson in the unpredictability and uncontrollability of radical ideas in a free society, Prevent has unleashed furies and divisions where none previously existed. Its supporters—including those who work on it—claim they are working to fight terrorism and keep people safe. Who could disagree with that? Meanwhile its critics dismiss the whole thing, labeling Prevent's advocates government stooges or patsies.

Chief among critics is CAGE, an advocacy group for former prisoners, especially those in Guantanamo Bay.* A perfectly legitimate endeavour, however, CAGE has also campaigned on behalf of people subsequently convicted of terrorism, and their director Asim Qureshi supports stoning for adultery, 'as long as all due-process elements are met'. (All supporters of stoning who also present themselves as in some way 'progressive' mumble this sort of watery proviso.[28]) Several well-meaning liberal groups keen to fight legitimate cases of unfair treatment against Muslims and brandish their own credentials have jumped into bed with CAGE. CAGE would have long vanished into obscurity

---

* Members of CAGE have reason to be upset: Moazzam Begg, the outreach director, was held for three years in Guantanamo Bay and then released without charge; and Cerie Bullivant, CAGE's spokesman, spent two years on a control order, which was eventually quashed in court.

had it not been for Prevent, which has provided it with an opportunity to position itself as the voice of an authentic Islam fighting a docile, state-controlled religion, sometimes with scant regard for the truth. A case in point is the story of Ifhat Smith, who claimed her son had been 'interrogated' by Prevent officers, and 'treated like a criminal' because he had used the phrase 'eco-terrorism' in school. She told Sky News Prevent allowed 'state-sponsored abuse of muslim children' and spoke at anti-Prevent events supprted by CAGE. 'Prevent is allowing state-sanctioned abuse of Muslim children,' she told Sky News in December 2015.[29] She took the school (and government) to court over this. She lost the case. The 'interrogation' was a ten-minute chat, was not referred to Channel, and the child was swiftly sent straight back to class. Then there was the case of the young boy who was apparently called in for writing 'terrace house' in class, which worried teachers thought said 'terrorist'. CAGE said the incident illustrated how 'legalising Islamophobia is a growing international trend'.[30] In fact the school was worried because the child had also written 'I hate it when my uncle beats me' and involved the police as they were worried about his safety. This also had nothing to do with Prevent. Yet in interviews for this chapter, I heard both these stories several times as incontrovertible proof that Muslims are being unfairly targeted.

This powerful argument—that we are an *authentic* voice—supported by a mixture of real and exaggerated stories has to some extent allowed the opponents of Prevent to dominate the debate about it within Muslim communities. The people who defend Prevent, or who at least want to do something to stop people supporting terrorists, have not been as aggressive or vocal as those opposed to it. That's not the only reason the programme has become controversial. When a group or ideology is singled out in society it creates several difficulties, and can even exacerbate the original problem. Prevent was designed to work with Muslims, partly to ensure they were not isolated or segregated from the rest of British society. But the result has been a decade-long laser focus on British Muslims, and a self-perpetuating obsession with Britishness, identity, Islam and terror. No other group has had so much money, interest, polling or political commentary dedicated to it. In 2015 alone there were 2,500 different pieces of academic research that directly addressed the subject of radicalisation, of which more than 400 were about the United Kingdom.[31] More than any other group in Britain, poor Muslims are expected to choose. Choose if they're pro-Prevent or anti-Prevent, choose if they're British or a Muslim, choose what they think about the concept of an Islamic caliphate or Sharia law. They aren't afforded the luxury of not thinking about this stuff like most of us. For American Muslims, the situation is arguably worse still. In addition to promising 'extreme vetting' of US Muslims and to create a Muslim database, President Donald Trump pledged to make US prevention work focus solely on Muslims, changing the name of Countering Violent Extremism to Countering Islamic Radical Extremism.

No wonder Muslims sometimes feel under siege. They live constantly under the spotlight. Under the guise of stopping terrorism, Prevent, and its associated cottage industry 'counter-terrorism', which is even mildly glamourous, accidentally made some sections of British Muslims feel singled out, or even directly under suspicion. President Trump appears set on achieving the same goal very intentionally. The UK experience suggests this is not a very smart move. Aside from the fact that this may be unconstitutional and that there are significant threats to US security from non-Islamist groups (as of February 2016, right-wing extremists had engaged in terrorist attacks in the United States twice as often as radical Islamists since 2002), such a move is likely to backfire. When people are afraid of speaking their minds, fearing they might get referred to Channel or arrested, those ideas don't disappear, they just find new modes of expression that are usually out of sight, unchallenged and unchecked. Perhaps worse, ideas voiced in this way can often appear more exciting for those who hear them. This is particularly true since, in line with many radical groups, the ideology itself is only one aspect of why people join. There is also the allure of being involved in a notorious, international terrorist outfit, which for young men in their teens and early twenties can be a powerful draw.

The major problem for Prevent is not where it is now, but where it might end up. Prevent was originally justified as a response to an unprecedented terrorist threat, but the threat will change. Although radical Islamism is currently in vogue, in ten years what is considered a threat to liberal democracy will be slightly different again (already 15 per cent of Channel referrals are far-right related, and there's even been a couple of far-left referrals). Radicalisation, in all sorts of unpredictable directions, is on the rise. The question of what the state should do in response will become both more important and more controversial.

Although laws to outlaw speech that directly incites violence or targets groups with extreme hatred are compatible with a free society, as a general rule, governments should not be in the business of telling its citizens what to think, even indirectly. And it should avoid focusing solely on one group of people, in the way President Trump appears to be doing. The tendency for governments—keen to protect their citizens—is to view more ideas as dangerous, to establish more censorship, to set up initiatives like Prevent. To ban ideas, to ban online videos or even entire groups of people. Consider the programme's trajectory: It started in 2003 as a very limited effort to stop al-Qaeda extremists using violence. By 2011 it had become a concerted effort to tackle all sorts of non-violent extremism and encourage Britishness. Four years later it had become a statutory duty for all schools, universities and health services. And at the time of writing, the UK government is planning to introduce an 'Extremism' bill that would give it more powers to challenge ideas deemed in conflict with British values, which it defines as 'active or vocal opposition to democracy, the rule of law, individual liberty and mutual respect and tolerance for different beliefs and faiths'.[32]

Could people in this book one day end up being referred to a Channel Panel? Public servants told to watch out for the signs of psychedelic radicalisation? Children taught about the dangerous recruitment techniques of transhumanists? It might sound ridiculous, but threats to freedom are usually trivial in isolation, yet accumulate over time and become pervasive. And once you have a word for a problem, especially a scientific-sounding one like 'radicalisation', the phenomenon it describes takes on

form. People who work in the field routinely speak about
the 'process of radicalisation', about kids getting 'radicalised' at this university or that website, and how to 'apply
a de-radicalisation procedure'.[33] Former prime minister
David Cameron calls Islamist extremism a 'disease', while
President Trump's former national security advisor General Michael Flynn has even likened Islam to a cancer.
Government efforts to 'prevent' terrorism and 'safeguard'
vulnerable people will have a tendency to always ratchet
up: Who doesn't want to help a vulnerable person avoid a
disease? Any time there is a terrorist attack the first impulse is to call for more prevention. But it's not possible to
stop them all. Attacks like the terrorist attack in London
in March 2017, just a man armed with a knife and a rental
car, show this. The phrase 'prevention is better than cure'
is certainly true in medicine. But the lesson we can learn
from Prevent is that it's far less easy in the realm of ideas.

But governments should not remove themselves entirely from the marketplace of ideas. They do have a role:
to help people become more discerning, sceptical and
to think critically, especially when they are young. This
is doubly true now given this marketplace is increasingly
populated with false news, lies and propaganda. If Prevent
teaches people how to think for themselves, not what to
think; if it guards against smothering ideas or movements
outside the norm under the guide of 'safeguarding'; if it values outspokenness and radicalism; and if it avoids accidentally creating a culture of self-censorship, then it can be
the friend of liberty. But it won't be easy. Encouraging citizens to be critical, sceptical and discerning will of course
also mean they will be awkward, stubborn and rebellious.
People who live in free societies are destined to be forever

infuriated by radicals—whether Islamist, far-right, libertarian or whatever else—who will use that freedom to say annoying or difficult things. Fortunately, there's nothing un-British, un-American or illiberal about criticising our way of life, defying the status quo, being a troublemaker or holding uncomfortable views. That's the very thing that distinguishes life in liberal democracies from the docile submission required by Islamic State.

Grillo vs Grillo

There is a leaderless and ownerless movement
You can find it by searching for the word
non-association
A network of directly connected people
We are the Web multitude, live now on our
webcams
Everybody counts as one, everybody counts as
one, everybody counts as one.

Five Star Movement anthem

The show *Grillo vs Grillo* begins with comedian Beppe
Grillo arguing with a life-size hologram of himself onstage.
The real Beppe then wanders into the audience, poking
fun at nervous spectators, his chaotic mop of curly white
hair just about visible from the cheap seats where I'm sitting. He energetically reappears onstage, picks up a guitar
and begins strumming, puts it down and paces the stage,

cracks jokes about electronic dildos, brandishes an internet-enabled Barbie doll. Hologram Beppe looks on.

Every one of Beppe's shows in Rome has sold out. Beppe is one of Italy's best-known comedians and has been for over thirty years. But he's also the leader of a political party called the MoVimento 5 Stelle (the 'Five Star Movement'). Technically speaking Five Star is not actually a political party, it's a 'non-association', governed by a 'non-statute'. It's *not* a party, Beppe often says, and I am *not* the leader, simply the megaphone of the people's will. Five Star is a 'non-', unlike anything else, a radical, internet-powered anti-establishment movement that has swept across Italy. The capital 'V' in 'MoVimento' stands for *vaffanculo*, which translates to 'fuck off'.

When Beppe co-founded the Five Star Movement in 2009 via a post on his popular blog, he had a simple message: Italian politics is corrupt, elitist and closed. 'Politicians are parasites,' he said at the time. 'We should send them all home!' He promised to use the internet to open up the tired old political establishment ('like a can of tuna'), introducing direct democracy, radical transparency and an end to corruption.

There are two Beppes. There's the direct-democracy visionary—played tonight by Hologram Beppe—who thinks the internet will sweep away representative democracy, political parties, ideologies and even religion. It will all be replaced with frictionless, corruption-free politics.[1] He believes political parties and their leaders were useful once, when people had no way to voice their concerns, and no way to coordinate political action. Media companies once used to be necessary to find, gather and present information to the public. But these hierarchical organisations accumulated power in the hands of the few, who invariably became corrupt and self-interested. Beppe thinks the internet has changed all that. People can now coordinate themselves without parties, and find information and news without the filter of self-interested editors. Five Star candidates are selected online by members, and local 'Meetup' groups, coordinated via a website, get together to choose their own policies. With the internet, you don't need leaders. Hologram Beppe promises an internet-enabled civic revolution.

There's also the real-world Beppe: the former accountancy student, star of popular yoghurt adverts, and award-winning satirist; the rabble-rousing comedian who calls former prime minster Matteo Renzi that 'little dwarf from Florence', for whom Silvio Berlusconi is a 'psycho-dwarf'. He pits the good, honest, ordinary citizen against the out-of-touch professional political class. He vows to represent the pure people, the 'we', against the morally corrupt elite, the 'them'.[2] An authentic and honest voice in a nihilistic political world of spin and self-interest. The solutions to problems are simple, promises Real Beppe. It's just a case of putting into effect the will of the people.[3]

This message resonated with millions of Italians. In the 2013 parliamentary election, a quarter of Italians voted for the four-year-old non-party Five Star, probably the best debut performance of any political party in Europe since the Second World War. At the time of writing they are the second largest party in Italy.

Digital Populism

Beppe Grillo is the personification of two major trends in politics. The first is that people are turning off the mainstream. Citizens aren't voting like they used to (certainly not for the main parties, whose vote share is falling across Europe) and trust their politicians less and less, seeing them as a distant and privileged elite.[4] He is tapping into all-time-high levels of frustration and distrust of the political system across Europe and beyond.[5] He is part of a populist wave. Populism, which can be either left or right wing, is an approach to politics that replaces one simplistic dichotomy (left and right) with another (the people versus the elites). The populist claims to represent the people against corrupt and self-interested political classes. It's a style of politics as much as a coherent world view: an explicit rejection of the culture and language of a professional political class.* Across the democratic world, parties and movements of all persuasions now wag their fingers at this amorphous lump they dismiss as the 'establishment'. Capitalists, socialists, liberals, Communists, anti-Semites and Islamophobic one-man parties all promise to rid us of snobbish out-of-touch politicians. There is even a new party in Slovakia called Ordinary People and Independent Personalities.

The second trend is the rise of digital politics. Millions of people now use the internet to engage in politics, and think it can help make politics faster, more transparent, smoother and more honest. Digital aficionados have

---

* The single most common background of Labour MPs in the 2015 parliament is defined as 'political organiser'.

long predicted that the internet would transform politics. In the 1990s Net activists wrote cheerful forecasts about emancipated, informed citizens voting with gadgets in a world of online consultations and live-streamed debates. A Jeffersonian democracy, a Greek agora, was just around the corner, about to expel the tired old fools who couldn't keep up.[6] Harley Hahn, an influential technology expert, predicted in 1993 that we were about to evolve 'a wonderful human culture that is really our birth right'. Nicholas Negroponte—former director of the illustrious MIT Media Lab—declared in 1997 that the internet would bring about world peace and the end of nationalism.

The Messiah has taken an unexpected form. The internet was supposed to make politics an Athenian paragon of informed citizens. Those McLuhanites, hubristic *Wired* editors and illustrious Media Lab directors did not expect the most successful digital politician of the age to be a sixty-five-year-old comedian, a man who used to smash computer monitors live on his television shows. They did not expect a man who routinely tells the entire establishment to fuck off.

The show *Grillo vs Grillo* was an exploration of the two sides of this complicated man: the comedian and the digital visionary. Beppe is the future of politics, using the internet to bring new people and ideas into civic life. He is also a tub-thumping professional comedian who insults his opponents. What is the relationship between the two sides of Beppe? Is democracy in the digital age really going to be any wiser, smarter or kinder than it used to be?

At the end of his two-hour show, Real Beppe walked up to Hologram Beppe and they embraced. As they did, both vanished and the lights went out. Wooooosh! A third

Beppe appeared floating in mid-air, another hologram, this time a deity dressed in white. On Beppe's prompting, the crowd shouted 'Vaffanculo!' in harmony and laughed.

Beppe Was Right!

Giuseppe 'Beppe' Grillo was born in 1948 in Genoa, where his father owned a welding factory. As a young man he performed with a guitar in local bars, but fans preferred his pre-show patter, and he evolved into a successful stand-up comedian. By the late 1970s he had a prime-time show on the state broadcaster RAI. Always a controversialist, in 1986 he made a joke live on air about the then socialist prime minister Bettino Craxi and his inner circle, suggesting they were a corrupt kleptocracy. He was ostracised from television and returned to the comedy circuit.

Six years later, a toxic mixture of public debt, political scandal and revelations of endemic corruption led to the collapse of the First Italian Republic. Craxi, along with one-third of his colleagues in Parliament, was convicted of accepting bribes, and fled to Tunisia, disgraced. Beppe was right! He returned to prime-time television in 1993, and his comedy shows became more explicitly political, combining environmentalism, anti-corruption and criticism of big business.[7]

After a show in 2004 Beppe was approached by a tall, austere-looking man called Gianroberto Casaleggio, an IT specialist who ran a medium-sized web consulting firm of middling success. Casaleggio (who died of a brain tumour in April 2016, while I was writing this chapter) thought the internet was the answer to the problems Beppe was complaining about. He told Beppe he could build him a blog and make it the most popular website in Italy within two years.[8] Using that blog, Casaleggio said, they could start a movement that would transform Italian politics— not by forming a party themselves, but by using the Net as a platform for new political ideas. Casaleggio initially told Beppe it would cost him €250,000. Beppe politely refused. ('I thought he was mad,' Beppe later said.) Undeterred, Casaleggio returned the following week and offered to build and run it all for free so long as he could recoup his money by selling advertising space and merchandise on the site. This time Beppe agreed.

In 2005 this unlikely duo launched www.beppegrillo .it and Beppe started blogging frequently about debt, 'capitalism without capital', speculation, corruption, renewable energy, sustainability and, increasingly, the power of the Web.[9] The blog quickly become the most popular in Italy, a watering hole for millions of fed-up Italians. After all, who was running the country now? Craxi's close friend, multibillionaire Silvio Berlusconi.*

No one could control the Net, Beppe told his followers, not even Silvio Berlusconi. Beppe suggested to his supporters that they should use another website, www.meetup .com, to coordinate offline meetings, 'Meetups', to discuss his ideas. There was no grand plan at this point, just a notion that ordinary citizens might become more politicised. Hundreds of Meetup groups started to appear, calling themselves Amici di Beppe Grillo ('Friends of Beppe

---

* When a magistrate ruled in 1984 that Berlusconi's three television networks were broadcasting illegally, Craxi quickly changed the law to get them back on air again.

Grillo'). In contrast to the lack of grass-roots civic activity in Italy's main political parties, thousands of people—most of whom had never been much involved in politics before—started meeting every week or two, and, without prompting from Beppe, began doing things: monitoring local councils, coordinating campaigns and holding rallies.[10]

In 2007 Beppe announced 'Vaffanculo Day' on his blog, asking people to demonstrate in the streets and sign a petition demanding a ban on politicians with criminal records serving in Parliament.[11] V-Day took place in approximately 200 squares across Italy.[12] (A second took place the following year.[13]) Beppe crowd-surfed in a red dingy on top of the thousands who'd turned out in Bologna's main square. No one had ever seen anything like it. Eugenio Scalfari, founder of the respected newspaper *La Repubblica*, wrote an editorial titled 'The barbaric invasion of Beppe Grillo'.[14]

V-Day helped convince Beppe that Casaleggio was right: The internet really could turn Italian politics on its head. With nothing but a blog and www.meetup.com they'd mobilised 2 million people and secured 336,000 signatures. Something big was happening to politics, and not just in Italy. In 2008 author Clay Shirky published *Here Comes Everyone*, which put forward the argument that the internet dramatically lowers the cost for people to organise and collaborate. With Facebook, Flickr and blogs, he said, there was no need for large formal organisations. (US internet penetration rates had grown from 21 per cent in 1997 to 75 per cent in 2007.) Shirky's thesis, which Casaleggio and Beppe both read closely, was being borne out by events. Around this time the Occupy Movement in the United States started to use the Net to coordinate offline sit-ins and occupations; the Pirate Party, founded by Rick Falkvinge (whom I'd later meet, see Chapter 8), was using internet-enabled direct democracy to score stunning victories in Germany, Sweden and Iceland; and Tommy Robinson was setting up a Facebook group that would turn into the English Defence League.* Barack Obama—an outsider in 2007—was elected US president in 2008 thanks in part to his active social media following. Anything seemed possible.

Beppe hoped the signatures and mass rallies might force the political classes to listen to his ideas about corruption, but V-Day was largely ignored by the Italian establishment. In response, Beppe and his *amici* started inching towards power.[15] The 2008 local Italian elections featured a handful of candidates endorsed by Beppe. He still hoped to work with the existing parties and publicly stated he was considering running for leader of the left-leaning Partito Democratico (PD). 'If Grillo wants to become a politician,' sneered Fassino, a leading member of the PD at the time, 'he must found a party, set up an organisation, go to the polls. Let's see how many votes he will take. Why he doesn't do that?'

In September 2009 Grillo posted an announcement on his blog:

On 4 October 2009, a new national Five Star Movement will be born. It will be born on the internet . . . The parties are dead. I do not want to found 'a party', an apparatus, a structure of intermediation. Rather I want to create a movement with a programme.[16]

---

* There were failures too, including ruck.us, which promised to replace party politics entirely, and Americans Elect, a plan to nominate a third-party candidate via some version of an open Web primary.

Five Star promised it would be different from the large, professional political parties that dominated Italian politics at the time. Candidates eschewed mainstream media, refusing to give any interviews. Their (very short) policy document contained a mix of traditionally left- and right-wing ideas, including a promise to abolish Telecom Italia and other monopolies, adherence to the Kyoto environmental protocols, and obligatory (but free) Italian lessons for foreigners. Beppe proposed introducing a single flat consumption tax and getting rid of income tax, was ambiguous about Italy's continued membership of the single European currency, and critical of large-scale immigration.[17] Above all, Five Star promised to rid Italian politics of its endemic corruption. It refused state funding, proposed to cap its MPs salary at the average national wage, and pledged to publish all proposed bills online three months before approval to allow for public comment. Only candidates without a criminal record could run (which ruled out Beppe himself, as he was convicted of manslaughter in 1981 following a car accident), and they promised to serve no more than two terms, to prevent any creeping professionalism.[18]

The engine behind it all was the local Meetups. Each was (and still is) run by one or several administrators. Dozens of Meetup groups were being set up every week, and thousands of Italians, usually in groups of around a dozen or two, were getting together in bars, cafés, bedrooms and kitchens to discuss Beppe's latest blog, propose ideas, agree on initiatives and, during elections, get out the vote. Many had never been politically active before and were excited by what felt like a new way of doing politics. And for some it was a stepping stone into a political world they'd assumed was blocked to them. Meetups also selected candidates for election, and they could develop their own locally focused policies, as long as the candidate's suggested policies did not contradict those set out in the non-statute. Most, if not all, of Five Star's candidates for elections were drawn from these Meetups.[19]

Tying everything together was the blog, which Beppe registered as the official headquarters of the movement. Five Star members could vote on key ideas and issues on the blog, which its MPs would have to follow. Candidates put forward from the Meetups to stand for election were voted for on the blog too, in online primaries (providing they met the criteria above, which was checked by a small group called 'the Staff' based at Casaleggio Associates' offices).[20] The number of votes received determined their position on the party list.*

Beppe was giving voice to years of quiet rage about pervasive corruption, nepotism and cronyism.†[21] His supporters remembered Craxi. They remembered that he installed his brother-in-law as mayor of Milan, while promising to restore morality to Italian politics. They'd heard rumours

---

* Italy's elections work on a candidate list system. Citizens don't vote for a candidate; they vote for a party. The party chooses a list of candidates, and the proportion of votes received determines how many candidates are elected. The higher on the list, the better the chance of getting elected, which vests a lot of power in the party machine.

† Duncan McDonnell, author of *Populists in Power*, explained to me that trust in politics was so low in Italy that populist politics was already mainstream when Grillo arrived. This means Grillo had to out-do even the populists (people such as Marco Pannella of the Radical Party, Umberto Bossi of the Northern League, Antonio Di Pietro of the Italy of Values and even former prime minister Silvio Berlusconi).

about Berlusconi's Bunga parties. They'd read Gian Antonio Stella's and Sergio Rizzo's *La Casta* ('The Caste'),
a book that exposed unbelievable levels of privilege and
wastefulness of Italian politicians.[22]

What could be more different to Craxi or Berlusconi
than a party of enthusiastic young newcomers with zero
political experience, led by a comedian? What else to do
but scream *vaffanculo*? That's exactly what millions of Italians did.

In the regional elections of 2010 Five Star managed 7
per cent of the vote; in the following year's local election
it scored 10 per cent in some places. In 2012 it elected a
mayor in Parma. Later that year, just ahead of the Sicilian
elections, Beppe swam the Messina Straits that divides
the island from the mainland as a stunt and told the *Financial Times* that Five Star was a response to 'a system
of political diarrhoea'. They won 15 per cent of the vote.
By the end of 2012 there were 500 Meetup groups.[23] Beppe
himself often joined the activist front line, taking part in
protests, including against the controversial TAV train line
linking Turin and Lyons, and getting himself arrested in
the process.

Although this was a stunning rise, the serious analysts—the ones who wrote for newspapers like *La Repubblica*—agreed Beppe wouldn't fare so well in the following
year's national parliamentary elections. People are fed up,
we can all agree on that, but this is a man who swims the
Messina Straits. A jester!

In early 2013, 1,400 enthusiastic Grillini—little Gril-
los—drawn from the Meetups, submitted their CVs to
Beppe's blog, and 30,000 members voted for who'd get on
the ballot in the election. Five Star presented candidates

in every single electoral district in Italy.* In line with the organisation's 'non-statute', Beppe and the candidates refused to give any interviews with mainstream media.[24] Instead, Beppe went on a 'Tsunami Tour' of packed, excited piazzas.[25] And beneath the radar, tens of thousands of Meetup activists—all volunteers—were meeting online and off, canvassing voters.

Italy is used to democratic upheavals. After the collapse of the First Republic and Craxi in the early 1990s, several parties disappeared entirely. But no one could quite believe it when the results came in on 25 February 2013. Five Star received 26 per cent of the vote in the Chamber of Deputies and 24 per cent in the Senate, making it the single largest party in Italy. (They did not 'win', as both the centre-left and centre-right parties formed an alliance, and so secured—only just—more votes.[†]) Days later, 163 Five Star MPs—54 senators and 109 deputies, none of whom had ever held national political office before—headed to Rome. 'Beppe Grillo's enormous tidal wave crashes on the Italian political system, revolutionising it forever' wrote a stunned *La Repubblica*. A combination of anger at the status quo, endemic corruption, smart use of new technology and a charismatic figurehead had propelled this fledgling movement from the weird fringe of Italian politics to the heart of the establishment in just over three years.

---

* Only Five Star members who'd been part of the movement since at least September 2012 were eligible to vote. The 30,000 figure should be compared to the 3.1 million participating in the analogous offline initiative of the Parti Democratico the same year.

† To avoid endless unstable coalition government, the largest party or coalition of parties also receives an electoral boost in terms of seats in the Parliament.

At a stroke Five Star radically changed the composi-
tion and feel of the Italian Parliament, which, until that
point, was dominated by a familiar cast of professional
middle-aged male politicians. In the Chamber of Deputies, all the Five Star members were under thirty-five and
a third were women.[26] It included one housekeeper, seven
unemployed people and fourteen students. There was
thirty-four-year-old Alessandro Di Battista, who worked
on human rights in Congo and Chile, twenty-six-year-old
beach entertainer Giulia Sarti and Maria Edora, an easy-
Jet stewardess.[27] They quickly became known for their
unconventional style: refusing the title 'honourable' as is
standard for deputies and senators, wearing trainers, 'occupying' the roof of the lower house in protest over a proposed bill and even physically confronting other MPs.[28]
They refused to enter into a formal coalition with the Partito Democratico, preferring to remain outsiders.

The ever primed, coiffed and impeccably dressed Silvio Berlusconi, whose centre-right coalition came second,
said they looked like 'guys from a squat'. But the guys from
the squat were taking over.

Meetups

Six months after the 2013 election I was sitting in the stuffy
John Snow Lecture Theatre at the School of Hygiene and
Tropical Medicine in central London, surrounded by sev-
enty Grillini.* I had written a short report about the Five

---

* This term is sometimes used—especially by parts of the Italian
  media—in a derogative way to denote obsessive or brainwashed

Star Movement for Demos, the think tank I work for. London-based Five Star activists had seen the report and invited me to attend one of their famous Meetups, to see how life at the grass roots really looked.

'We are famous for our internet use,' Nicola Marini, the thirty-eight-year-old co-organiser of this meeting, told me. 'But the real engine is the Meetups.' This Meetup was for European supporters of Beppe. It was a celebration of the recent electoral success, and a chance to plan for the fast-approaching European Parliament elections in May 2014.[29]

The American journalist Murray Kempton once wrote that political meetings are 'not places where you come away with any trace of faith in human nature'. But when I arrived at the John Snow Lecture Theatre on Saturday afternoon, it was a hive of optimistic activity. Four recently elected MPs had flown in from Rome, and in the opening session they presented to the group what they'd done, explained decisions they'd taken and asked the Meetup for advice about the decisions that lay ahead. There was a session dedicated to reaching voters for the European elections the following year. Activists sat in a large circle, passing a rented microphone around, proposing ideas and voting on them. In keeping with Beppe's hatred of leaders and hierarchies, there are no formal leaders at the Meetup (although dominant characters usually emerge, often the organiser) so everyone gets a chance to present ideas and discuss them.[30] As a result, unorthodox ideas, often drawing on whatever diverse skill sets and interests are available, get put forward. In 2014, for example, the European

---

fans, but I use it simply to describe people who consider themselves supporters or members of the movement.

Meetup decided to investigate a proposal of the Italian government to sell overseas buildings they owned. Members of the Meetup put together an inventory of all Italian-owned buildings in Europe, and shared it with a Five Star senator, Laura Bottici, helping her to challenge the government.

Tens of thousands of Grillini pass two or more evenings a month doing this, excited by the promise of a new type of politics. Grillini are distrustful of political parties but have channelled frustration into action rather than apathy.[31] It's not perfect, of course. The lack of rules means the quality of meetings often depends on how motivated and talented the organisers and activists are. Some Meetups get nothing done and in certain towns there is more than one, and they don't always get along. (In the Sardinian regional elections in 2014, activists fell out and were unable to present a single list, so Beppe refused to certify it, which meant no one from Five Star appeared on the ballot.) But when it works, it's quite a beautiful thing. Spontaneous, organic, civic activism—democracy in action.*

Into Europe

On 25 May 2014, thanks to the work of the European Meetup supporters I'd met in London, and hundreds of

---

* I was made a little jealous by all this. I spend much of my week working at the UK think tank Demos, grappling with how to bring more people into politics. For twenty-five years we have written pamphlets and run countless seminars and workshops trying to work out how to engage new faces in politics. And here were the Grillini, just getting on with it, thanks to a couple of websites and, above all, knowing that their efforts might actually lead to something changing.

others like them who campaigned vigorously, the Five Star Movement enjoyed another stunning success at the polls. They won 21 per cent of the European parliamentary vote in Italy, and came second only to Prime Minister Renzi's Partito Democratico alliance. Seventeen MEPs headed to Brussels. (Nicola Marini ran for the European parliamentary election that year for the Sicily and Sardinia region, although missed out on being elected by just 200 votes.)

When the Five Star MEPs arrived in Brussels, no one knew what to make of them. Other MEPs would often ask if they were left wing or right wing; they would always reply: neither.[*] Thirty-one-year-old Ignazio Corrao delivered Five Star's inaugural speech in the Parliament wearing bright red Converse trainers, criticising the EU's preference for 'business as usual', arguing for more citizen involvement in decision-making, and attacking the proposed Transatlantic Trade and Investment Partnership (this deal, known as TTIP, had seemed a shoo-in at the time but collapsed after the election of Donald Trump).[32]

---

[*] Most parties in the European Parliament join a political bloc, an alliance with similar parties from other European countries. As a new party that refused to be categorised, it wasn't obvious who Five Star would ally with. The Green Party—probably their preferred partners—didn't appear to want them. In the end, they had only three options: Europe of Freedom and Direct Democracy (EFDD), a Eurosceptic grouping that included the UK Independence Party; a right-wing group that included Berlusconi's party; or going alone, which would have meant missing out on the funding and political weight that comes with being part of a bloc. After a vote on Beppe's blog, 78 per cent went for EFDD. 'I am extremely pleased,' said UKIP leader Nigel Farage. 'We will be the people's voice.' This partnership made some Grillini nervous. Although they agreed on the need for more direct democracy, on issues like government spending or the environment, they were very different indeed.

In October 2015 I travelled to Brussels to see how the Five Star MEPs—mostly anti-establishment activists used to the can-do Meetups—were fitting in to the infamously bureaucratic, committee-obsessed European Parliament. Ignazio agreed to let me shadow him around for the day, and I met him on the seventh of the seventeen floors that make up the Alberto Spinelli building, the largest in the Espace Léopold complex, where he and the other sixteen Five Star MEPs are based. Their airless hallway was festooned with posters that hint at their activist roots:

No TAV [the proposed train line]
No MUOS [a satellite system]
#NoAusterity
#RIPdemocracy

In Ignazio's office there was a *V for Vendetta* mask and a poster that read 'Live every day like the last day.' There was a pull-out bed in there too. 'I sleep in that sometimes,' he said.

Ignazio is tall, slim and has long dark hair. He's handsome but also slightly nerdy, which gives the effect of a movie star playing the part of a shy student. He was carrying a bag that had a 'War is not the answer' sticker on it, and wore a scrappy green duffel coat that he kept on the entire time I was with him, including during meetings. Someone like Ignazio doesn't quite fit in here. The European Parliament buildings feel like they've been designed with the express purpose of sucking any reforming vigour out of newcomers: Corridors in every direction take you to hundreds of unmemorable meeting rooms. Whenever I come here I get lost, and no one ever seems able to help because they're lost too. Before the days of mobile phones, people must have been stuck here for days.

Ignazio's life consists of endless committees and political group consultations, ad hoc meetings and plenary votes. He's a member of several commissions and committees, each of which scrutinises the work of other EU bodies, proposes amendments to laws or regulations and writes reports. Ignazio's first commitment of the day was to sit on a committee about human rights. From there he rushed to a committee about development, where he was one of twenty MEPs who needed to vote on a draft paper about the role of authorities in developing countries. The committee chair read out a series of 'amendments' and 'compromises' to this draft paper, and after each, MEPs voted whether to agree, disagree or abstain on key passages.*

'Amendment 19,' said the committee chair. 'In favour?' Twelve hands raised 'Against?' Two hands raised. 'Abstain?' Three hands raised. 'Adopted! Amendment 20. In favour . . .' He slugged through thirty of these amendments that had been suggested by members of the committee and diligently voted on each, knowing how to because he and his team had spent a couple of hours beforehand preparing. Sitting next to him was a member of his political bloc (EFDD) from UKIP (who voted in more or less the

---

* Because of the way the European Parliament works, there are usually as many translators present as languages being spoken. These unsung heroes circle committee rooms in raised glass boxes, each containing two of them, who speak four or five languages so well that they translate whatever is being said into whatever languages are needed in real time. The colossal task of translation is one of the reasons everything at the European level is so slow, expensive and bereft of humour. Translators will always tell you that humour just doesn't translate.

opposite way to Ignazio). Ignazio casts hundreds of votes like this every month.

All this just to change a few words in a report? Ignazio learned from the Meetups that small, sometimes tedious, efforts like this are one way to have some impact, even if it is marginal. Ignazio, whose bugbear is corruption (like many of the Grillini), carefully reads and amends language in proposed legislation, recommendations or reports to ensure anti-corruption work is included.[33]

Will this make any difference? I asked his assistant, Luigi. 'We've learned to measure our impact in years, not months,' he said.

After lunch, Ignazio waded through another interminable meeting about public commons, which was a messy exchange of 'roadmaps', 'defining principles' and 'definitions', in which nothing whatsoever was concluded. From there we rushed through those endless, airless corridors to the development group, where Ignazio serves as rapporteur for the 'Corruption in Development'. He gave a presentation about the fight against corruption and an EU initiative to tackle international money laundering.

Ignazio works incredibly hard. During the week he deals with all this parliamentary business. At the weekends, like many Five Star MPs or MEPs, he usually heads back to Sicily or Sardinia to meet with his local Meetup, to tell them what he's been doing and to ask for their advice. 'Their anger and frustration keeps me motivated. It reminds me of why I've been elected,' he told me.

Parties and movements that are explicitly anti-establishment, like Five Star, can be obstructive when they reach positions of power. Even though they are frequently accused by the media of being intransigent and stubborn, Five Star MPs have shown a willingness to work with other parties in the Italian Parliament. By 2015 one study found that Five Star MPs were just as likely as their counterparts in other parties to work collaboratively when proposing legislation.[34] The same is true in Brussels, where they work with others across the political spectrum, and make sure they work harder than everyone else. Fabio Massimo Cataldo, the long-haired, bearded, rock music fan and thirty-one-year-old leader* of the EFDD, told me they have surprised everyone in the Parliament. 'They didn't expect us to be such well-educated, can-do people. They expected us to be extremists. We are not here to destroy Europe, but to rebuild it.'

I wondered whether Ignazio was working hard because I was following him. So when I got back to London, I checked the website www.mepranking.eu, which determines, based on various measures, how hard every one of the 749 MEPs work. At the time of writing, Fabio was the third hardest-working MEP in the entire Parliament, Ignazio the fifth. Eleven of the seventeen are in the top hundred.[35]

Beppe

Spending time with Grillini—the Meetups and the MEPs—persuaded me that Beppe really has started an internet-powered revolution. The Grillini are an impressive bunch: generally hard-working, smart, enthusiastic and

---

* A position he held jointly with UKIP leader Nigel Farage until the latter resigned in July 2016.

sincere. True, some Grillini are rude, stubborn, incompe-
tent, opportunistic or obstructive, but the same is true of
all political movements. One of the great myths of politics, usually perpetuated by those already in power, is that
politics is such a difficult and specialised business that it
should be left to experts. In truth, it's a generic occupation,
which relies on active, motivated and honest citizens, and
MPs drawn from the wide pool of people they are supposed
to represent. Beppe's promise—which sounded ridiculous
in 2009 when he announced the birth of Five Star on his
blog—to use the Net to bring fresh faces and ideas to politics and replace hierarchies with a new leaderless model,
has actually worked. In the summer of 2016, for the first
time since the office was established in 1870, Rome elected
a female mayor: thirty-seven-year-old Virginia Raggi, of the
Five Star Movement.

But what about the other side of Beppe? Not the hologram-
matic cyber-utopian, but Real Beppe, the one who says the
ruling classes are 'dead and should be buried with a loud
raspberry'?

In February 2016, after several months of trying, I
managed to secure a rare interview with him, and travelled to Rome to meet Beppe and one of his advisors,
Marco Morosini. We met in the restaurant (closed to the
public) of the hotel he always stays in. I quickly realised
how famous he really is. There was a small crowd outside
as I walked in, hoping to get a glimpse of the man. The
day before, he had had to sneak out wearing a horse mask,
but of course everyone knew it was him.

Beppe wandered in late—he enjoys daily siestas—waving his smartphone. 'This,' he said, as he sat down, 'this is what changes everything!' He was wearing a nifty-looking blue puffer jacket and jeans. He's the antithesis of bland. Before I'd even asked a question, he picked up the small spoon that came with his espresso, and starting staring at it, making it bend. He then looked at me, and then back at the spoon, and then back at me, and laughed.

I asked him what he thought was the appeal of his movement, and what was prompting so many people to get involved in this new type of politics.

This was his answer, which is worth quoting in full: 'Because voters delegate one person. But with us you vote for projects, ideas, something that directly concerns you, your place, your culture, your environment, you decide how your budget is distributed, yes or no, I want to know how my taxes are spent. This is politics! Here is an exceptional fact. In Marseilles, a forty-four-year-old man, who worked for the Treasury, with two sons, a wife, a family, an IQ of seventy-five, gets admitted to the hospital for something in his leg, and they run a CAT scan on his brain just to make sure he's OK. And they discover he has no brain! His head is full of water; just a thin membrane of brain! What does it mean?! He was a person who conducted his life always doing the same things. Everything was planned, someone told him what to do, and he did it. So what does this mean? That millions of people who have a brain prefer a life of directives, with no freedom, no creativity. This is nowadays the split between men.'

That was a good story. Beppe told the exact same story at his show *Grillo vs Grillo* later that night.

I asked him about some of the tensions that a direct-democracy movement like Five Star creates. When people get to vote on everything, things don't always work out.

'It isn't strange that a comedian starts a movement and then gets back to being a comedian . . . I've returned to my job. I have no political power; and never had it. This is strange, if I was talking of someone else and not about myself, I would think that this is strange. No one's ever done anything like this.'*

I couldn't get a handle on anything Beppe was saying. He skilfully danced around subjects with grand statements; he set off on exciting tangents destined never to return; he of-course-ed his way past inquiries; he flattened objections with colourful and unprovable axioms.

Populism is a *style*. It's a revolt against the boring, slow and often professional approach of modern politics. As the traditional left–right divide (and party loyalty) weakened from the 1970s onward, politicians coalesced toward the middle. They were forced to appeal to an ever broader coalition of possible voters, something Bill Clinton called 'triangulation': the task of finding policies that the largest number of people agree with. And as media scrutiny became more intense—thanks in part to the Net and the manic twenty-four-hour news cycle—politicians became further incentivised to avoid risk. The result is that today senior politicians are flanked by a small squadron of press officers, focus-group researchers, PR advisers and speech-writers, all of whom are supremely talented in the

---

* Beppe announced shortly before the interview that he is planning to reduce the amount of time he is spending on politics, and go back to focusing more on his comedy.

art of saying things that are impossible to disagree with. Politicians have become specialists of inoffensive bland. From left to right, most politicians dress, look and sound the same, ponderous cardboard cut-outs of one another.

Populists, often quite intentionally, dress, look and sound different. They reject the drabness of established and professional politics. The populist's answers to problems are obvious (do what the people want) and the populist's delivery is funny, outrageous, unprovable. And it's usually spoken, very intentionally, like an ordinary person.

'*Vaffanculo* is a warrior word,' Beppe told me.

'There is no left and right anymore,' he said.

'The EU is a non-place, it's a like a big supermarket. It is doomed,' he said.

'Technology is an anthropological revolution,' he said.

'If everyone in China is a socialist, from whom do they steal?' he said in 1986. That was the joke about Craxi that got him banned from TV.

Each of these tiny parcels of emotion and wit provoke and stir. And each could fit into a tweet, sent out to his millions of fans. Beppe isn't a paradox! The rabble-rousing opponent-insulting comedian is in fact the ideal politician for a digital age. Blogs, Facebook and Twitter are the perfect platform for someone like him. With its word-count limits and networked sharing, there's no time for boring business of negotiation and compromise online. Digital technology is dichotomous and interactive, a series of discrete packets: 0/1, Like/Don't Like, My Guy/Not My Guy, Evil/Good.[36] It incentivises simplicity and rewards pithiness. Slogans and memes are its currency.

Surrounded by competing news, busy social media threads and updates, politics is increasingly about grabbing attention.[37] And online content that uses extreme words, either positively or negatively, is more likely to be shared than content composed of boring sensible words.[38] According to a 2015 academic study of Beppe's blog, posts using more intensive anti-establishment vocabulary attracted twice as many comments, and two and a half times more unique commenters.[39] No wonder he calls Silvio Berlusconi a psycho-dwarf. It guarantees retweets, shares, comments and coverage.

Put another way, in language any digital advertiser would understand, populist politics is clickable and sharable content.

The digital prophets assumed that limitless information and total connectivity would make us more informed, less bigoted and kinder citizens. But the internet is an overwhelming smorgasbord of competing facts, claims, blogs, data, masquerading propaganda, misinformation, investigative journalism, charts, different charts, commentary and reportage. All this information is not making us more thoughtful: it's making us more emotional. In our busy lives, we will pay attention to the one person making more noise than anyone else, we only have time to click on that funny thing at the top of our feeds, or the thing our friends—who think like us—have posted.

It's not the slow, informed and careful politicians who have thrived online; it's the populists from across the spectrum. It's the people with the simple, emotional, shareable messages. It's people like Beppe.

Dutch anti-Islam politician Geert Wilders, who's compared the Qu'ran to *Mein Kampf*, is the most followed politician on the Dutch social networks. Bernie Sanders was propelled to within an inch of the Democratic Party

nomination with help from his online #feelthebern fans
and online donations. But the biggest shock of all (to pollsters and mainstream newspapers anyway) took place in
2016 when billionaire magnate, ur-populist, professional
simplifier and Twitter addict Donald Trump was elected
forty-fifth president of the United States. This should not
have surprised anyone. Like Beppe, Trump is the perfect
politician for the digital age.

His content is wildly popular online. On 29 November
2016 President Elect Trump posted on Twitter: 'Nobody
should be allowed to burn the American flag—if they do,
there must be consequences—perhaps loss of citizenship
or year in jail!' This was retweeted 74,000 times. It was
also in direct contravention of the US Constitution. It
wasn't quite as popular as his tweet of three days earlier,
however, which was retweeted over 100,000 times: 'Fidel
Castro is dead!' But even that paled in significance to his
tweet the day after he won the election on 8 November:
'TODAY WE MAKE AMERICA GREAT AGAIN!' (his
capitals). This was retweeted 355,000 times. With colleagues at my think tank Demos, I ran a small piece of
analysis on Trump's twittering, and collecting all of his
and his Democrat opponent Hillary Clinton's tweets between 1 January and 16 June 2016. Trump's tweets averaged
4,318 retweets from other users; Hillary Clinton's average
was 1,556. (Beppe Grillo's was 4,701.)

It didn't matter that Trump repeatedly lied, exaggerated or insulted his opponents. What mattered more
was that his message was out there, being shared and
retweeted far quicker than any careful denunciation ever
could. Outrage sells, and journalists are secretly addicted
to Trump, and to his compelling outbursts. According to

one US-based analytics firm, Trump received around $5 billion in free media coverage over the election cycle as cable news gobbled up his headline-grabbing tweets and outlandish suggestions—twice the amount Hillary Clinton received.[40]

Politicians evolve to suit the media of the day. They became more telegenic after the television was invented: John F. Kennedy famously trounced the pale and nervous-looking Richard Nixon in a television debate, but those listening on radio thought Nixon had won. Tony Blair and Bill Clinton—the masters of the easy sound bite—were perfect for the twenty-four-hour news cycle, with its endless repetitions. In the same way the media is increasingly driven by clicks and shares, so today's digital-savvy politician has to compete for people in an attention-poor era. The entertainers, the professional simplifiers and the emotionally outraged are the new masters.

The love affair between populists and social media goes deeper than just being outrageous, emotive or simplistic. Populists claim to be the voice of the people, fighting a corrupt, powerful and professional elite. The internet is the ideal direct line to those honest, decent, hard-working people, circumnavigating the self-interested establishment parties and media. Every populist, whether now or in the past, believes they speak for the downtrodden and quiet man on the street, the silent majority. They always think they possess some version of what the philosopher Rousseau called the *volonté générale*—a vague, mystical notion of the people's will, to which a leader can attach himself. (Shortly after I left, Beppe announced a new Web platform that would replace the blog, called Rousseau.[41])

It's a dangerous thing to believe, since it can justify anything. In mid-2016 the *Washington Post's* fact-checker blog examined Donald Trump's testable statements, and found 70 per cent of them were dishonest.[42] In response, Trump revoked the *Washington Post's* press credentials 'based on the incredibly inaccurate coverage and reporting of the record-setting Trump campaign'. He posted that on Facebook (of course) saying he had 'no choice' but to take his message *direct* to the American people via social media. (In December 2016 he tweeted 'If the press would cover me accurately & honorably, I would have far less reason to "tweet." Sadly, I don't know if that will ever happen!' That one was retweeted 38,000 times.) This is a particularly effective technique when trust in the mainstream media is at a record low: in 2016 only 32 per cent of Americans (and only 14 per cent of Republicans) said they trust mainstream media, down eight percentage points from the year before.[43] When I asked Beppe about the repeated criticism from Italian media about Five Star, he replied that criticism from the Italian media was 'like a medal'.

Leaders who believe they are in possession of the people's will and up against vested interests are able to justify avoiding reasonable checks on their power. Beppe's blog is hosted on a server in Casaleggio Associates' very ordinary-looking office in Milan, from where 'the Staff' run the blog and enforce the rules. Beppe owns the blog along with the name and logo of the movement, which means, legally speaking, he and the Staff can do whatever they want with it. (Amazingly, while I was researching this, no one seemed to know precisely who the Staff are, although they are thought to include Beppe, Gianroberto

Casaleggio (until his death), Gianroberto's son David, Filippo Pittarello,[44] a small number of lawyers, technology experts and communications specialists.[45])

Shortly after the blog was set up, Beppe called it 'the tool that we have for creating true democracy'. But there are unconfirmed reports that David Casaleggio writes most of the blog posts as well as running Beppe's Twitter feed.[46] And although each post typically receives thousands of comments, no one ever replies; in fact, if supporters do write back on the blog, the Staff can just delete it with a click.[47] One study, based on an analysis of deleted comments, revealed that many of them contained politely worded criticism.[48] It all feels very democratic, but there is still someone in charge. Only now, they're sitting behind a computer screen in another city.

There have been at least fifty votes on Beppe's blog since 2005, allowing members to express their opinion on everything from the alliance with UKIP to who Beppe should meet, and elected representatives follow whatever decision is reached.[49] It's an admirable example of direct democracy in action, and far braver than any other political party. But the Staff decide what questions are put to an online vote, and the way they are worded. Federico Pistono, an activist and technology specialist who founded both the Verona and Biella branches of the Amici di Beppe Grillo, told me he'd been drawn to the movement by the promise of creating a more sustainable economy and environment powered by direct democracy. But he's been disappointed. 'This is a facade of democracy,' he told me. 'Democracy is also about deciding what you are voting on. Voting itself is the final bit. If you're presented with two bullshit options by the Staff, that's not really a democratic choice.[*] And the online votes can be overridden anyway. The day I watched *Grillo vs Grillo* the Italian Senate was voting on a proposed bill to allow same-sex civil partnerships. On the blog, Five Star supporters overwhelmingly voted in favour. But a clause in the bill permitted people in civil partnerships to adopt each other's biological offspring. This potentially controversial clause had not been included in the vote that took place on Beppe's blog. So a few days later, Beppe decided the vote would be non-binding, and said MPs should vote according to their own conscience.[50] Several upset Five Star supporters turned up at the beginning of *Grillo vs Grillo* to disrupt the start of the show, saying he had done this to score political points against the government.

Perhaps it's just a very small staff trying to enforce some semblance of order and discipline over what is a very jumbled movement. But since 2013 several leading figures have left, been expelled by a blog vote or prevented from using the logo. Many of them have complained specifically about the Staff's (especially Casaleggio's or Beppe's) control over the movement, the lack of internal democracy and lack of communication from anyone in charge.[51] (Federico Pistono told me he contacted the Staff often, but never

---

[*] There are other, more advanced systems to allow users to contribute to online discussion, such as the Pirate Party's much discussed 'Liquid Feedback', although this has had its own, slightly different problems. Under Liquid Feedback, a member can make a proposal and if 10 per cent agree it passes to a voting stage, at which point others can submit counter-proposals, and people can transfer their vote to someone they consider more knowledgeable. Rick Falkvinge, the founder of the Pirate Party, explained to me that the idea of Liquid Feedback was to combine direct democracy with expertise and specialism.

received a response.) By late 2015, of 163 MPs elected in 2013, 37 had left—9 of whom had been expelled.

Il Duce

It's easy to assume Five Star is the product of Italian exceptionalism—a revolt against Craxi, against Silvio, against La Casta. But every democracy is experiencing a growing distrust of political elites, declining confidence (and vote share) of the large left and right political parties, and frustration about slow, unresponsive governments and professional elites. Rising numbers feel politics has become too distant, too complicated, too professional and too closed. And they're right. Politics in many Western democracies is a stage-managed soap opera of manufactured outrage: one long and uninspiring who's-up-who's-down show. Thoughtful discussion and big visions are almost entirely absent because anything popular with people is populist. Anything detailed is egg-headed or academic. Anything unusual is radical. Anything forthright is extreme. The whole business of politics is an exercise in risk aversion, since saying anything interesting or unusual disqualifies you from office, which is why most politicians look, sound and indeed are similar.

The internet offers hope: an increasing number of people engage with politics online, and from there enter 'real-world' politics. Whether it's signing petitions or starting new political movements, the internet has dramatically lowered the cost of entry into politics, and diminished the power of media editors and political organisations.[52]

There's much to celebrate in that. Young people in particular see the Net as an effective and important place for political debate and action, generally viewing it as representing progress for democracy.[53] Of course there are plenty of problems—including boring technical challenges—of using digital tools for political activism.[54] But used carefully and with healthy scepticism, digital tools could liberate our ailing democracies. Beppe has shown how it can be done. At the time of writing there are well over 1,000 of these Beppe Grillo Meetup groups, with over 150,000 members, dotted all across Italy and beyond.[55]

The internet might bring more people in, but it doesn't automatically follow that it makes politics any better. The great conceit is that when armed with technology, we will make better decisions, find answers to tricky problems, resolve fundamental conflicts of interest, end corruption and all get along better. Blogs and Web primaries and www.meetup.com will not smash hierarchies, influence, self-interest and power.[56] These things simply reconfigure with new forms and names like the Net or the Staff. And the notion that digital politics will be more informed and thoughtful is even more unlikely. Beppe is a warning shot about what the internet is doing to politics: it brings in new people and ideas, but also simplifies complicated issues, and convinces people they are in possession of the obvious answers.[57] It makes it easier than ever to believe that you are in possession of the truth, the voice of the people, against the corrupt elite. In this world, your opponents can't simply hold a principled difference of opinion. They must be bad. They must be incoherent babblers, sinister Machiavellians, politically correct elites or hoodwinked buffoons.* That makes compromise more difficult, since compromise relies on the acceptance of principled differences of opinion in good faith.[58] According to voting records, the US Congress is now at its most ideologically polarised since records began.[59] It makes for emotion-fuelled certainties, for angrier, more polarised politics: where attention-grabbing and controversy-generation are incentivised over plodding, unshareable deliberation.

Representative democracies, with their checks and balances and layers of powers between the people and law-making, were partly a protection against the furious mob taking over.[60] As the speed and ease of our digital lives grow, the sluggishness of representative democracies will become even more frustrating. Representative democracy is in many ways pathetically out of synch with other societal trends. As consumers, we are told that we are always right and *deserve* to have anything we want. As citizens, individualism and human rights declare each of us is sacrosanct: we should marry who we wish, sleep with who we choose, believe whatever we want and say whatever

---

* In summer 2016 a group of politicians, writers and celebrities set up More United, a digital platform to crowdfund for candidates, and to stop politics becoming more polarised. It was a very decent effort to push back against increasingly polarised politics. 'We'll do this by using the power of the internet to transform the way politics is funded, making it easier for moderate, progressive MPs to get elected and creating a new centre of political gravity in the UK,' Caroline Criado Perez, one of the organisers, said. 'This isn't about left or right. This is about a common, internet-generation purpose to make the UK a more progressive country.' Typical of web-based initiatives, it implies there is an obvious and 'correct' answer for political problems. ('Values', More United UK, http://www.moreunited.uk/beliefs.)

we believe. As digital netizens, we demand access to the world's information at the click of a button. Yet in our political lives, arguably the most important of all, the best we can expect is a single vote every few years. And we must accept the result and delegate our political choices to someone else we've probably never met.

Direct democracy is now more plausible than at any time since ancient Athens because the internet allows the people to have their say quicker, cheaper and more visibly than ever before. It's an irresistible force. But used excitedly with blind utopian fervour, carried on a wave of passion and revolutionary zeal, digital politics could easily become just as autocratic as its analogue cousin.

Italy's most infamous populist was Mussolini. He also claimed that his Fasci di Combattimento was not a party but a movement, and that corrupt political parties were the problem. He also saw himself as a saviour who could deliver his people from the establishment of the day. He didn't have the internet, of course, but did use modern communication to get beyond the straitjackets of left–right political ideologies. Mussolini also promised a new, purer type of politics, one that could rescue civic activism from its torpor. By whipping up furies and frustrations, promising utopia and denouncing opponents as enemies of the people, it degenerated into violent fascism. Mussolini killed his opponents, Beppe just insults them. He's no fascist. I think Beppe is a true a believer in the emancipatory power of the Net. But it's not surprising that some journalists have noticed the troubling similarities.[61]

When I put it to Beppe that he had been compared to Il Duce, he just laughed and shrugged his shoulders.

'You cannot compare a thing like this! Even if Mussolini was an extraordinary comedian, it is *him* who resembled *me*, in being a comedian!' I couldn't work out what on earth he was trying to say. It was obviously meant to be some kind of joke. It wasn't as good as the one about Craxi.

6

Temple of Duhm

Day 1

As the sun rises over the Portuguese countryside I find myself standing in a circle on top of a hill with a group of strangers, nervously grasping hands, my eyes tightly shut. We are gathered around a collection of enormous 'sacred' stones, a candle, a ceramic bowl filled with water and a crystal. A woman in white robes is humming something incomprehensible.

This is no futile sun salutation. This is a 'Ring of Power'. We are trying to stop the war in Syria using the power of our thoughts.

I arrived at Tamera the night before, after a two-hour train journey from Lisbon into the heart of Alentejo, a region known for its vast open countryside—it's the bread basket of Portugal—but also for desertification and erosion due to the extreme heat. A serene German called Bernd met me at the train station at Funchiera, which is the nearest town, and we trundled slowly through twenty miles of poorly lit and barely tarmacked roads in his tatty old Mercedes, finally arriving at an isolated 350-acre site miles from anywhere.

When a tiny band of Germans arrived here in 1995, it was just a dilapidated farm plot, with nothing save a few orange trees, an olive grove, an oak forest and abandoned buildings. They had little money, no drinking water, no animals and no food, but an ambitious plan to create what they called a 'healing biotope'.[1] A template of how man could live in harmony with himself, his fellow man and his environment.[2] Now they are 150-strong, having survived rainless summers, freezing winters, flooding, planning problems, five deaths and a dozen births. They've turned a scorched dustbowl into a functioning free-love commune that has transformed the local water ecosystem and reinvigorated animal and plant life. Bernd dropped me off at the welcome centre, and wished me luck.

The Ring of Power was the first item on the printed agenda distributed to the forty of us who had arrived that evening to attend Introduction Week. Once every three months or so Tamera allows members of the public to live here for a few days, and learn how it works. You have to pay, of course: it cost the forty of us €350 each to attend Introduction Week, plus €30 per day for food and accommodation (40 × €350 + [40 × €30 × 5] = €20,000).[3]

Tamera is split into two sites. On the western side, there is the seventy-acre 'Campus', which is where all the visitors stay. That's us on the Introduction Week, plus thirty or so people who are volunteering in the gardens/kitchen, and another couple of dozen attending other seminars and courses put on here. The Campus is visitor-friendly: it has a bar, a café, an open kitchen, a large communal eating area, a 'cultural centre', a bookshop, a guest house (an extra €28 per night), male and female dorms and a large auditorium.

The 150 Tamerians who actually live here full-time are over on the separate eastern side, which is three times larger than the Campus. Dotted among the sprawl of lakes, agriculture plots and plant-life reserves are small villages where twenty to thirty residents, aged between four weeks and eighty years, live together in cluttered caravans, huts, yurts and shacks. The whole site has the feel of a half-finished holiday campsite because Tamera is currently designated by the Portuguese planning authorities as agricultural land, which prevents any major construction work. The small number of decent buildings are mostly located in a part of the site called Grace Village, including the grandly named Institute for Global Peace and the Political Ashram. Grace Village is also where the two founders live: a seventy-two-year-old psychoanalyst called Dieter Duhm, and his partner Sabine Lichtenfels, a self-declared medium in her midsixties.

After the Ring of Power, everyone on the Introduction Week walks to the largest of the seminar rooms on Campus, an airy room with laminate wooden floors and forty chairs in a circle, for the more orthodox introduction to the place.

Shoes are not allowed in the seminar room, which causes a small pile-up of hopping and bending over around the door. Once that's successfully navigated, Monika, a senior Tamerian in her early sixties with blonde hair, flowing clothes and crystalline blue eyes, strides in radiating calm, welcomes everyone and we each introduce ourselves.

Monika has lived in Tamera full-time since 2000. She will be our guide for the week, along with Maria, a nineteen-year-old who's lived here all her life.

Everyone has their own reasons for making the trip to this remote European outpost, but they are all fairly similar. Visitors are mostly well-off Westerners dissatisfied with what the modern world offers: not knowing your neighbours, trashing the environment, buying stuff that doesn't make you happy, sex everywhere but where you want it, smartphone addiction. In one way or another they think Tamera might give them something more meaningful. Chris, a tree surgeon from Scotland, was inspired to visit after reading about Tamera's work bringing wildlife back to the local area. Laura, a middle-age woman from Spain, is searching for somewhere to live that feels 'more like a real community' than her home city of Madrid. Mario, an atheist from Italy with a string of failed relationships behind him, wants to explore polyamory and free love. At least half of those at Introduction Week are contemplating becoming fully fledged Tamerians who live here all year round, and are here to find out how.[*]

---

[*] There are four or five stages before someone can become a Tamerian. First, becoming a volunteer or a guest, like us. Then one can become a student and undergo an intense study of the basic philosophy of the place. If the community thinks you fit, you become a 'joiner' ('Einsteiger' in German), then a 'co-worker' in training, before finally a full Tamerian. The stages are not very clear-cut and rarely formally enforced. If you have in-demand skills (which currently include a forest gardener, web designer, business manager, IT specialist, project manager and electrical engineer), it would be slightly quicker. There is also a separate status of 'specialists', some of whom are hired to advise on specific topics, and unlike all other workers in Tamera, receive a salary.

Monika says over the week we will learn how Tamera 'cooperates' with animals, generates its own energy, how free love works and how they plan to create that 'healing biotope' that, she says, will save the world. Today she will give us the basics of life here, and a potted history of the ideas behind the whole project.

Tamera is the brainchild of a German psychoanalyst called Dieter Duhm. He had been involved in the 1968 left-wing student movements that swept across Europe, but was confused by their failure to transform the world. In 1972 he published a 'bestselling' book called *Angst im Kapitalismus*, which argued successful revolutions are only possible if we reprogramme our thought patterns first.* Like many failed 68ers, Dieter concluded Marx had it wrong. It wasn't the material world that needed reshaping: it was the mental one. Set upon exploring this further, Dieter left his wife, turned down an offer of a professorship, and went travelling to research alternative communities that were trying to break out of 'modern' social conditioning and moral constructs.† Heavily influenced by Wilhelm Reich, an Austrian psychoanalyst who believed that

---

* The only reference to it having been a bestseller appears on Dieter Duhm's website. It was not on the annual bestseller lists of the magazine *Der Spiegel* or the periodical *Buchreport* in the years 1972–84. It might have been an unofficial bestseller in leftist circles, but not in the mainstream.

† There were many alternative communities being formed around this time. Dieter's visits included Poona, an ashram in India. It was set up by Bhagwan Shree Rajneesh (aka Osho) in the 1960s to help people let go of egos and boundaries, including sexual. In 1981 Osho moved to the United States to continue his work, but his ashrams were investigated for a series of crimes, for which his personal secretary was ultimately convicted, and he was deported.

neurosis was rooted in sexual conditions (and who even
Freud thought was too obsessed with sex), Dieter concluded unresolved sexual desire, jealousy and a lack of
trust were the underlying reasons for the world's problems.[4] Every social utopia of the past had failed, he wrote
in 1975, because that dishonesty causes squabbling, envy
and sexual repression, which are then mirrored in the dys-
functional organisations we create.

Between 1983 and 1986, under the leadership of Dieter and his new partner Sabine, fifty people moved to a
large house in the Black Forest in Germany in order to figure out how to create a 'trusting community'. They called
their little commune the 'Bauhuette', which is German for
tool shed. Monogamy was replaced by free love and polyamory. They sat in freezing rivers to test their endurance,
and performed theatre dressed as Nazis (this is known as
'psychodrama': a psychotherapy tool to use role play as a
means to self-reflect). They lined up rows of chairs facing
each other and talked for seventy-two hours straight. And
after dinner every evening they would pile up to the attic
and sit in a large circle to hold a 'self-performance forum',
where each person would tell the whole group everything
they feared, wanted and fantasised, often in an exaggerated or dramatic way.[5]

The vision was to smash down conventions and create
a transparent, envy-free community. German newspapers,
churches and political parties did not share Dieter's view
that this was a vital social experiment. A series of investi-
gations in 1985–6 painted the group as a bizarre sex cult,
and their landlord asked them to leave. Some went on to
found the Centre for Experimental Culture Design just
outside Berlin (which is still going strong today, under its

German abbreviation, ZEGG). Dieter, Sabine and a handful of others headed to the Canary Islands before going on to found Tamera in 1995.

'We are building a trust-based community,' says Monika, putting into practice Dieter's theories and ideas 'to create a model that's an alternative to all major areas of life, based on trust, mutual support, and responsible participation'.

To that end Tamerians do not live in nuclear families, but rather as a wider community. Adults usually live alone or in shared single-sex accommodation or vans. About thirty children live in Tamera too, most of whom were born here. From the age of four they live together in the Place of the Children, accompanied by an adult, not always the parent. Some children have several mother and father figures who are not necessarily the biological parents (although it is usually known who the real parents are—'I think we always know if we need to know,' Monika says). There is also a school and a kindergarten, where the children are home-schooled, according to the Portuguese national curriculum. Though there are a handful of Portuguese, a couple of Brits and Israelis, nearly everyone in Tamera is German, which creates occasional communication problems with the Portuguese authorities, who intermittently visit the site, although Monika says they have a good relationship.

Sex and eroticism is a public not a private affair. Although many Tamerians have a 'primary partner', nearly everyone has multiple sexual relationships. They don't call this free love, rather 'love free of fear'. There are a number of 'love zones' scattered around the site, which are small huts expressly set aside for having sex.

'Trust comes through radical honesty,' explains Monika. This is mainly achieved through daily forums, modelled on Dieter's forums from the Bauhuette days. Tamerians sit (also in a large circle) and are guided by a forum leader. One person steps into the middle and says anything that's on their mind, including who they'd like to sleep with. The others then 'mirror' back: saying what they think in return.[6] Free love and transparency are, she says, key to Tamera's survival as a sustainable commune. It's what creates trust, and that's why they've survived so long.

But the place cannot function on free love alone. Tamera is run by a frequently shifting constellation of committees. The main decision-making body was until recently a 'government' that consisted of three members, but that changed in 2016 to a 'carrier group' of about fifteen, and then to a 'planning council' of twelve.[7] They make the big decisions about how the money is spent, resolve any major disputes or disagreements and determine what the year's priorities should be.

Lunch is cauliflower, cabbage soup and rice balls—Tamera is a vegan commune—which was planted, ploughed, dug, cooked, served and cleaned by a squadron of tired-looking volunteers in their twenties who all look like they do yoga. The food is laid on a large common table in the Campus, with instructions to all one hundred visitors who eat together (the Tamerians eat separately in their little villages) to grab a large bowl and plate of food and take it back to a table to share with those around you. Do not—and they really insist on this—*absolutely do not* get food only for yourself. That would be individualistic. The resulting anarchy is a combination of confusion and inequality. Some tables end up with far too much food, while others barely have any.

I sit with Mario and Hannes, a cosmopolitan and convivial engineer from Munich. They are both here because they believe that the norms and mores—especially monogamy—that characterise sexual behaviour in the outside world don't really work for them. Both have wound up feeling guilty when they've been attracted to people outside of their relationship, and both are eager to find out exactly how free love plays out. So immediately after finishing lunch the three of us set out in search of one of the love shacks Monika mentioned earlier.

The Campus is a complicated assortment of dirt paths that cut through bushes and brambles in every direction, leading variously to freshwater showers, small hills, tidy rows of compost toilets, camping areas and the little Tamerian villages. Gossiping as we wander, lost, up and down the paths in the warm autumn sun, we finally chance on a wooden shack tucked away behind some densely packed trees.

Inside is a dusty, slightly worn, double mattress on a wooden pallet resting on four heavy-duty grey industrial breeze blocks. There's a window, a shabby dreamcatcher and a table with some oil, condoms and a roll of toilet paper. I have a sense that the shack has been recently used.

Hannes looks a little deflated. 'It's not very romantic is it?' he says.

That evening I arrange to meet Monika in the Campus bar to interview her, and hopefully fix a time to meet either of the founders, Dieter or Sabine.

Monika greets me warmly, buys me a drink and absolutely insists that I ask her any question I want. 'No subject is off limits,' she says.

I asked about the role of women in Tamera, since they seem particularly prominent. Women are very important in Tamera, she says. We get deeply involved in all the social relationships of the community, and take a key role in helping support a couple deciding whether or not to have children.

'Do you encourage polyamory?' I ask.

'You do it as you want,' she says. 'But around here there are so many possibilities, so many attractive people, why should you be restricted to one?' It's true. Everyone in Tamera *is* good-looking. Presumably free-love communes are more fun if you're attractive.

'What about your personal life?' I ask.

'I am married and live together with my husband in Grace Village. But I also have sexual encounters with other men. We want to build the template of a life form based on trust. As long as you have to betray your love partner because you fall in love with another, the result will not be peace, but war. To overcome jealousy, we need to change our thinking habits, our actions, our complete life. Recently I had a wonderful sexual encounter with a twenty-one-year-old. This is such a taboo in our society. But it had a deep meaning for him. He experienced total acceptance by a strong motherly woman. For him this creates a beautiful basis for his love towards women in general, and for me it is a change in my view on the meaning of my role as a woman this age.'

I ask about how young people get along with free love. Given the openness towards sexuality, and the fact that children are brought up here, it is a subject that many of the Intro-Weekers are slightly nervous about. I'd read before arriving that young Tamerians attend something called Love School, where they can speak to adults about sex.

She tells me: 'I learned through this project how the generation gap can be overcome in such a beautiful way. Children in the wild age of puberty are so soft and gentle when they find adults whom they can trust. Love School for youth is a sensitive and responsible task for men and women mainly in their twenties and thirties who accompany them through their encounters and love experiences. In the outside world, people's first sexual encounters are usually bad and shameful. Young people in Tamera celebrate this together with friends in a beautiful way.'

This seems both worryingly vague and overly hopeful, I think. I make a note to look into this more when I return home.

After the interview, I stumble back to my accommodation via a dirt path, helped by torch and moonlight. I'm staying in one of the small number of guest rooms near the welcome centre. Although extremely basic by modern standards, out here in Tamera these guest rooms are the height of luxury since they have a (shared) power shower and a normal bathroom. The guest rooms were in high demand, but I'd convinced Monika I needed a table, chair, light and plug socket so I could record the day's events each evening.

I sit down on my small wooden desk and start writing.

Day 2

At breakfast, which is a surprisingly tasty cold porridge-gruel, I speak to a group of six young Israelis. 'We live in a place with no peace,' says David, a handsome man in his late twenties from Tel Aviv. Politics has repeatedly failed to resolve the Israeli–Palestinian conflict, he adds. 'We are looking for hope.'

At the other end of my table Petr, an Austrian in his early forties with an immovable grin and unusually loud voice, tells everyone within earshot, which is almost all one hundred of us, that 'we create our own reality.' As proof he says he once went without food for *two years*. When pushed on this utterly stunning claim he says in fact he *did* eat, but only rice milk, bananas and chocolate. Not having been able to drink anything like my usual strength or amount of coffee, Petr's voice is a catalyst for my fast-developing withdrawal headache.

Today is animal day. Maria walks us over to Terra Deva, which translates to 'the Land of the Spirits'. This hectare of enchanting forest, ponds and small valleys is right in the heart of the site and is considered the most sacred place in Tamera. Monika calls it a 'research' area where Tamerians investigate how to regenerate the land.

Heike Kessler is one of five caretakers of Terra Deva. She's a jovial, slightly rotund, blonde Tamerian with an uncommonly cheerful face. She's also Maria's biological mother. Before she lets us enter Terra Deva, Heike stops at a large oak tree near the entrance gate and asks us to gather around it in a circle and close our eyes. (We seem to do everything at Tamera in circles.)

'I greet the beings, invisible and visible,' says Heike, in a thick German accent. 'We ask for permission to step into the area. We are coming in peace.'

After a short pause, she nods and smiles. 'I have a feeling we're invited.'

Tamerians believe that animals and humans, by virtue of sharing the same DNA, are able to communicate. It's just a question of plugging into the right resonance, of connecting to the correct wavelength. In his 2001 book *The Sacred Matrix*, founder Dieter Duhm writes that 'the same consciousness pulses through a molecule, a galaxy, a worm and a human being. Internally they all react in the same way, and they are connected with the same dream of existence.'[8]

Among other Tamerians Heike is renowned for her ability to connect to the right wavelength. Last year Tamera had a problem with wild boar, which were invading the site and destroying the vegetation. Heike meditated, prayed and felt something. She spoke to the animals, and they spoke back.

'Don't come into our land,' she told the boar, offering them a separate bit of land they could dig and eat and wreck to their hearts' content. But in return, they had to promise to leave the vegetables alone. She wrote a little contract in German and wedged it into the parcels of land she wanted them to avoid.

'It worked!' she excitedly tells us all.

'How did you know?' I ask.

'They let me know by leaving their footprints close to *but not directly on* the plants.'

The boar apparently left the vegetables alone too, which Tamerians took to be a minor miracle, proof that animals and humans can cooperate. 'An amicable agreement with wild boars has developed', wrote Dieter in his 2014 book *Terra Nova*. (They claim to have a similar arrangement in place with rats too.[9])

This year a new boar family has turned up and, judging by the roughly dug-up vegetation across Tamera, have decided to disregard the treaty.

'This new boar is ignoring our prayers and meditation,' says Heike, slightly exasperated. 'The boar said to me "We will keep coming until you understand our message. You have to change." So I asked the boar how, and she told me to wait.'

She's still waiting. Someone suggests she might consider having a word with the mosquitos too.*

Heike invites us to walk around Terra Deva alone; perhaps we can feel some resonance too. It's an enchanting place, with a fairy-tale feel to it. But I don't feel anything.

As I wander around the forest trying to work out if Heike is talking in metaphors, and why a wild boar would understand German of all languages, I spot Hannes sitting alone and looking pensive in a love shack. Unlike the first one this is a little more appealing. There are no wooden pallets or breeze blocks. It's just a small clearing in the trees, about four square metres, with a tasteful mattress. It's set back away from the paths, and there are stunning views looking down onto the trees and rivers.

'Now *this* is more like it,' says Hannes, looking cheerful. 'This is where I come alive sexually.'

In the afternoon seminar we all share some of our own projects. One person works for a similar community in Scotland, called Findhorn. Another talks about her project studying alternative education systems. One of the group doesn't have any projects but does have a little ukulele,

---

* Monika emailed me a few weeks later and said that it had rained and the soil had softened: 'the wild boar finds enough food outside of the gardens and accepts the rules again. She shows up with her four little ones, more and more fearless as a becoming member of the community.'

and he sings 'I Don't Want to Live on the Moon' by Ernie
from *Sesame Street*:

> Well I'd like to visit the moon
> On a rocket ship high in the air
> Yes I'd like to visit the moon
> But I don't think I'd like to live there.

After dinner—a delicious aubergine curry, and I think
we're slowly getting the hang of the food arrangements
too—I walk down to the site shop to take a look at what's
on offer. Along with a variety of crystals, precious stones
and books on spirituality are Dieter Duhm's and Sabine
Lichtenfels' extensive writings. There is also a book in
German called *Aus dem Gefängnis* ('From Prison') by an
Austrian man called Otto Muehl. Muehl was the leader of
the most notorious and authoritarian sect of recent years,
called the Aktionsanalytische Organisation (AAO).

Muehl founded AAO in 1972 as a radical social experiment in free love and communal living. Each of the
500 members had a number denoting their position in
the organisation's hierarchy. Everyone had to sleep with a
different person each night, and Muehl could sleep with
whomever he wished. Children were routinely humiliated
in front of hundreds of adults in mass forums, and diktats
from Muehl were religiously followed. Shortly after the
commune collapsed in 1990 Muehl was convicted for sexual
relations with minors (classed as aged under fourteen), rape
and forced abortion, and sentenced to seven years in prison.

Dieter spent time at the AAO in the mid-1970s and
described it as a 'revolutionary experiment', writing that

it was 'the only project that had a relatively truthful way of dealing with the number-one topic' (sex), although he's also written that he was unhappy with much of Muehl's behaviour, in particular the amount of control he had, and repeatedly distanced himself from Muehl.[10] Not sufficiently distanced, though, to stop selling his book.

I make a note to ask Dieter about this. But in the bar that evening Monika tells me it won't be possible to interview Dieter, and Sabine is also too busy because she's on a 'pilgrimage' walking across Portugal talking about water retention. But, she adds, Dieter will be doing a public Q&A on day 4, and in view of my position as a writer, she would be happy to pass on any questions I have.

Day 3

Tamera is part of a growing movement of communities that call themselves 'eco-villages'. Eco-villages are typically made up of between fifty and 150 people who try to live together in an environmentally, socially and economically sustainable way. They are usually an effort to develop ways of living that don't trash the earth, and some have a spiritual element too, such as trying to create a way of life that people find meaningful. Although such communities have always existed, the eco-village movement formally started in the 1970s. In the mid-1990s the Global Ecovillage Network was founded to encourage the growth of the model. According to the Intentional Community Directory there are currently 2,255 eco-village communities around the world, spread across seventy countries and covering everything from a network of remote villages in Sri Lanka to the very popular Cristiana in Copenhagen, a self-proclaimed autonomous commune of 850 people founded by hippies, squatters and anarchists in 1971.

Uncertain times often stimulate 'back to the land' movements like this. The seventeenth-century Diggers, with their dreams of small, independent, egalitarian agricultural communities, began during the great political and social unrest of the English Civil War.[11] During the anxiety and strains that followed the Napoleonic Wars, social reformer Robert Owen imagined 'villages of cooperation' that would be economically and socially self-sufficient.[12] The 1970s saw a surge in communal utopias (approximately 750,000 Americans lived in communes during that decade), some members of which were disappointed hippies, but many were explicitly driven by a fear of an impending apocalypse and energy meltdown, including the New Atlantis Commune and the Genesis Project.[13] These are uncertain times too. According to the Intentional Community Directory, over 300 new eco-villages were founded in the first ten months of 2016.

For a commune to reach full autonomy is extremely difficult. In the 1990s a group of researchers at the Centre for Alternative Technology in Wales calculated it would take 600 adults to create a reasonably modern functioning community that doesn't depend on the outside world. (They worked out that 220 different roles would need filling in eleven general sectors—agriculture, crafts, arts, sports, estate management, services, health, education, commercial, technical and industrial—and each role would usually need more than one person.) Intentional community-building like Tamera is not easy. It takes a lot of work to make these places succeed, including plenty of technical know-how. In 2006 Dylan Evans, a successful academic worried about imminent societal collapse, decided to build a small self-sufficient community in the Scottish Highlands. His dreams of a friendly, meaningful and harmonious commune quickly evaporated in a fog of tedious digging, damp yurts and lazy free-riding idealists. After months struggling, Dylan had a breakdown and eventually wound up in a psychiatric hospital.[14]

In the mid-2000s Douglas Baillie, a handsome polymath in his early forties, was working in a well-paid job in the United Kingdom as an optical physicist at Heriot-Watt University. But he become increasingly worried about the environment—climate change, fossil fuels running out, declining biodiversity—and wanted to use his scientific background to help. One summer he visited Tamera, and fell in love with the place. After a couple of years visiting periodically to offer technical advice on their work building solar panels, Douglas gave up his job, sold his home and moved to Tamera full-time. Now he is one of their chief engineers and lives in the Solar Village with his two young children (one of whom is in the Place of the Children) and thirty other Tamerians, many of them engineers and scientists like him. 'It was a difficult choice to leave it all behind,' he admits, as he walks the Intro-Weekers to the Solar Village. 'Now I have only thirty euros in the bank. Either I'm extremely poor, or I live in paradise.'

It's a very humble village: a collection of caravans and shacks that surround an open-air kitchen, a table-tennis table, a seating area and a single building the size of a school classroom. There's a couple of largish workshops full of heavy-duty machinery and tools, where Douglas and others at the Solar Village spend most of their day researching how Tamera can become self-sufficient in energy, food and water.[15]

Douglas shows us his 'solar kitchen'. It consists of a Scheffler mirror, which is a twelve-foot by eight-foot fixed-focus solar reflector that captures direct sunlight and reflects it onto another smaller mirror, which in turn reflects it onto a stone that heats under the pots and pans. The mirror moves automatically to follow the course of the sun with the help of a mechanism built from bicycle parts. During the hot Portuguese summer it works as well as a conventional gas cooker. On cold or overcast days, the kitchen runs on biogas, generated by kitchen waste, which, when mixed with warm water, emits methane that is used to power a small flame.

For three years, says Douglas, the Solar Village has survived entirely on sun and biogas. But not today. It's overcast and Douglas explains that something is clogging up the biogas system. That morning the village chef bought a small canister of natural gas to make sure the Solar Villagers have a hot meal tonight. Douglas seems upset by this. 'We're not all committed,' he mutters several times under his breath. 'We should have eaten raw food tonight.'

On the more complicated projects, Douglas works with a German inventor called Jürgen Kleinwächter, a specialist in renewable energy. Kleinwächter invented something called the Energy Power Greenhouse (EPG), which Douglas and a couple of others helped build and install in Tamera. The EPG uses Fresnel lenses to heat vegetable oil in pipes mounted inside the greenhouse. The hot oil is piped into a low-energy Stirling engine to heat air. When air is heated it expands, and that expansion moves a piston, which creates mechanical energy that can be turned into electricity.[16] The vegetable oil—which is still hot—is then piped to the kitchen to warm water, before heading back to the greenhouse to be reheated. There are no emissions or waste: the vegetable oil never leaves the system, it just endlessly flows, transporting heat.* 'It's a different way of thinking,' explains Douglas. 'We're part of a cycle.'

Even more impressive is Tamera's water-retention landscape, which we explore after lunch. The whole of southern Portugal has very long, dry summers, and although rain falls in winter it usually runs off, leaving the region very arid. Water shortages are not due solely to lack of rain: it's also that rain doesn't settle in the ground because it runs off concrete, tarmac and patios, which depletes natural aquifers. When Tamerians first arrived in 1995, their main worry was whether they would have enough drinking water, and some years they did not. Yet even in this year's blazing hot summer there is plenty of water to go around. Since 2007 Tamerians have been working with Sepp Holzer, a renowned permaculturalist, to develop landscapes designed to keep rainwater in the ground through strategically placed lakes, ponds, wells, water terraces and rotational grazing ponds.[17] As a result, the soil in Tamera has become more abundant, vegetation is growing and the wildlife is more varied than in the surrounding areas. A European Union case study of Tamera found that benefits included increased carbon storage, improved water quality,

---

* Due to some technical difficulties, the EPG wasn't working the day we were there. The fact that both the EPG and the Solar Kitchen, both excellent in theory, weren't working on the day I was there was either exceptionally unlucky or suggests the technology does not work as well as they claim.

increased productivity, greater diversification, increased biodiversity and stabilisation of the groundwater table.

This is more like it, I think to myself. They might talk to animals, but they're also building water-retention landscapes, biogas cookers, Stirling engines and solar pulses. They're experimenting with serious, potentially workable technology.

Walking around the Solar Village I realise how reliant I am on all sorts of complicated and quite fragile systems (infrastructure, finance, communications, transport) that I barely understand at all. For tens of thousands of years, humans learned and passed on the knowledge and skills necessary to survive: how to hunt, harvest, find water, generate heat and make shelter. I can fix a printer, send an email and drive a car, but I have no idea how clean water comes out of my tap, and wouldn't know what to do if it one day stopped.

Somehow, somewhere deep in our collective subconscious, I wonder if that's stress-inducing. There's a certain calmness at Tamera: perhaps it's the feeling that they are not helplessly dependent on others for life's basic necessities. I resolve to learn about energy production when I return home, which of course I never do.

After lunch Monika asks me for the questions I want to ask Dieter. I deliberate for a while on this. The Solar Village was impressive, but I couldn't see how it would be scaled up to anything more than a small group of people living out on the land. The Tamerians I'd met all seemed very friendly and open, but Otto Muehl's book had made me nervous about any cultish or controlling tendencies. So I write the following on a scrap of paper and hand it over to Monika:

Doesn't the history of tribes and man's role in tribes suggest violence is a 'natural' state of man and any return to it will fail?

Your literature and writing mainly talks of man and woman. What about transgender people?

How do you deal with conflict and have you ever thrown anyone out of Tamera?

Yours is a global plan. But what about the billions of people who follow, for example, Islam or Christianity and have a very different view about sex?

How many members of the community have you had sexual relations with?

That evening, chiselled Tamerian jaws and bendy yoga bodies flow back into the bar on Campus to listen to a talk by Martin, a young Tamerian in his midtwenties. This evening is dedicated to the current political process in Colombia. Martin says Tamera has been supporting a 'peace community' there called San José de Apartadó who are worried the international community will forget about them if the Colombian government and the guerrilla group FARC agree to a ceasefire. Tamera has been running a campaign (which included sending spiritual messages) to encourage politicians to include a specific paragraph in the treaty about protecting peace communities.*

After the talk, Monika tells me my questions don't really work, and so won't be passed on to Dieter after all.

---

* To ratify the agreement, the ceasefire deal between the Colombian government and FARC was put to a public referendum. Every opinion poll suggested that it would comfortably pass. A few days before I arrived it failed by a whisker: 49.8 per cent to 50.2 per cent, on a very low turnout. I think Tamerians blamed themselves a little for this.

Day 4

Jules is a boisterous consultant in his fifties from Newcastle who leads a double life as a 'spiritual hippy'. He is also a fine connoisseur of hearsay and gossip, which he has a knack of collecting. A little older than most of the Intro-Weekers, he is determined to get to the bottom of what Tamera is really about. He has heard, he tells me, that at 7.15 a.m. every Tuesday-thru-Saturday, Dieter or Sabine hold an hour-long seminar called God Point for Tamerians in which political and social issues are discussed.

God Point isn't on our printed Introduction Week agenda, but at just before 7 a.m. Jules and I walk the one kilometre from the Campus to the Political Ashram—a wood cabin in Grace Village—to find thirty Tamerians sitting with pens and paper readied.

Dieter, wearing tracksuit bottoms, a wool beanie (it helps his sensitive skin, which he developed after a bout of shingles a few years ago) and Crocs shoes, is sitting on a table at the front next to Monika. Although now seventy-four and slightly frail, Dieter still has something of the imposing, handsome and confident forty-one-year-old leader who led fifty people to the large commune in the Black Forest in southern Germany in 1983.

Jules and I are shuffled into a corner and a translator is scrambled for us. The wooden floor and walls, twinned with German voices, give God Point a Lutheran quality. This must be how those early Protestants once gathered, in secretive wooden huts, passing around contraband copies of the vernacular bible. That reverie is broken when Monika plays 'The Gambler' by Kenny Rogers over a sound system by way of a welcome. And it's not the Luther Bible that Monika proceeds to read out and discuss; it's selected passages from Dieter's book *The Gospel Then and Now: Thoughts from the Sea of Galilee.*

Dieter sits next to her, listening carefully, and then discusses the passages, which touch on his core philosophy, in further detail. This was my chance to make a little more sense of the place.

Tamera isn't just about creating an autonomous community that's environmentally sustainable. It's about changing the world. There is, says Dieter, a 'deep' structure of reality beyond the superficial one we see. That deeper reality can be accessed if we awaken our consciousness through spiritual thought, meditation and 'meaningful encounters' with the world around us. Doing this, you can tune in to the world's consciousness, the 'morphogenetic field', which is a bit like mood music for the earth, created by the sum collective of human thoughts and behaviours. According to Dieter, the planet's morphogenetic field is currently trapped on violence towards men, women, children and nature (and has been since humans abandoned tribal life in favour of agriculture around 8,000 years ago).[18]

But that field can be changed. Dieter explains that the ultimate purpose of Tamera is to create new information and new thoughts that can be sent out into the morphogenetic field, and tip it onto a more peaceful setting.[*][19] He

---

* He took the idea of morphogenetic fields from the British author and biologist Rupert Sheldrake, who came up with the idea of 'morphic resonance', which argues that memory is inherent in nature. This suggests that molecules and cells have a sort of collective memory of all the things that had happened to their ancestors, which also

imagines several communes (other 'healing biotopes') all over the world, like Tamera. We are small, says Dieter, but more important than size is how comprehensive and complex these healing biotopes are and how many elements of life are united within them. Free love, water retention, Terra Deva, it's all part of the same project to create a new, unified model of life. Evolutionary fields develop not according to the 'survival of the fittest', writes Dieter, but the 'success of the most comprehensive'.[20]

Anything is possible once you connect to that deeper reality. You can talk to animals, like Heike. You can spontaneously heal without modern medicine.[21] You can end the war between FARC and the Colombian government. 'We can move mountains with this power!' says Dieter, in a warm, baritone voice. 'The new culture, the new possibility: it isn't just a dream.'

A member of the God Point audience raises his hand: 'The discussion we had last night about Colombia was phenomenal. I could have cried. Then the thought came to me: through the Ring of Power we really have the possibility to change something. We've had successes, we can have an influence, we know little of these workings, but in this moment, the possibility opens, we can change something in Colombia.'

Over another round of porridge—which seems to get tastier every day—Jules and I tell other Intro-Weekers what we heard.

---

allows for telepathy-like communications between different organisms. Scientists dismiss the idea as lacking any empirical evidence, but it is popular among many New Age thinkers.

Straight after breakfast Dieter gives his set-piece Q&A to everyone at Tamera. This is the highlight of the Introduction Week, the chance to hear the great man himself. Everyone on Campus gathers excitedly in the main auditorium. The four Qs are tee-ups, asked by Maria, Monika's young assistant. (One is: 'I'd like to return to the powerful engine of love, eros, sensuality. I've only just realised how huge they are. What is the anchor to think new thoughts and not be washed away by this power?') His As involve more morphological field building and the possibility of changing the mind of the president of Colombia. Humans are organs of an overall organism he says, warming to his theme. So if I move this glass (which he picks up), I move the whole world, even if just a tiny amount. 'Once you create a space of resonance, anything is possible,' he says. 'It's just a question of whether we have the right visions.'*

There is no opportunity for questions from us. On concluding Dieter stands up and swiftly exits stage left. 'Thank you for the beautiful questions,' he says.

Dieter's speech sorts the believers from the sceptics. Intro-Weekers are now divided. One of the group, an English woman, is incredulous that Dieter didn't mention that free love has a long history in women's rights movements. And that he seems oblivious to the fast-growing sex-positive movement, of which she is a part. 'They don't know what's happening out there in the real world,' she tells me, shaking her head. I'm more struck by how unoriginal it all is. Dieter's promise of accessing a deeper reality

---

* The other three questions from Maria were: *What is the purpose and goal of Tamera? How do I know my work here in Tamera has an effect? For building the frequency, is community needed?*

and affecting the universal consciousness to change the world is standard fare. Deepak Chopra, multimillionaire icon of New Ageism, has written more than eighty books that say essentially the same thing as Dieter, and has sold tens of millions of copies.

But those already keen think Dieter is wonderful, profound and brilliant. 'It touched me *so* deeply,' says Petr, in his loud voice. He is convinced that Dieter's message doesn't only feel good; it's scientific to boot, and spends some time explaining to me that Dieter's arguments are backed up by hard evidence. To my mind, that's not correct. True, modern science is as ridiculous and sounds as implausible as anything Dieter says. Multiple dimensions and universes are now seriously discussed in academia, while quantum physics has established that at the atomic level matter exists in multiple states and is not fixed until the moment it is observed.[22] Modern science makes a mockery of our senses, but it is done according to a commonly agreed set of standards. Dieter, however, regularly cites people who are roundly discredited in scientific circles. In his books he calls Wilhelm Reich—a man whose theories are widely debunked and who invented fraudulent machines called orgones to stimulate sexual prowess—a 'great pioneer of modern life research'. He approvingly quotes Erich von Däniken, author of the sham book *Chariots of the Gods?* about tribal contacts with extraterrestrial beings. And although it calls itself a 'research centre', Tamera's studies are not done rigorously by any academic standards: there's no study design, formal collection methods or proper evaluation.*

---

* Research appears to mainly mean self-reflection and trying stuff. 'This is not a sect, this is *serious research*,' one member told me later.

I have no problem with reinserting the spiritual and divine into a world that has become quite devoid of mystery.[23] But theosophy like Dieter's tends to a very particular type of New Age vagueness. His books, for example, include the following:

> Being seen means being loved.

> We will see how everything in the world is in a constant state of 'doing' and how this 'doing' is controlled by information that we are constantly producing.

> My circumference and the circumference of the universe are identical.

> There is no objective time or space, for everything is contained in everything. Everything exists at one point. These points are everywhere. The panorama of the world unfolds from every point into all directions of space and time. Past and future are held in the present at every point.

The notion that Dieter's circumference is the same size as the entire universe's is obviously nonsense. But it's profound sounding nonsense; it feels like it might reveal something meaningful. It is therefore easily mistaken

---

When one handsome German said he was learning about sexual partners, it was couched as a research enquiry. 'Free love and free sexuality opens many research questions,' he said. In his book *Terra Nova*, Dieter says the validity of his views about sexuality 'has become clear through many years of research'.

for profundity.* We tend to judge as profound that which we fail to grasp. Obscurity can inspire awe. One can find whatever it is they are looking for in sentences that are so devoid of any clear meaning.[24]

The issues of control and coercion lie at the heart of any form of communal living. Who is in charge? What power do they have over other members? This is particularly important in Tamera given the central role of sexuality and young people. Otto Muehl's book being sold in the site shop gave me further cause for concern. Short manufactured visits are rarely sufficient to get to the bottom of these sorts of fundamental questions, so when I returned to London, I sought out any stories related to Tamera, looking in particular for news related to abuse, control or any other form of coercion or cultish tendencies. I interviewed English and German experts on new religious movements, and even commissioned a German researcher to spend two days finding and translating every German language story written about Dieter Duhm and Tamera going back thirty years. As far as I was able to determine, there are no credible stories about Tamera being a cult or engaging in sexual abuse. And I could not find any former Tamerians claiming they had been forced to stay against their will or do things against their will. That doesn't mean it's not happening. It's

---

* In 2015 Canadian researchers randomly generated phrases from tweets posted by Deepak Chopra. The phrases retained syntactical sense but were clearly mumbo jumbo (e.g., 'we are in the midst of a self-aware blossoming of being that will align us with the nexus itself'). Two hundred people were asked to rate how 'profound' these meaningless statements were. The average score came out at 2.6 out of 5 (in between 'somewhat profound' and 'fairly profound'). The authors of the study called it 'pseudo-profound bullshit', and noted its growing popularity.

certainly a strange and unorthodox place, but if Tamera is a sinister sex-cult, they are uniquely good at keeping it secret.

That's not to say it's a perfectly free and open-minded place however. Control and power are not always in the written rules, rather they are found in the subtle ways that ideas, norms and common wisdoms are created and upheld. Although Tamera claims to be breaking free of narrow materialistic thinking, and to have escaped what they consider dogmatic Western rationalism and scepticism, they've created their own unchallengeable assumptions.[25] Later that day, Monika talks us through each of Dieter's (several) books, which she lays out carefully on the floor. Monika never calls Dieter 'Dieter': it's always 'Dieter *Duhm*'. She describes his ideas as 'visionary', and calls his book *The Sacred Matrix* 'something like our bible'. His influence is everywhere in Tamera. His quotes are pinned on the walls and painted on murals. One of his smaller books, *The Decision*, a bite-size guide to life, is found in every compost toilet, attached to a piece of string.[26] Younger Tamerians repeat Dieter's quotes, lines and metaphors mechanistically with little deviation. It is simply assumed to be true, for example, that bringing children up in a commune-like environment is better; although most child psychologists would disagree, especially given how hard it is to protect them (including on the issue of sexual consent). It is taken as obvious that free love is better for one's psychological well-being, despite there being no actual evidence in psychological studies to show that the denial of free love adversely affects mental or physical health.

According to Amanda van Eck Duymaer van Twist, a specialist in new religious movements at the London School of Economics and author of *Perfect Children*, thought-conformity is very common across communities like this. The culture of radical transparency so often found in communes, she explains, doesn't always lead to open-mindedness and debate. Public forums are decent therapeutic practice but are also a means of policing social conformity, sometimes accidently. They magnify the effect of peer pressure, which often results in a powerful but subconscious tendency towards loyalty. Speaking out against the prevailing thinking can come at the cost of your social standing in the community. (The most tragic and infamous example of this is the story of the Jonestown Massacre, where, in 1978, over 900 adults and children committed suicide in their commune in French Guyana under the direction of the leader, James Jones.) The more closed the group, the greater the risk that independent critical thinking will be replaced by groupthink. When groups of people surround themselves with like-minded fellow believers—in a similar way to how Pegida supporters create echo chambers online—it's remarkably easy to become cut off from different ways of thinking.[27]

While nothing stands out from my time at Tamera, the possibilities for subtle control in this sort of environment are endless. Six weeks before I arrived, one senior Tamerian in her thirties called Vera gave birth to a son. A few days earlier, the father of Vera's son had another child with another woman, with whom he has a less close relationship. 'Maybe this was a plan not made by us. Maybe something wants to be born that is beyond our intelligence and our planning,' she tells me over coffee. Vera had been living with the father—highly unusual—in a fairly monogamous relationship.[28] After the births, she decided to move out and back into communal living, with fifteen other men and women.

Tamera is a confusing place. Part ridiculous, part slightly worrying and part hugely impressive. Perhaps truly radical experiments in living, the ones that rip up the rulebook and start again, need to be a little crazy in order to un-shackle themselves from wider social norms. And every time I thought I had worked out Tamera's flaws and its problems, something always seemed to happen that pulled me back in, and made me wonder if they were onto some-thing after all.

After lunch, we have a session on free love, and dis-cuss trust and sex in our large circle. One of the quiet Germans, a timid man called Klaus who'd not said a word all week, pipes up.

'I'm in my twenties, I'm still a virgin and I'm very ner-vous around women. I have no idea what to do about it. I need help.'

Klaus's honesty prompts a new dynamic in the room. We split into smaller groups (one for men, one for women) to discuss the points raised.

'I'd like to thank Klaus for his bravery,' says one man in my group. 'It's given *me* the bravery to say—and I haven't even told my friends this—that I'm attracted to men as well as women. But I'm also terrified of contact with both.'

We all nod.

'I would also like to possibly explore sexuality with other men but don't know how to do it,' adds another.

'OK, I've not said anything yet,' says a third, a hand-some and friendly German in his midtwenties. 'I have no idea how to deal with women either. I can't approach them. I always think they won't like me and so I stand back. My life is driven by fear. I'm trembling to speak in front of everyone, but thanks to Klaus I thought I had to. Fear is ruining my life and I need to do something.'

For this he receives a spontaneous round of applause.

Klaus has stimulated an avalanche.

'I can't deal with my jealousy,' says a fourth.

'I'm feeling so guilty for having had sex with a woman I don't like. What's the man's role today?'

'I'm having sex to deal with my depression.'

'Don't worry Klaus, I was twenty-five when I lost my virginity.'

'Me too!'

'I was twenty-five too!'

There are a lot of men walking around in the world looking confident, but who are suffering on the inside. Openness and honesty in especially sexual matters remains something rarely discussed in most of society, certainly among men, and that's causing all sorts of problems. Men are struggling with personal and professional expectations placed on them, and are far less likely than women to talk to anyone—either friends or a therapist—about it.[29] And by several measures we're not doing brilliantly well at our close relationships in the Western world. In the United Kingdom around four in ten marriages end in divorce, and over 1 million people report being in 'extremely unhappy' relationships.[30] In the United States almost half of married couples ultimately divorce, and one in five married couples have sex less than once a month.[31] Many of the men on Intro-Week are here because they're looking for help, or maybe just someone to talk to. At the end of the session, which runs on into dinner, we all hug. Two people tell me they are planning to go back home and set up men-only discussion groups.

Day 5

Despite having been overwhelmed with information from Monika, Heike, Douglas, Dieter et al., by the final day I still haven't seen enough of how Tamerians actually live. Monika, who I think has persuaded herself I'm deeply impressed with Tamera, agrees to give me a final tour of the whole place before I leave later today.

'Our applications for building permission are stuck with the authorities,' she says, as we walk through constellations of wooden shacks and run-down caravans. 'Therefore we still have to live very temporarily.'

Everyone is fed up with living in caravans. People have few possessions: some have battered television sets, a few books and second-hand clothes. They aren't completely off-grid here, but everything is just a little worn out. In addition to living in temporary accommodation, the typical Tamerian day can be long and hard. It often starts with some form of meditation (although some attend God Point). Then, depending on the role, it's on to the day job. Monika shows me the pottery workshop, with two people hard at work designing a sculpture for the community centre. In the sewing workshop, three women are repairing clothes and making new ones from scraps. We walk over to the Institute for Global Peace, which looks like a typical open-space tech start-up office. But no one's talking. Half a dozen faces are squinting determinedly into their laptops, replying to emails, redesigning the website, etc. From there we head to a large white yurt with a polished wooden floor: a place, Monika explains, for meditation, 'dream' research and spiritual prayers.

It all feels very full-on. The loss of privacy, the inde-
terminable explorations of your own and everyone else's
bodies and feelings and emotions and jealousies and neu-
roses must sometimes be exhausting. Constantly worrying about the water supplies and energy production might
be satisfying, but also very draining. Since the 1970s the
failure of communes has been the subject of serious academic study. Many collapse at the first sign of difficulty,
especially when members know that modern comforts are
easily accessible.[32] Those governed by rigid social hierarchies are often embroiled in sex scandals or accusations
of financial misconduct, while egalitarian communes typically result in a degeneration of interpersonal relationships
on which the community's endurance depends.[33] 'The dark
side of cooperatives and communities has been endemic
since the modern movement got going in the early 1970s',
writes the academic Roger Hallam in *Diggers and Dreamers*, a guide to modern communes, noting the 'horrendous
situations of power abuse and the embarrassing degeneration of places which were supposed to be examples of alternative idealism'.[34]

Yet Tamera hasn't failed. I found no physical coercion
or overt indoctrination. The founders are obviously still
sources of the vision, but much of the daily business has
been handed over to a younger generation. No one is here
against their will; in fact every Tamerian seems thrilled to
be part of this project.[35] (Even former Tamerians—and dozens have left Tamera over the years for various reasons—
who spoke to me off the record didn't have anything bad to
say about it.) It's hard not to admire their dedication, their
willingness to stick at it, their openness and optimism.

Here they still are, twenty-five years on, thriving in their own way, avoiding the fate of most communes.

In return they are getting something meaningful: simplicity, sustainability and community, all of which seem in short supply elsewhere. Despite all our progress, growing numbers of people consistently report feeling lonely, anxious and depressed, or think that life is meaningless, and these problems are most concentrated in highly unequal societies with strongly materialistic and individualistic values.[36] Even though there is some inequality—Dieter's house is nicer than the rest—it does feel like everyone is somehow in it together.

Something else about the Tamerians was very distinctive, but it took me a while to figure out precisely what it was. I never saw anyone glued to a smartphone. According to one recent report, the average Brit checks his or her phone *fifty times* every day. It's a modern epidemic, now so ubiquitous that we barely see it (we're usually too busy checking our own phones). I am constantly checking Twitter to see if my latest witty remark has been retweeted, following the very latest up-to-the-second news, aimlessly listing around Facebook, or sending and receiving unnecessary text messages. I don't particularly want to do any of these things, but I can't seem to help it. A growing number of writers and psychologists are picking up on the dangers of too much online stimulation. One recent study from Japan found that young people are struggling to develop relationships with anything but their phones.[37] Within five years, I reckon internet addiction will be a widely recognised disorder. No one here seems to suffer with nomophobia ('no mobile phone phobia'). No one in Tamera is frantically and pathetically checking if their last tweet went viral. I envied them for that. When Monika told me that there was Wi-Fi in the bar area, I went out of my way to avoid it.

Tamera combines this back-to-the-land, almost tribal, simplicity, with a more modern individualistic impulse: that we happy few can change the entire world and everyone in it from our yurt, and fulfil all our sexual desires while we're at it. That would normally seem solipsistic, but at Tamera you don't need to feel guilty because you're working for world peace. For some people, that's a very attractive mix.

But Tamera hasn't succeeded either.

Just before I head back to London, Monika tells me Tamera's spiritual attention is currently homed in on being more 'embedded' in Portugal, which she thinks will help them receive building permission from the planning authorities. 'It *will* happen, if there are no outer obstacles, and we put our geistic [mind and spirit] focus on it,' she says.

This is extremely important, she says, because at the current population of 150 they depend a lot on the outside world, and can't grow without planning permission. They want to make Tamera fully energy autonomous, but only about half the energy they use—lights, heaters in the guest house, powering the Wi-Fi, refrigeration, irrigation system and so on—is generated by the Solar Village and the solar panels that decorate the site. The rest comes from the Portuguese national grid. They only grow 25 per cent of what they eat, and the rest they buy in from local organic farmers. Approximately half their income comes from outsiders like us Intro-Weekers paying to visit. Over the winter, some Tamerians go out into the real world to earn money to plough back into the project. They're not aiming at complete autonomy, says Monika—they want to remain connected with the outside world—but she says that if Tamera is to become a 'healing biotope', sufficiently complex and comprehensive to change the morphogenetic field, it needs to grow to about 500 people.[38]

But studies of villages, tribes and early human settlements has found that tight-knit communities rarely grow to that size because there is a brain (and time) limit on how many relationships humans are able to maintain. This phenomenon is called Dunbar's Number, after Robin Dunbar, the British anthropologist who calculated this cap to be 150 people. That's exactly the size of Tamera. If it grew too much, formal rules and hierarchies would be necessary, and the social structure that holds this place together—the God Point seminars, the forums, the relationship-building and the conformity of thought about 'love without fear' or morphological fields—would break down.

It's impossible to know what life is really like here in such a short space of time. But I have a feeling that, like most utopian dreams, Tamera is trapped, destined to forever strive but never arrive. Of course, that's part of the appeal: to be in a perpetual state of happy struggle, with the end always just over the next hill.

That's a good place for Tamera to be. If Tamerians were ever able to properly test Dieter's theory of changing the world through the Ring of Power and the morphogenetic field, it would fail. And then what would become of this radical social experiment with its unusual theories, its beautiful forests and water retention, its optimistic, hard-working free lovers, its men's circles and bad Wi-Fi, its uncomfortable forums and accidental closed-mindedness, its vegan dinners and love shacks, its solar kitchen and happy wildlife? Better that it stays trapped between failure and success, a small beacon and a warning for those from the outside who look at the modern world and wonder: Can't we do something better than this? Can't we start again and try something different?

7

The Activists' Paradox

Only a very particular type of person becomes a committed activist. To stick your head above the parapet commits you to a life of early mornings, cold exhausting afternoons and evenings lost to tedious organising. That angry-looking person marching, chanting and waving a banner is usually damp, sleep-deprived, hungry and worried about getting arrested. Most ordinary people soon tire of this thankless life, but the activist is obsessive and determined. They always conclude that even if the prospects of success are limited, it is worth the effort. There are benefits to this life, of course: the thrilling victories, the camaraderie of purpose that comes with confronting 'the system', the powerful social and emotional ties. But by Einstein's definition of insanity—doing the same thing repeatedly and expecting a different result—the activist is slightly mad.

Slightly mad was, at any rate, how I was feeling early one freezing morning in May, as I approached the United Kingdom's largest coal mine along with 300 direct-action, climate-change activists. These activists believe the 'softly softly' approach to climate change hasn't worked; that the familiar NGOs like Greenpeace, Friends of the Earth and the WWF, with their legal lobbying and palatable messages about flying less, are too supine, and that our best hope to stop catastrophic climate change is to physically prevent fossil fuels being burned. Even if it means civil disobedience.

Ffos-y-fran, which is just outside Merthyr Tydfil in South Wales, is a gaping 178-metre-deep hole in the ground, owned and excavated ten hours a day by the mining firm Miller Argent. When Ffos-y-fran was first opened in 2006 it sparked considerable local protest, and was appealed all the way up to Welsh Assembly.*

Fifty of us in my group—Block C, all wearing red, with the phone number of legal advisers written on our forearms—slowly scaled the Ffos-y-fran perimeter fence. At the other side of the site, Blocks A, B and D were doing the same. Clambering into the mine was surprisingly easy. But I'm naturally a rule follower, a queue-abiding type of person, so breaking the law took some mental effort. Indra, a veteran of the environmental movement who's in my block, has been arrested eighteen times on 'actions' like this. She breezes over the fence with a smile on her face.

We marched up the muddy dirt path toward the lip of the mine, surrounded by overflow of discarded soil, which contrasted with breathtaking views of the Welsh Valleys.

---

* In 2015 Miller Argent submitted a plan to open a similar plant at nearby Nant Llesg. Almost 10,000 local activists signed letters of objection asking Caerphilly County Borough Council to reject the plans, which they did. But Miller Argent has appealed the decision. At the time of writing, this is still ongoing.

One of us played a trumpet and periodically someone raised a chant:

> Activist: Whose mine?
> Block C (together): *Our mine!* (x5)

I was chanting too of course but was very conscious that, on a purely legal basis at least, Ffos-y-fran was definitely *not* our mine. It was Miller Argent's. Ahead of us would be Miller Argent's private security, along with the police, to remind us of this unfortunate fact. Aggravated trespass—which basically means stopping people from going about their business, such as chaining yourself to machinery—carries a maximum sentence of six months in prison and a hefty fine.

'So what's the plan if the police try to stop us?' I asked the man walking next to me.

'Well *my* plan is to run past them and chain myself to the machinery,' he said.

The ground was wet and muddy and very slippy. I wondered how fast I could run in my boots.

Of all the movements deserving of attention in the twenty-first century, climate-change activism has arguably the most persuasive *casus belli*. Greenhouse gases released into the atmosphere as a result of burning fossil fuels are causing the earth's temperature to rise.[1] (I began writing this chapter on the warmest September day in over a century.) If temperatures continue to increase, the overall net effects will be catastrophic.[2] Based on current projections, by the end of this century the sea could be three feet higher. Large swathes of the globe will become un-inhabitable. Extreme weather will be commonplace, as will food shortages and drought. Thousands of animal and plant species will become extinct. By 2050 as many as 250 million people could be climate-change refugees.[3] According to *Nature* magazine, we're rushing toward some awful mass extinction by 2200.[4]

While unanimous consensus is impossible, the vast majority of scientists agree we need to quickly limit the amount of fossil fuels we burn.* And although there has been progress—including an estimated $2 trillion invested in clean energy since 2004, and a recent slowdown in the growth of greenhouse gas emissions—every year brings more bad news.[5] In 2015 we destroyed 20 million acres of tropical rainforest, which reduces the earth's ability to absorb carbon dioxide and produce oxygen. Since 1995 the atmospheric saturation of carbon dioxide has continued to increase, along with global average temperatures and sea levels.[6] February, March and April 2016 were all the hottest ever on record.

Future generations will look back at twenty-first-century denizens, the wealthiest, healthiest, most informed and literate bipeds in the history of the earth, and wonder how we became so stupid.

In response to this overwhelming and existential threat, one might expect tens of thousands of people to march on places like Ffos-y-fran, demanding change. But even though this was the largest ever trespass of a coal

---

* In order to maintain a global temperature increase below 2 degrees compared to pre-industrial levels it is estimated that we could release up to 565 gigatons of carbon dioxide into the atmosphere. Energy companies have already identified fossil-fuel resources that would equate to five times that amount.

mine in the United Kingdom, it was still small. More people had turned up to an industrial park in rainy Birmingham three months earlier to listen to Tommy Robinson tell us—once again—that he didn't want the United Kingdom run by Islamic fundamentalists. And he was slightly disappointed by the low turnout.

As we trudged closer to the ridge of the hill, I was thinking about those statistics: three feet higher, 250 million climate-change refugees, and 'mass extinction'.

Why aren't there more of us? All radical groups ask themselves how to go from a small band of motivated believers to one that millions of people get behind. But it's most acute for the direct-action climate activists because climate change is a uniquely awkward problem. It is what academics call a 'tragedy of the commons', which refers to the overuse of unregulated, finite, shared resources. No one has the obvious incentive to act responsibly unless everyone else does.* (Why give up that much-deserved holiday, if no one else is?) And because the consequences of climate change are still a few years away from having a direct effect on our day-to-day lives, most of us are not motivated to take the risks and costs associated with direct action.

The nature of the problem—vague, indirect, international—creates a second problem. Becoming a climate activist is a *choice*. It's not thrust on people in the same way that being frustrated with Italian politics might push you

---

* The classic example is fishing. If everyone fishes the lake to maximise their own haul, sooner or later, there will be no fish at all for anyone. But no one has the incentive to voluntarily limit their activity, since other fishermen might not act likewise and catch the fish you left. Everyone acts rationally, and yet all end up with something none of them want.

to Beppe Grillo, or a psychedelic experience might trigger some awakening. Because it's such high-risk, low-reward activism, deciding to get involved in direct-action climate activism is a very conscious, and in many respects quite irrational, choice. The result is that climate activists in liberal democracies have become a self-selecting group of very similar people—usually educated, well-off people who can afford the time and risk—who have decided to opt in. Like every group of like-minded people who spend lots of time together, climate activists have created a powerful shared subculture—ideas, language, received wisdom, behaviour and even dress codes—that helps keep them bonded and committed to the cause.

But does that subculture also act as a ceiling on growth, making people feel activism isn't really for them? You might have heard it expressed like this: I'm all for the environment, but those eco-warriors are *weird*. That's the climate activists' paradox. Are they saving the planet, or accidentally enabling the rest of us to destroy it?

All subcultures have a founding moment. The activists' can be traced roughly to the early 2000s and the Climate Camps, which were a series of eco-villages and camps established alongside large protests, including at G8 summits and at big power stations.[7] They were organised by anti-capitalist activists, including Earth First!, probably the most well-known radical environmentalist group in the world, and notorious for its militant direct action.

The Climate Camps were described by participants as a 'space of resistance' because, in addition to being run on renewable energy sources, these enormous camps—often several hundred strong—were effectively self-governing anarcho-communes. 'Affinity groups' of three or four like-minded people would often work on a particular project related to the camp, making decisions among themselves. Everyone was also part of a larger 'neighbourhood', which would come together in plenary meetings to make decisions. Each neighborhood sent a spokesperson to a General Assembly, where all major decisions were taken. 'It was unbelievable,' John Jordan, one of those involved in setting it all up, told me via Skype from France (where he was occupying a large site trying to prevent a new airport being built). 'An enormous, functioning community, without hierarchies. And it worked.'

Activists came to see climate change as the inevitable by-product of a capitalist system that promotes endless consumption, the pursuit of profit and corporate interests. Capitalism would always lead to the world being exploited.* Climate change needed 'system change,' those involved said at the time. They concluded that government and business won't change the system because they're too invested. It would be down to the activists.

Climate Camps initiated and cultivated a generation of young activists into the culture and language of anarchic organising, anti-capitalist thinking and collective decision-making. Several went on to found or run many of today's direct-action movements, including Occupy London, UK Uncut and the organisers of the Ffos-y-fran trespass.

---

* This is the reason all sorts of anti-capitalist movements tend to see each other as allies, and why you will typically see movements that have little in common marching together. Free Palestine flags are often found at anti-austerity marches. They all see themselves as somehow fighting the inherent oppression or injustice of capitalism.

The camps ended in 2010, through a combination of exhaustion, internal political disagreement and a simple desire to try something new. But Earth First! in particular continued to play a leading role in the direct-action movement, bringing activists together at 'gatherings' and 'moots' every year to plan how to continue the struggle.

In November 2015 world leaders in Paris agreed to limit global warming to under two degrees compared to pre-industrial levels. The Paris deal was greeted with much fanfare and celebration. But not for EF!, who thought it was a weak compromise.* Indra, who's been involved with EF! since the 1991 protests against the extension of the M3 motorway (which is credited with kick-starting the direct-action anti-roads movement that swept the United Kingdom in the 1990s, notably the Newbury Bypass protests), organised an emergency meeting of activists to figure out how to keep the pressure up.[8] In February 2016, after learning about this 'moot' at a book fair for radical anarchists I'd attended a few weeks earlier, I made my way to the Centre for Science and Art in the small Gloucestershire town of Stroud. I arrived to find around fifty activists, from the messy network of overlapping direct-action causes that emerged from the Climate Camps, including Reclaim the

---

* Earth First! members often say among themselves that 'the earth is not dying, it's being killed and the killers have names and addresses'. During the 1980s it was notorious for its direct action, including 'tree sitting' to prevent logging. One offshoot of the movement was the Earth Liberation Front, which supported direct economic sabotage. (In 2001 the Earth Liberation Front was described by the FBI as a serious terrorist threat.) There are no leaders at EF!—it calls itself a 'convenient banner' under which others can work. It coordinates, brings people together, shares knowledge and helps create networks of like-minded groups.

Power, Fuel Poverty Action and Plane Stupid, all trying to figure out how to make 2016 a year of mass civil disobedience. (Activism is very disparate. People come and go, join a group, go to one demo and then disappear again.) 'We didn't expect Paris to achieve anything anyway,' Indra told me, as she welcomed me in. 'They never do.'

Journalists aren't usually permitted to attend moots but I was allowed on the condition that I did not write about specific individuals or plans. Mobile phones and cameras were banned during the weekend. Surrounded by a mix of young graduate activists and veterans like Indra in their forties and older, I sat through workshops on how to build 'solidarity' with other movements; we drank tea from enormous urns; we read home-printed leaflets about upcoming events; we ate vegan food prepared by volunteers; we spent ninety minutes learning how to spot undercover police officers; we concluded that capitalism in any form was incompatible with environmental sustainability; we sat on chairs facing one another in pairs and said 'What if everything we do is never enough?' for two minutes to help us avoid 'activist burnout'; and we pinned the locations of different protests taking place across the country onto a large map of the United Kingdom.

Some attendees were visibly nervous that I was there, and very few were willing to speak to me. There is a strong culture of secrecy and suspicion among direct-action activists. Donal, who runs something called the Undercover Research Group, held a session at the moot about undercover surveillance, and explained why. In 2011 it was revealed that a long-term activist in these circles—Mark Stone (aka 'Flash'), a much-liked member of the network, a regular at Climate Camps and EF! meetings, a man who made himself useful when it came to driving—had been working for the Metropolitan Police all along. He'd even been involved in sexual and long-term relationships with activists. 'That sent large reverberations around the movements, and really affected those who'd come to know him,' Donal said. 'It was hard to believe the Met would embed someone with us for that long.' After Mark Stone (whose real name was Mark Kennedy) went public, several similar stories also broke. Ever since, everyone has been very nervous about newcomers. (Donal later told me it was not possible to rule out there being an undercover police officer at the EF! moot, and almost certainly corporate spies who would report back to power stations.)

Just as I was leaving, a man told me to keep an eye on 'Reclaim the Power', a grass-roots organising network for 'taking direct action on environmental economic and social justice issues'. They were, the man said, planning a major trespass in Wales called End Coal Now that would kick off a series of large direct-action protests around the world called Break Free. You need to get there, he said. They will be holding a huge camp, just like the old Climate Camps.

End Coal Now

After weeks of secretive meetings and a quick workshop tour, at 4.30 a.m. one blustery Saturday morning two lorries carrying marquees and half a dozen smaller vans with food and activists turned up unannounced at a large patch of common land just in front of Ffos-y-fran's perimeter fence, off a B road between the villages of Fochriw and Dowlais Top. Within an hour they had erected a large marquee and hammered a few handwritten signposts into the soggy ground. By the time the Welsh police showed up three hours later, one hundred volunteers were pottering around an impressive and well-functioning campsite, complete with working toilets, a media tent, kitchen, and a battery-recharger van.

On arrival everyone was asked to fill in a short questionnaire about how willing they were to get arrested. Based on their response, each person was put in an affinity group with a handful of like-minded people. Ever since the police infiltration of the environmental movement, affinity groups have become de rigueur because they are harder to disrupt (no affinity group knows what the others are doing), as well as giving people a meaningful and active way of participating.[9] At various points over the three-day camp I saw affinity groups huddled together agreeing on how far they'd go in the mine and what they'd do if arrested. The first thing I saw when I arrived was Indra, deep in hushed conversation with four other people who made up her affinity group.

Activists had travelled from all over the country to get here. One group had cycled from London and their arrival was greeted with loud cheers. There were the climate clichés, of course: hemp bag carriers, tie-dye, dyed hair, alternative-medicine practitioners, etc. But I also met teachers, solicitors, students, civil servants and professors, capable people deeply worried about the environment who had carefully weighed up the moral case for shutting down Ffos-y-fran. By Monday lunchtime it was an environmentally friendly, smooth-running, anarchistic camp of 300 people. Jobs posted on the pinboard (the night shift on the gates, checking for police, vegetable chopping and the dreaded toilet clean) were always promptly filled. 'If you see a job that needs doing just go ahead and do it,' a tired but friendly woman with dreadlocks told me in the welcome tent. 'You don't need to ask anyone.'

Gliding serenely across the site with a clipboard and walkie-talkie was Danni Paffard. She strongly denied that she was the leader, and said 'facilitator' was more accurate (activists hate the word 'leader'). That was technically true: there were lots of different roles being filled here, and over the weeks of organising this action, many different people assumed various leadership roles at different times. It's a very fluid system of organising. But for the day of action itself, Danni was definitely something of a key figure. Not in charge in the sense of being able to tell others what to do, but all difficult questions seemed to gravitate to her (which she always patiently answered). Danni's a seasoned activist, although she's only in her late twenties. Soon after graduating from Oxford University, Danni attended Climate Camp in 2009 and then helped found both UK Uncut in 2010 and No Dash for Gas in 2011, which later became Reclaim the Power. She was convicted of aggravated trespass in 2012 and then again in 2015 when, along with twelve others, Danni cut through the wire at Heathrow's perimeter fence and chained herself to the runway to protest against the proposed addition of a new runway.[*] 'Activism is my life,' she told me. 'This is just part of who I am now.'

---

[*] It took the police six hours to remove them. In early 2016, after a two-week trial, they were all found guilty of aggravated trespass and entering a security-restricted area of an aerodrome, but avoided jail.

The same could be said for most people at the camp. In fact, I started noticing that an awful lot of people at End Coal Now looked, dressed and talked a lot like Danni. It was an overwhelmingly white, middle-class, left-wing graduate affair. There are no statistics on the demographic make-up of direct-action activists. But the work that has been done on the broader environmental movement finds that most come from a very narrow cross section of society. A 2014 US study of nearly 300 environmental organisations (191 environmental non-profits, 74 governmental environmental agencies and 28 leading environmental grant foundations) found that their presidents and chairs were more than 70 per cent male, and that fewer than 4 per cent of their board members came from ethnic minorities. A similar study found that nine out of ten American environmentalists are white, and 78 per cent are college-educated.[10] In 2015 the head of Friends of the Earth called the UK environmental movement a 'white, middle-class ghetto'.

This problem haunts the activists, because they see anti-racism and environmentalism as part of the same (anti-capitalist) struggle. But there have been occasional tensions within the climate movement about the dominance of white graduate types. When the planned Paris Climate Talk demonstrations were cancelled after Islamist terrorist attacks in the city, UK activists invited several French activists to attend the London demo instead. A group of indigenous activists called Wretched of the Earth were asked to lead the march and wear 'traditional clothing'. But they turned up with banners that the more established charities found controversial ('Still fighting CO_2lonialism: your climate profits kill', read one). Some wore all black clothes and covered their faces with masks.

Worried about potentially negative press, the organisers decided that it would look better if the march was led by people dressed up as animals: polar bears, elephants, lions, antelopes, etc. But the Wretched bloc wrestled their way to the front anyway, which resulted in skirmishes among activists. It got so heated that each side called the police. Tisha Brown, a black climate and anti-racist campaigner who was part of the Wretched bloc, told me how she'd been marching with these people for years, and yet suddenly found herself surrounded by hostile animals. 'I got shoved by a *giraffe!*' she told me, when I later interviewed her in central London. 'There's a strange assumption that people of colour can't be environmental activists.'

Everyone at Ffos-y-fran was aware of the diversity issue. They just don't know how to fix it. 'We worry a lot about it,' Danni told me. 'But we haven't quite figured it out. This isn't a problem we're going to crack overnight. We've tried to make spaces welcoming and inclusive to different people, but it's not enough. Building a broad-based social movement is crucial. We need to meet people where they're at more, link up different struggles and put justice—environmental, economic and social—together at the centre.' Part of the problem is that very few people are likely to have the money and time to spend campaigning at Ffos-y-fran for three days. But a bigger part is the natural tendency all movements have, especially those that are high-risk, to create a self-reinforcing subculture that outsiders find alienating.

The activist subculture has several key components, ranging from language to dress code to dietary habits to decision-making procedures. It is perhaps most obvious in the way people talk. I quickly picked up, for example, some of the commonly used phrases that describe activist wisdoms and established truths. Using them establishes the speaker's credentials, that they are a member of the club. That they get it.

'Space' (n.): Refers to a room, or indeed any other location, either physical or metaphorical. *This is a great space to have a meeting.*

'Action' (n.): Shorthand for 'direct action'. Any demonstration, protest, march or similar protest-type activity. *The Ffos-y-fran action will be huge.*

'Intersectional' (adj.): Refers to the idea that different types of oppression relate to each other. Discrimination on the basis of gender, class and ethnicity are not independent of the other, but underpin and support each other. Black women may face both racism and sexism. First proposed by Kimberlé Williams Crenshaw, an American civil rights activist and professor of law.

'Cultural hegemony' (phrase): First proposed by Marxist theorist Antonio Gramsci, it argues that the ruling classes control the culture of society, which they use to make sure their world view becomes the accepted cultural norm, making the status quo appear natural. It is also a useful way to explain why your movement is insufficiently large. ('Mainstream media' or 'MSM' is one variant of this.)

'Social licence' (phrase): Describes the intangible sense of whether a company has (usually tacit) approval

within the local community or society at large to operate. *We need to weaken Miller Argent's social licence by
making the local community realise the damage they are
doing to the environment.*

'Cis' (adj.): Shorthand for 'cisgender', denoting or relating to a person whose self-identity conforms with the
gender that corresponds to their biological sex, i.e.,
not transgender. It is considered a better term than
'normal', which implies that transgender or other less
common forms of gender identity are abnormal. *The
Greenham Common protesters were mainly composed of
people self-defined as cis non-men.*

The subculture is also marked by its dislike of all types
of hierarchy, whether patriarchal, economic or organisa-
tional. They are viewed as being inherently capitalistic or
corruptible. There are no leaders in activist circles: decisions are reached by a 'consensus-based' system, which is
essentially a democratic process where a large group decide together through a set of hand gestures what they
want to do. When a proposal is discussed, people twinkle
their fingers in the air pointing upward if they agree or
vote yes, point down for no, point straight in front if they
aren't sure, and cross their arms on their chest for a 'block',
which is designed to halt debate. For many newcomers,
getting involved in decision-making can be thrilling and it
is a reasonably decent leaderless way of making decisions
among large groups of people.

This is all extremely laudable. After all, the goal is to
create a welcoming and inclusive movement. No other
group I spent time with invested the same amount of time

or effort into trying to get people involved in decision-making or being more diverse. It's hard not to admire the intention or the effort. The problem is that activists confuse ends with means: they have elevated the procedure and language to the level of a religious sacrament. Consensus-based decision-making, for example, is now so firmly set in the culture of many anti-capitalist movements that it cannot be questioned, even though it sometimes leads to stalled meta-discussions about decisions about decisions about decisions. (Not to mention that hierarchies do still exist: people who know the rules of the game or are well-known faces still exert far more influence than others, it's just less visible, which arguably makes it worse.)

When laudable goals are expressed through language, the result is usually an obsession with procedure and language rather than results. Everyone here very carefully, very deliberately, used the correct hand gestures and appropriate words. And yet nearly everyone was still a white graduate type. The tragedy is this: anyone who turns up to a direct-action meeting from a different background, someone who isn't a university graduate already involved in anti-capitalism—in other words the very people necessary to make this movement truly diverse—will find similarly aged and identically dressed adults talking in received pronunciation about 'intersectionality with non-cis people' and see solemn fingers being twinkled. They will most likely immediately conclude that this is not a movement where they would be welcome. Traditional right-wing voters worried about the environment would, in theory, share much in common with activists. But they might not see past the obsession with intersectionality or anti-capitalist tropes about open borders and corporatism. This is why direction-action environmentalists seem to elicit such disdain from their opponents. It's not the ideas or the argument they object to, so much as the *type* of people they are. It's a visceral dislike rather than an intellectual one. Only later would I realise what a cruel irony that is.

The Action

The night before the trespass, affinity groups were put into one of the four blocks, each of which was given a location in the mine. All I knew was that I needed to be in the main tent at 7 a.m. and that I should prepare to be arrested, and that everyone should wear red so we could create a visual image inside the mine, signalling a 'red line' that climate change must not cross. My block, Block C, was tasked with going into the heart of the mine and disrupting machinery.* Danni reminded everyone of the 'action consensus': the document that sets the tone for the action. Treat the workers with respect, stay calm, don't escalate any confrontations and don't damage the machinery.

A small legal team set up by activists gave us advice about what to do if we were approached by the police. In fact, said the lawyer, a police liaison officer has already turned up and is standing at the main gate to the camp. 'Do not speak to him,' she repeated. 'He's not our friend.'

Monday night was bitterly cold. The camp was set up high on the Darran Valley, which is at an altitude of about

---

* There were two likely charges: walking around the outskirts of the mine would be 'trespass'—a civil offence—while chaining oneself to machinery and preventing it from being used would be the more serious criminal offence of 'aggravated trespass'.

500 metres, and the icy wind made the inside of the tents frost up. Most people gave up trying to sleep at about 6 a.m., by which point a police helicopter was circling overhead. ('They're doing that on purpose,' Indra told me.) By 7 a.m. affinity groups were huddled around the main tent, clustered into the four blocks, sharing tea and handing out packed lunches. A couple of police cars and loitering police liaison officers were stationed at the entrance, but they were soon swamped. A sea of red was forming: several were dressed head to toe in red boiler suits.

I was starting to feel a bit nervous when some good news filtered through. Two small affinity groups had climbed the perimeter fence at 5 a.m., lain on the main dirt road in and out of the mine and linked arms through long metal pipes made of old lamp-post shafts, which they were connected to by carabiners.[11] The arm tubes would make it difficult for police cars or security guards to get in and out. We had a bit of breathing space.

At 7.30 a.m. everyone was ready. Danni shouted the block order so there wasn't a stampede: B then C then A then D, and wished us all good luck. Someone had brought a speaker system and played music as each block waited for the green light. As Block C set off, the 'Imperial March' from *Star Wars* blared out. Everyone laughed.

Over the fence, and on we marched, through the mud and stench of machine oil mixed with coal, up along the dirt track. Finally, the ground levelled out, and I got my first proper view of the site.

Open-cast mines are remarkable places, unlike claustrophobic underground mines. The scale of Ffos-y-fran was staggering, a crater hundreds of metres in diameter. A winding road snakes around the perimeter. Down and down dig the monster machines, getting a little lower each year. Dumpster trucks ferry the loads back up to sifting machines and from there it's transported to either Aberthaw, Wales's largest coal-fired power station, or to Tata steelworks in Port Talbot.

We passed one of the heroic advance teams lying on the floor with their arms in tubes. They were four members of Christian Climate Action. One of the group was an eighty-year-old local whose father had worked in the mines in Merthyr. I sat down and interviewed a horizontal Alice Hooker-Stroud (who is also the leader of the Green Party in Wales). 'We believe that God created the earth,' Alice told me. 'God created the earth and we're trashing it! If we worship God, how can we trash the earth?' Jesus was an activist, said Martin, another member of the group. 'Jesus always challenged society. He got arrested. St Peter got arrested. St Paul got arrested. They were executed by the state. So . . .'

I did not want to get arrested, and definitely not executed. I held my breath as we turned the corner into the machinery area where, so we'd been told in last night's briefing, the police would be waiting for us.

But they weren't. No one was, except a handful of staff in their high-vis jackets and helmets leaning casually on Miller Argent's motionless Caterpillar trucks and JCBs. The block was surprised and relieved, but it made perfect sense. Activists often thrive on police presence. If the police are aggressive in their methods—which they sometimes are—it creates a new reason to protest. (And can sometimes end up with a violent confrontation.) They had obviously decided against it.

It suddenly dawned on everyone that we had free rein of the United Kingdom's largest open-cast coal mine, and could do whatever the hell we wanted. At the bottom of the mine, we joyfully reconnected with the other blocks, who'd had a similarly smooth walk down.

We all joined up to create a single hundred-metre-long snaking line across the main pit path, and one of the media team flew a drone mounted with a camera overhead and took aerial shots. Others set up huge inflatable 'cobble-stones' that had large red lines down the front.[12] A handful scrambled on top of the Caterpillar excavator machinery for selfies. Someone started a football match. Red umbrellas with large black letters when put together read 'No New Coal'. The sound system, which had invaded with us, blasted out 'Nine to Five' by Dolly Parton. One wrote 'Catastrophe' over 'Caterpillar' and hung a large 'End Coal Now' banner across the monster machines. Shutting down the mine was definitely the priority, but like Zoltan, getting good photos and selfies was a close second.

Such was the excitement and backslapping that I almost missed the two miners who stood watching us clamber over their work machines. They weren't hostile. In fact they understood quite well why we were here. But they weren't exactly overjoyed either. 'That is un-be-liev-ab-ly dangerous,' grunted one miner in a thick Welsh Valleys accent, pointing at an activist swinging from a digger. 'If I did that, I'd be fired on the spot. You can't climb on those machines! Christ. If one of them slips they'll need an ambulance.' I asked them what they thought of the movement and its aims. 'I think it's misguided,' the safety-conscious miner replied. 'I'm all for clean energy too, but this lot are against everything. We need to keep people's homes heated and the lights on. Until there are other ways of doing that, we need to keep going. Otherwise we'll just ship in the coal from further away and that'll be even worse for the environment.'

'I'll bet some of them used steel to bike here,' added the second miner.

'Hey, you know what? We could have done them a deal!' replied the first.

'Haha!'

Activists are always caught in this hypocrite-or-fanatic bind. It's difficult to unplug entirely from the modern world. They want to have a holiday and also need a laptop. When they do they're hypocrites. If they go off-grid or refuse to fly, they're fanatics.

The activists understood Merthyr Tydfil's problems. They knew it used to be a bustling, successful centre of iron mining and that it now ranks as one of the worst places to live in the United Kingdom. They knew that Ffos-y-fran has created jobs and a community fund.[13] The coal industry is dying, and the activists chanted that they want better (greener) jobs for these miners and called for more government investment in the region. Similarly miners don't want a dead earth or sea-levels rising by three feet or mass extinction. The two groups shared a common goal, and yet they were miles apart. The two miners watched as a group of graduate activists in their twenties danced to drum and bass music, posed for pictures on the miners' work machines and tweeted those pictures out with clever hashtags.

The miners knew some of them would whizz back to London and get back to their well-paid jobs of the future.

They would have noticed, no doubt, that one was playing a bongo drum, one was dressed as a clown and another had a hula hoop.

So what do you do once you've taken over the country's largest open coal mine? Not very much. After about an hour, the euphoria of success was slowly and then very quickly replaced with boredom. Direct action—occupying space or a building—isn't much fun. There's nothing to do except sit it out.

At 1.30 p.m., a consensus decision-making council was called, and everyone formed a large circle. A forty-five-minute discussion ensued to discuss options and twinkle fingers. Half decided to leave, half to remain. I walked back up onto the top of the ridge to watch what was happening from above. Police vans were entering the site. Danni radioed the information over to the remaining activists, and another quick meeting was convened. Everyone agreed it was time to go. By 5 p.m. everyone was out.

'Such a success,' said Danni a little later on the Reclaim the Power blog. 'One of the most beautiful and powerful things I've ever taken part in.' In many ways it was. No one was arrested, it was peaceful, respectful, there was plenty of media coverage and above all 4,000 tonnes of coal stayed in the ground that day.

For around seventy people, this was the first time they'd taken part in an 'action'. On the way back to London later that day I spoke to some of them. 'It was amazing,' said one, a civil servant with his face still painted red. 'Far more welcoming that I'd expected. I'd definitely do it again.' (Danni told me a few weeks later that a few of them had since become more closely involved with the movement.)

As promised, End Coal Now kicked off a series of similar actions that took place that month all over the world. Straight after Ffos-y-fran, Danni headed to Germany, where, along with thousands of others, she shut down Vattenfall Welzow-Sued coal mine, which is one of the largest in Europe. Other actions took place in Newcastle Coal Port Australia, March Point oil refinery in Washington State, in Indonesia, Nigeria, Brazil, Turkey and a dozen other places.

But this all took so much time and effort. End Coal Now alone cost around £16,000 to put on (all raised in donations), entailed dozens of 'roadshow' meetings, forty volunteers working round the clock and three freezing days in the Welsh Valleys. Four thousand tonnes sounds like a lot, but on a typical day around 23,500 tonnes of coal are extracted from UK mines.[14]

Impressive though it was, I left Wales with an uncomfortable feeling that Miller Argent would make up for the loss. For direct action to have a serious effect on the climate, this sort of event needs to happen every other day. It needs tens of thousands of people, not just a few hundred. But how? The tragic thing about activist-ism is that it feels almost inevitable. It's inevitable that only activists get sufficiently motivated by abstract global problems to risk arrest; inevitable that they create a tight subculture; inevitable that this subculture keeps the movement motivated but smaller than it could be.

There is no obvious answer to this paradox. But part of the solution might be to think about activism in a slightly different way. Whether we like it or not, most people get motivated not by global issues, but by problems in their immediate neighbourhood.

Nimbyism and Activism

'Nimby' stands for 'not in my back yard', a pejorative term for protesters concerned only with themselves and their immediate surroundings. Activists are the pros: they roam the country, joining causes and taking risks. They are the people for whom being *an activist* is part of their identity and social life. It's like being a 'hacker' or a 'foodie': not just something that you do, but something that you are.[15] Nimbys are different: They are the ordinaries who are upset about something in their own back yard. They don't have a subculture. They're just angry.

Historically, these groups haven't cooperated much. As the activist is shutting down a coal mine, the Nimby is writing to their local councillor about the wind turbine that's just been erected near where they take the dog for walks.

But what if Nimbyism served as a way into activism, piercing the subculture and turning activism into a mass hobby rather than an elite sport? A mass movement of Nimbys might sound like an oxymoron, but it's already happening. In several Western democracies—notably the United States, Australia and the United Kingdom—there is a fast-growing crusade of people who are helping to tackle a global issue: the anti-frackers.

'Fracking' is shorthand for hydraulic fracturing, the process of blasting a mix of water, sand and chemicals at

shale rocks hundreds of metres underground. Tiny fissures
in the rocks contain trapped gas, and the process releases
that gas into pipes, and on to a refinery. In the United
States, where this industry is most advanced, fracking
makes up roughly half of all gas extraction, has created
thousands of jobs and driven down energy prices.[16]

It turns out the United Kingdom has potentially enormous reserves of shale gas deep underground too, and
since 2008 the British government has awarded dozens of
licences to companies to start exploratory drilling. In 2014
then–prime minister David Cameron said the government
was going to go 'all out for shale'.[17]

Although fracking is more environmentally friendly
than coal, it's far from perfect. The gas it releases is still
a fossil fuel, so burning it might be incompatible with the
United Kingdom's target of reducing carbon emissions by
80 per cent by 2050. But more significant are the localised
risks. In 2014 New York banned fracking after a two-year
study into its impact on public health, noting in particular
the risk of water and surface spill leading to local drinking-
water contamination and heightened risk of earthquakes
in the area.[18] (Poor regulation in Wyoming resulted in fifty
times the safe level of benzene, a flammable fuel component, in the local drinking supply.[19]) It's also an eyesore,
damaging areas of natural beauty and animal habitats, and
can be extremely loud.

Independent studies have found that the risks associated with fracking can be managed, and advocates argue it
will create thousands of local jobs and improve the United
Kingdom's energy security. Yet since 2011 the United Kingdom has been frack-free because local Nimbys got angry,
and then got organised, with the help of activists. And

when activists and Nimbys work together, something can really happen.

In April 2011 the energy company Cuadrilla started test-fracking in Lancashire and shortly after there were two small earthquakes. Anti-fracking groups in the area formed and started to campaign against it. In 2012 Cuadrilla received a licence to test a site near Balcombe, a sleepy, middle-class village in West Sussex. Activists from Reclaim the Power and the local anti-fracking groups held a large camp and managed to get the locals on-board.[20] Seeing the scale of local opposition, Cuadrilla gave up on Balcombe and turned back to Lancashire, scoping out a new test-drill site just outside Blackpool. In August 2014 twenty anti-fracking demonstrators in their fifties, sixties and seventies—calling themselves 'the Nanas', dressed in yellow tabards and matching 1940s headscarves—occupied the site for three weeks. Cuadrilla took them to court and were awarded £55,000. Cuadrilla said that they'd pick a person at random to fine if no one was willing to act as the named defendant. One of the trespassers, Tina Louise Rothery (who was fifty-two at the time), put her name forward.

Tina Louise doesn't look like an activist. She looks like a grandmother, which is what she is, although she has the energy of a teenager, twinned with an encyclopedic knowledge of all things fracking. Ask her if she takes sugar in her tea and five breathless minutes later she'll be explaining why the latest peer-reviewed paper proves that fracking isn't so environmentally friendly once you factor in transport costs. Along with her quieter and more organised older sister Julie, Tina has become the face of the anti-fracking movement in the United Kingdom.

Back in 2011 both Tina and Julie—neither politically active—were angry about the bank bailouts that followed the financial crash and read about the anti-capitalist Occupy camp that had pitched up in the City of London. Tina visited on a whim and ended up spending much of the following three months there. When Tina and Julie heard about Cuadrilla's plans in their home county of Lancashire, they both joined the local campaign group. A natural and fluent public speaker, Tina quickly become a de facto spokesperson for them and started travelling the country to talk about it. At one coordination meeting in early 2014, members of several anti-fracking groups—there were well over one hundred by this point across the UK—were sitting in a large circle discussing tactics, when they realised they were all older women.* So they decided to form a new group. Ever since, Tina and the Nanas have been a roving band that turn up every fortnight or so to anti-fracking events all over the country, and Tina often attends three or more each week. 'If the Nanas are turning up, it's an event to look forward to,' Tina told me when I caught up with her in Manchester at a Unite Against Fracking conference, where she was greeted with cheers and 'I am Tina Rothery' T-shirts.

'We have an average age of about sixty-two,' Tina told me, as we sourced some tea and sat down during one of the short breaks.

---

* In fact they were asked to sit in a circle by a camera crew from *Vice* magazine, who was following them. In that circle, they got talking, and had the idea of creating a new group of older women who could help the movement grow. *Vice* accidently and unknowingly helped start the Nana movement.

'Fuck off!' said Julie. 'Janice? Ginette? Bette? Maureen? Ange? It's more like forty-five.'

'OK, yeah it's not quite sixty-two,' said Tina, chastised by her older sister.

The Nanas were Nimbys; that's what makes them notably ordinary. Maureen, who's in her sixties, felt the earthquakes that followed Cuadrilla's first test-fracking in 2011 and went online to figure out what on earth had just happened, and got worried about her grandchildren's drinking water. Ange, Janice and Bette have almost identical stories, and they all told me they don't see themselves as campaigners or activists, just ordinary mothers or grandmothers who were worried and wanted to do something. 'I still cannot believe I actually did that!' Maureen told me, recalling that time her and the Nanas turned up at former prime minister David Cameron's house in Oxfordshire on a tank Vivienne Westwood lent them, wearing tabards that said 'The Oven Gloves Are Coming Off'.

The difference between the activists with their subculture and the Nanas with their tabards is critical, since it determines the likelihood others will join. Contrary to popular belief, people don't commit to a cause based solely on a rational or objective consideration of statistics and facts. If they did there would have been 10,000 people at Ffos-y-fran, not 300. People also sign up because they think it will be fulfilling or because their friends are in it or because it looks like *their sort of thing*. Powerful subconscious and subliminal forces drive our choices about the movements we join, which the sociologist Erving Goffman called 'cultural framing'. They include things that on first sight appear frivolous—language, dress sense, accents, social background, class, skin colour and a thousand small things—but which help people find self-realisation, belonging and fulfilment.[21] (And because humans have well-documented preferences to club together with like-minded or like-looking people, the effect is multiplied and self-reinforcing.[22]) This is why the subculture is so important, and partly why the activists at Ffos-y-fran were so homogenous and limited in numbers. The cultural framing created a ceiling. Although a similar dynamic was at play in other groups I followed, it was most pronounced here. Even their attempts to mitigate the problem through micro-procedure and carefully selected language was itself part of the frame. By contrast, the cultural framing of the name Bette or Tina or Maureen is an ordinary and concerned grandmother, not a university-educated professional activist.

'I've never seen an issue that's got so many people involved in environmentalism,' Jamie Peters, an anti-fracking campaigner at Friends of the Earth, told me. 'And most of them haven't done any sort of activism before. Activists subconsciously build hierarchies. But with anti-fracking you feel completely at home.' It's true: I heard the Nanas speak knowledgably about toxicology, legal rights, radioactivity decaying times, isotopes, planning law, Halliburton, acidification, soft squeeze and hydrofluoric acid. But it doesn't put you off. The anti-fracking movement is not inclusive because its supporters use the word 'cis' instead of male or female; it's because they happen to be naturally welcoming. Consensus decision-making is very attractive at the theoretical level, but at the subconscious level cups of tea and home-made scones will beat it every time.

It is impossible to judge for sure how successful anti-fracking has been. It's a very imprecise science. But it has become the most vigorous part of the environmental movement. For the past two years Jamie from Friends of the Earth has been trying to compile a map of anti-fracking groups, but there are now so many that he's more or less given up. There are at least 300 he told me, and many thousands of people who are active. 'There is now opposition to fracking every time a licence is issued.' And above all, despite the government's promises and pledges, despite millions of pounds of investment, there has still been no fracking in the United Kingdom. In mid-2013, 44 per cent of British adults supported fracking in the United Kingdom, and by late 2016 that had fallen to 17 per cent.[23]

The anti-fracking movement in the United States has followed an almost identical trajectory. Its roots are not in environmental activism, but local people worried about the risk it poses to the local environment, especially the water. In 2009 residents in Dryden, New York, sitting atop the Marcellus shale formation, were getting pressured by oil- and gas-company representatives to lease their land for fracking. They started reading up on fracking and set up a residents association to campaign against it. Other associations were founded soon after, which started researching how to use local zoning regulation to prevent fracking. Julie Huntsman, a vet from the small town of Otsego, New York, organised presentations, a petition and a phone bank to call registered voters. Otsego became the first town in the United States to ban fracking using zoning ordinances. After Otsego, Springfield, Middlefield, Cherry Valley, Tomkins County and over 200 other municipalities in New York State did the same. By December 2014 New York's Department of Health published a report that concluded fracking posed serious risks to public health, and soon after the New York governor announced he would permanently ban fracking. Its original success was local, assisted by high-profile media coverage and a growing number of academic studies; it has since grown into a significant and potent nationwide movement. Public opposition in the United States to fracking is rising rapidly, from what was once virtually an unknown issue, to 40 per cent opposed in 2015, and then 51 per cent opposed in 2016.

After the Manchester event, I followed the Nanas to the World Transformed Conference in Liverpool, where they gave a talk to activists about how to campaign. World Transformed was a shadow conference organised by the Jeremy Corybn–supporting anti-capitalist Momentum movement alongside the official Labour Party conference. Workshops and seminars about 'politics, art, music, culture and community' ran over three days in the Black-E building, a large community and arts centre.*

---

* Momentum is a grass-roots movement that grew out of the successful campaign to get the unlikely radical, left-wing candidate Jeremy Corbyn elected as leader of the Labour Party. It is not formally tied to the party, but retains close links to Corbyn, and exerts an increasing influence on local Labour constituency parties. Critics have argued that Momentum has become an 'entryist' organisation for more radical left-wing groups and that its members are trying to aggressively deselect MPs that they deem insufficiently left wing (something Momentum denies). But even its detractors admit Momentum has injected new energy, ideas and thousands of new active members, especially young people, into the Labour movement.

Following their workshop they sat on the steps in front of the building, smoking roll-up cigarettes and practising their latest song, 'Bring Me Sunshine' with repurposed anti-fracking lyrics:

In this world where we live
There should be re-new-a-bles
Bring me sunshine
Bring me tidal
Bring me lo-ve!

A fresh-faced Momentum organiser suddenly burst out of the building and ushered us all inside the main hall for a surprise announcement. This turned out to be by Jeremy Corbyn, who the day before had been re-elected as leader of the Labour Party. After his speech—in which he spoke

---

Momentum and Jeremy Corbyn suffer from the same paradox as the activist because they belong to the same tribe. Had things turned out slightly differently Corbyn would have been at the Earth First! moot or in that mine. The man has serious activist credentials, having spent his life fighting unpopular causes with a small number of fellow believers, including for the Guildford Four. In a very similar way to the activists, Corbyn and his supporters have created a powerful subculture, and the more they are attacked by the media or other parts of the Labour Party, the more ardent it becomes. Because he's both an activist and a political leader, Corbyn's supporters treat him with an unusual mix of familiarity and reverence. He's 'Jez', he's one of us, he's a normal honest guy. Yet simultaneously his face is festooned across T-shirts, and his name is the subject of adoring poems. Momentum supporters wear 'Jez We Can!' T-shirts, attend 'Concerts for Corbyn' and tweet #WhatYouDoToJeremy-YouDoToMe. It's a movement of the devout and the believers. This is why the larger and louder his rallies, the lower his support in national opinion polls seems to be.

about the unpopular but ultimately vindicated struggle of
the activist—one of the Nanas, Amy, snuck past Corbyn's
security team and into his car as he was putting on his seat
belt. 'Can I give you this from the Lancashire Nanas?' she
said, handing him a yellow anti-fracking wristband. 'Oh
thank you very much,' said Jeremy, politely. 'You know, I
don't like fracking very much.' Amy took a photo and shared
it on Facebook. The next day (and unrelated to Amy's hero-
ics), the Labour Party announced it would ban fracking if
elected. Tina texted me that evening: 'A huge victory for us!'

But it was a short-lived victory. Ever since it was first
proposed, the anti-frackers fought tooth and nail to successfully persuade Lancashire Council's planning authority to reject Cuadrilla's application to test-frack. But in
2016 the government published new guidance that said the
secretary of state could overrule local planning decisions
about fracking. And in October 2016 Secretary for State
of Communities and Local Government Sajid Javid overturned Lancashire Council's decision, thus clearing the
path for fracking after all.

From Liverpool two dozen Nanas drove to Bucking-
ham Palace where they set up a twenty-four-hour vigil at
the Queen Victoria monument, asking for the Queen to
intervene. 'We know it's a waste of time,' Tina told me,
on the steps of the monument, 'but we want to show that
we have tried everything, all the democratic options open
to us, before we go crazy.' There they sat, all day and all
night, handing out scones, drinking tea on their granny
shopping trollies in the spitting rain, looking for toilets and
telling confused-looking tourists how awful fracking is.

Feeling rebuffed at every turn, they are ready to become more radical, and now increasingly link their local

Nimby struggles to the wider climate and anti-capitalism movement. 'The whole thing is rotten from top to bottom,' Tina told me. Linda, sixty-five, told me she's ready to chain herself to machinery if it comes to that. Debs, fifty-two, who needs a crutch when she walks, said she'll fight fracking to her 'dying breath'. Tina told me 'nothing' will make her give up. 'Even prison.' She continued to refuse to pay Cuadrilla's £55,000 fine, and in December 2016 Preston court concluded she didn't have the means to pay. One hundred and fifty supporters waited outside the court and sprayed her with champagne as she emerged victorious.

The Activists' Paradox

Activism—both direct action and the more conventional approaches—has already achieved a huge amount. The same month we shut down Ffos-y-fran, a record low of 6 per cent of UK electricity was generated from coal, down from 20 per cent only a year earlier.[24] In November 2015 President Obama used his presidential veto to block construction of Keystone XL, a planned pipeline between Nebraska and Alberta to shift crude oil. Our energy is getting cleaner: around 25 per cent of UK power came from renewables in the last quarter of 2015, and over the year a whopping £198 billion was invested in the global clean-energy industry.[25] Things are changing. The committed and dedicated activists can take some of the credit for this.

But it's not enough. By 2040 the amount of energy required to power our world will likely be around 50 per cent higher than it was in 2012. To meet this increased demand, the International Energy Agency forecasts yearly coal demand to grow 0.6 per cent every year between now and then.[26] In one rotten spell for activists in autumn 2016, carbon dioxide in the earth's atmosphere stayed above 400 parts per million for an entire month for the first time ever (which many scientists consider a point of no return for catastrophic climate change), the Living Planet Index projected that the earth could lose two-thirds of wild animals by 2020 and the UK government approved the construction of a new runway at Heathrow airport. Then Donald Trump was elected, appointed a former Exxon Mobil chief secretary of state, vowed to overturn Obama's veto of the Keystone XL project, expressed support for the Dakota Access Pipeline, and promised to resurrect the coal industry.

None of this will stop until tens of thousands of people are willing to do what the activists did in Ffos-y-fran. But for that to happen, activism needs to somehow break out of its subculture. The shared language, the common wisdoms about inclusion and intersectionality, the cliquey friendships and twinkling fingers might keep the movement coherent, especially when the whole endeavour is so thankless and risky, but at the same time, they surely alienate possible allies and new members.[27]

As the oil keeps flowing and the coal keeps burning and as the temperature keeps rising, I suspect in the coming years activists will become more desperate. I predict there will be more disruption, more trespasses and more extreme actions every year from now on.[*28] This is not sur-

---

* The book and movement *Deep Green Resistance* is an example of how far this could go. They argue for total industrial collapse—and then to rebuild again: 'We have better weapons. If you love this planet, it's time to put them all on the table and make some decisions.'

prising: civil disobedience has a long and distinguished past in all modern democracies. The most successful and important radical movements usually broke the law. Every country has its own heroes. In the United States the American revolutionaries, the abolitionists, the civil rights activists, the LGBTQ rights groups all used civil disobedience as part of their modus operandi. For groups who feel so strongly that a law or policy is extremely unfair, and that there are no reasonable alternatives, it has always been an important part of protest, especially in countries (or historical periods) without democratic rights. There are many cases where, although unlawful, large numbers of people have concluded that civil disobedience is morally justified, and ultimately forced changes in the law, such as Gandhi's non-violent resistance in India and the civil rights movement in 1960s America. But for climate-change activism to use civil disobedience with similar effect, it needs to become a mass movement: activists and Nimbys have to work together. Activists doing it alone will replicate the same problem: a small band of well-intentioned risk-takers who accidentally turn off the masses.

Activists can bring their experience, daring and know-how, and Nimbys can bring the numbers—the long tail of grandmothers, builders, unemployed people, personal trainers, bankers, shopkeepers, conservative voters—that are necessary. This is the dynamic that has helped turn anti-fracking into a powerful force, and it's the same dynamic that mobilised thousands of indigenous Americans against the Dakota Access Pipeline in 2016. When the pipeline—which allows crude oil to be transported from North Dakota to Illinois—was first approved, more than

200 Native American tribes allied and protested against the pipeline that ran across sacred land and would contaminate local drinking water. Led by these tribes—rather than seasoned activists—and relating to local drinking water, it became the site of enormous public protest. At its peak an estimated 10,000 people joined the protest campsites, many of whom had never been involved in environmental activism before.

The tragic part is that the activists know the paradox I've described above. They have a sinking feeling they're part of a subculture that ordinary people can't quite relate to. But what are they supposed to do? Just give up, and let the world burn? They are not the bad guys in this story. They have to keep going because most of us can't be bothered: we're too lazy, selfish, short-sighted or busy. We allow ourselves to be conveniently put off by their subculture. But the activist suspects that pretty soon ordinary people will start to feel the effects of climate change in their own back gardens, and know that when that happens more people like Tina and Maureen will mobilise. They will welcome the Nimbys of course, and happily watch their activist subculture get swallowed up in a mass movement that's big enough to turn the tide.

But they won't celebrate because they'll be lying awake at night worrying that it's already too late.

8

Looking for Liberland

Apart from small areas of both the Arctic and Antarctic and a lifeless patch of desert between Sudan and Egypt, there is only one piece of land in the world that is not formally claimed by any sovereign state. It's called Gornja Siga: a seven-square-kilometre patch of uninhabited swampland on the Croatian side of the Danube River. Ever since the break-up of Yugoslavia in 1991, and the subsequent Croatian war of independence from Serbia, the precise boundary between the two countries has been disputed. As it stands, the Danube River acts as the de facto border, but Croatia believes the true border should be the Danube's nineteenth-century course, which would give it several land parcels currently inside Serbia and put Gornja Siga inside Serbia. Although Gornja Siga is under Croatian control, the government won't publicly acknowledge it because to do so would weaken their claim to the much larger lands on the Serbian side. Serbia, quite happy with the status quo, doesn't want it either.[1] This overgrown and unremarkable little swamp is *terra nullius*. Under vaguely defined and loosely enforced international law, the first person who claims sovereignty over *terra nullius* can have it.

In 2014 a thirty-year-old libertarian political activist from the Czech Republic called Vit Jedlička was searching the globe for places where he might start a new country. When he learned about Gornja Siga, Vit made a large flag with help from his father (yellow to denote libertarianism, a black stripe to denote rebellion and a crest of arms) with a metre-long screw to secure it in the ground, wrote a statement and headed to Croatia with a handful of friends. On 13 April 2015, the anniversary of Thomas Jefferson's birthday, he arrived at Gornja Siga, planted his flag, and declared the swamp 'the Free Republic of Liberland'. Thus was created the newest country in the world, the third smallest, and the first based on the principles of radical libertarianism: voluntary taxation, almost nonexistent government, legal drugs and guns, and barely any restrictions on what you can say or do.

Grand plans like this often go one of two ways. They wither away and die barely noticed by anyone, or they take on a life and momentum of their own. Liberland looked like it was here to stay. The world's media loved the idea of a new country—and in the middle of Europe too!—and reported it widely. Vit was overwhelmed with donations and offers of support. Within a couple of months 200,000 people applied online for Liberland citizenship, many of whom said they'd move there as soon as possible.[2] (At the time of writing there are over 100,000 'eligible' applicants, who've filled in all the paperwork correctly.) In the hectic weeks that followed his declaration of independence, Vit assembled a cabinet of ministers, was voted in as president, published a short constitution and sent official-looking letters to sixty heads of state, ambassadors and foreign ministers. He then embarked on a series of 'diplomatic missions', visiting forty countries in twelve months, trying to convince them, without success, to recognise his micro-nation.

Gornja Siga/Liberland/the Swamp is both an ideal location for a new country and a terrible one. It's right in the heart of the world's most prosperous continent, located in a relatively temperate zone that's surrounded by fertile land, and close to the major cities of Belgrade, Zagreb and Budapest. But people in the Balkans are very wary of new countries. Between 1991 and 1995, thousands of people died in the war that followed Croatia's declaration of independence from Serbia. In Vukovar, just a few kilometres from Liberland, the houses are still riddled with bullet holes. When Croatia fully ceded, some older Croats near the border found themselves living in their seventh country, without ever moving house.* Understandably, the Croatian government did not taken kindly to Vit's quixotic plan. Worried he might undermine their land dispute, they quickly blocked the main road into Liberland, and now arrest anyone who is caught there. President Vit has been arrested twice for setting foot in his own country.

---

* Anyone over the age of seventy-seven in 1995, living in bits of eastern Croatia, including an area called Baranja (where Liberland is), would have lived in the following countries without ever moving: Austria-Hungary (1867–1918); State of Slovenes, Croats and Serbs (1918–22); Yugoslavia (1922–41); Independent State of Croatia (1941–5); Federal People's Republic of Yugoslavia (1946–91); Republic of Serbia Krajina (1991–5); Croatia (1995–present).

This is why the one-year anniversary conference to celebrate the founding of Liberland wasn't held on the promised land itself, but a dozen miles away in a rustic hotel in sleepy Lug, a small village in the Croatian region of Slavonja. The area is known for its agriculture, farming, traditional music and friendly locals. And also its relative poverty: Slavonja is the poorest of Croatia's four regions— GDP per capita is under 10,000 euros—as well as its least densely populated. Under a million people live in its 5,000 square miles of vast plains, valleys and mountains.

Sixty hard-line libertarians had travelled from across the globe to Slavonja to discuss the prospects for Liberland in Hotel Lug, a lonely white-and-red building, on a stretch of road from nowhere to nowhere else. Hotel Lug was the sort of place that closes when it wants. Vit had rented every room, along with the main hall, a super-heated tennis-court-sized space lined with sixty wooden chairs and a projector. But even this, the largest hotel anywhere near Liberland, wasn't enough for all the foreigners who had descended upon it, so Liberland volunteers had arranged accommodation in nearby hotels and sourced a minibus to ferry people around. I was staying twenty kilometres away, in somewhere even more remote than Lug.

Libertarians

I'd originally heard about this strange new country from a libertarian called Susanne Tarkowski Tempelhof, an anti-state fanatic in her early thirties from Sweden, whom I'd met at a technology conference in London. She told me she was trying to start her own nation that was based entirely online, and would soon be travelling to Lug to share ideas with radical libertarians like her.

Libertarianism is a vague catch-all term for people who support very small or no central government and want to promote individual liberty. Like most labels, this obscures a wide spectrum of beliefs. Moderate libertarians—such as the US Libertarian Party—tend to support some general taxation and limited nationalised public services. But Liberland is Mecca for libertarian's more radical strands, especially 'anarcho-capitalists', people who believe the state should be abolished entirely, replaced by individuals clubbing together to contract services from private companies.* Also in attendance at Hotel Lug were

---

* Anarcho-capitalists believe that the only morally just society is one where everything is voluntary, but unlike some strands of anarchism—such as anarcho-syndicalism or anarcho-communism, which is based on collective ownership and pooled assets—'an-caps' believe in individual property rights, capitalism and profit. An-caps don't think anarchists who believe in collectivism are true anarchists, since they argue that some form of central authority would be necessary to enforce it. The term was coined by Murray Rothbard, who was trying to combine Austrian economics with its preference for capitalist free markets, classical liberalism's emphasis on individual freedom and individualist anarchism's rejection of coercion and state power. Its basic tenet is that the state is abolished and groups of people club together to provide their own services from a free market. Strands of anarcho-capitalist thinking can be traced back to John Locke's natural rights; the mid-seventeenth-century English Levellers, with their model of a church of voluntary associating equals and self-proprietorship; mid-nineteenth-century anarchist thinkers Julius Faucher and Gustave de Molinari; Henry David Thoreau's 1849 essay *On the Duty of Civil Disobedience* (where the phrase 'That government is best which governs not at all' originated); and the anti-state liberalism of early twentieth-century America (often called the Old Right).

businessmen intrigued by the possibility of (legally) paying zero tax, two American fans of the influential free-market economist Ludwig von Mises, a handful of anarchists from Italy and several bitcoin fanatics. A British couple in their thirties—David (a poet and practitioner of the Israeli martial art Krav Maga) and Hannah, who described themselves as 'voluntaryists'—wanted see if Liberland was really viable. (Voluntaryism sounds kinder than anarcho-capitalism, but it's essentially the same thing.) Rick Falkvinge, the founder of the Pirate Party movement, and a well-known digital-rights activist, had flown in from his native Sweden. There were also a handful of local Croats, people who think Liberland could help the struggling region.

One person, however, was notably absent.

'Our president is in *exile!*' announced Damir Katusic as this rabble of freedom-lovers assembled in the main hall. The forty-year-old chief organiser, a local entrepreneur of sunny disposition, was looking stressed. Damir was born and lives in the next town, Osijek. At age fourteen, he was shot by the Serbian Army during peaceful protests at the beginning of the war of independence. ('Why do you hate governments?' someone asked him later. 'Because the state shot me in the anus!' he replied.) The day Vit planted his flag, Damir chanced upon an online article about it and realised 'Liberland' was just down the road. He jumped on his bike and cycled over to see what the fuss was about, only to be turned away by angry police. Intrigued, he started reading up on Vit's plan and has been volunteering ever since, trying to convince sceptical locals that Liberland is a brilliant idea for local business.

President Vit had tried to get into Croatia three times, once from Hungary and twice from Serbia, and was stopped each time at the border because the Croatian Ministry of the Interior had decided he was a threat to national security. 'Vit is just on the other side of the border, at a hotel in Serbia,' said Damir, looking at one of his two phones. 'It's a complete circus! The Croatian government is actually *scared* of us! They've let 650,000 immigrants pass through the country without passports on the way to Germany from Syria. And an EU citizen like Vit isn't allowed into Croatia?! This is crazy!'

The Nation-State Monopoly

Many characters in this book think, in one way or another, that modern capitalism and individualism is to blame for today's problems. Liberlanders are the refreshing opposite: they think we need more of both. And the biggest problem of all, the arch-enemy of freedom and prosperity in the world, is the modern nation state.

I'd never given much thought to the nation state before, considering it part of the natural order of things. But this political system, a blend of 'nation' (meaning people with common attributes and characteristics) and 'state' (an organised political system with sovereignty over a defined space) is in fact a fairly modern invention, a response to mass industrialisation, war and the first large-scale communications networks. Until the mid-nineteenth century most of the world was a messy sprawl of empires, unclaimed land, city states and principalities, which travellers crossed without checks or passports.* As industrialisation made societies more complex, large centralised bureaucracies grew up to manage them. Those governments best able to unify their regions, store records and co-ordinate action (especially war) grew more powerful vis-à-vis their neighbours. Revolutions—especially in the United States (1776) and France (1789)—helped create the idea of a commonly defined 'national interest', while improved communications unified language, culture and identity.[3] In 1750 hardly anyone in France thought of themselves as 'French'; by 1900, they all did.[4] With imperialistic expansion, this nation-state model spread across the world and the global economic slump of 1873 resulted in immigrants being asked to produce identification at borders and ports of entry, which become formalised during and especially after the two World Wars.[5]

By the middle of the twentieth century the nation state—a specific response to an industrial world—was the only game in town. One hundred and ninety-three of them now have a virtual monopoly on how the world is run, and, despite obvious variations, they all share similar features: a controlled border recognised by other nation states, strictly controlled rights and duties for citizens and a single, sovereign system of law that everyone inside those borders has—in theory—to follow, even if they disagree with it.

---

* The Icelandic Commonwealth (which existed quite happily and peacefully between 930 and 1262) had a private law system, and subjects could transfer allegiance between different chieftains. The Ottoman 'Millet' system allowed religious communities within the Ottoman Empire (which included the Greek Orthodox Church, Greek Christians, Jews, Armenian churches and Islam) to govern themselves according to their religious laws. In the eighteenth century, the Dutch and Swiss had no central government at all.

Liberland is trying to offer an opt-out of this monopoly. Everything has been designed to maximise individual liberty. For a start, it's a voluntary nation, which means anyone can join and leave as they wish (you can become a citizen either by buying it or earning 10,000 'merits', the country's currency).[6] It would be the first country in the world where nothing would be compulsory, where you can do whatever the hell you like, as long as it doesn't physically harm someone else (this makes it closer to anarcho-capitalism than libertarianism). But Liberland's truly revolutionary idea is voluntary taxation. Citizens—or little groups of them—will only pay tax if they want to, and only receive services they've paid for. Schools, hospitals, pensions, roads, sewage works, rubbish collection and the rest will be provided by the market, if people decide that's what they want and stump up the money. Enforcement of the law would come through dispute-resolution systems exercised under contract law, as agreed by those who entered into agreements, secured by a tiny police force and a handful of judges. There will be a political body to keep things ticking along, but it's been designed to be toothless and weak. Twenty representatives will be elected every four years to an assembly, and can only serve a maximum of two terms. Five per cent of the electorate can recall an assembly, and the same proportion can trigger a referendum on any law.

Through the Looking Glass

I'd never have guessed that no nations have recognised Liberland, or that the patch of land itself is still a deserted, inaccessible swamp. I walked into Hotel Lug, and into a parallel universe where a government in-waiting was getting on with the business of planning the imminent takeover.

'Good morning ladies and gentlemen, ministers, ambassadors and friends of liberty, it's my great honour to moderate this conference for you,' said Martin Panek, a timid, slightly awkward man in his early thirties in a suit. 'It was supposed to be moderated by the president, but, er, he called me Thursday to say he was denied entry by Croatia.'

Vit's four-foot-high smiling face was projected on the wall in front of us, beamed in via Skype, from his 'exile' in the Anne Caffe Hotel in Bezdan, twenty kilometres away in Serbia. Vit is an unassuming man, who looks younger than his thirty-two years. He wears a short goatee beard, which matches his strawberry blond hair, and has a Greek wrestler's build. He is also blessed with that rare condition of a face that rests on a smile.

'Without further ado,' said Jan, glancing at Vit's massive smiling face, 'er, I guess I will give the floor to the president—we're still waiting for a few more people to come in—OK. Ladies and gentlemen, the founding father and president of Liberland!'

Vit tried to welcome us, but the Wi-Fi was so bad that we struggled to hear him. Damir asked everyone to disconnect their phones to lessen the load on the bandwidth. I've never been to an event about our glorious technology-filled future where there hasn't been at least one major tech-related problem. But it did not deter Vit, who stop-started his way through some opening remarks:

'You're not only liberty minded people, you're also brave enough to step forward to be part of our new nation . . .'

'I'm very honoured . . .'

'Political systems taking away people's money and putting it into a big machine called the state . . .'

'It's hard to anticipate what our country will look like in two years . . .'

'We put forward our positive vision . . .'

'We know when private property is secure we end up with enormous amounts of prosperity and happiness . . .'

'Nobody can say this isn't Liberland . . .'

'Croatia is treating us differently, we are still the only ones who claim it . . .'

'I hope you will enjoy this event . . .'

'Or we will meet tomorrow for a boat trip . . .'

The audience clapped, a little confused, and Vit's image was replaced by the real-world Ivan Bertović, chairman of Youth Liberals Croatia, a tall, handsome Croat in his early twenties, who gave us a crash course in the history of small nations. Liberland can thrive, he said, as did the independent city state of Ragusa (modern-day Dubrovnik) between 1358 and 1808. Like Hong Kong, Liechtenstein, Monaco and Singapore do now. Then Sven Sambunjak, the 'Representative of Liberland in Croatia', a middle-aged, upbeat IT consultant, explained that Slavonja is so poor it needs Liberland.

Damir was variously rushing around with his two phones, organising minibuses and food, arguing with the hotel staff, smoking, making sure the projector was working and texting Vit. He periodically asked everyone from the front of the tennis court furnace to *please* disconnect from the Wi-Fi because the president can't follow what's happening.

We sat in rapt attention as Dominik Stroukal, a stragglyhaired professor of economics, explained that within fifty years of Liberland being recognised, Croatia would gain exactly 64 per cent GDP increase, because it would be a hub of innovation and economic growth. 'You don't want to throw that out for some small dispute over land!' he said, to approving nods.

Statecraft

All countries are agreed upon fictions, but new countries are supposed to meet a few basic conditions set out in the 1933 Montevideo Convention on Statehood: a permanent population, a defined territory, an effective government and the capacity to enter into relations with other states.[7] The United Nations generally discourages new territories forming from existing states, since it might undermine the international order (although it does happen: the newest country in the world is South Sudan, which came into existence in 1998*).[8] Because of Gornja Siga's *terra nullius* status, Vit's legal standing under this convention is unclear. 'A completely novel situation' wrote the esteemed *Chicago Journal of International Law* in its detailed examination of Liberland in July 2016, suggesting it had 'a shot' at statehood.[9] In the end, the most important consideration is the unwritten rule of international recognition. If enough

---

* South Sudan declared independence from Sudan on 9 July 2011 after a bloody civil war that had plagued the nation since 1962 (Sudan gained independence from joint British–Egyptian rule in 1956). A peace agreement included autonomy for the south and an independence referendum. Ninety-nine per cent voted in favour, and the UN unanimously recognised the new country.

other countries say you are a country, then you are.[10] This is why Liberlanders, and above all Vit, are doing all they can to look like a proper country, and act with the dignity befitting one.

Everything at Hotel Lug was designed and executed to that end, even if the resulting performance bordered on the ridiculous. In October 2015 Vit announced an architecture competition, inviting companies to submit proposals for how to build this 'high-density city nation'. Three architecture firms travelled to Hotel Lug to earnestly present their entries, which were all futuristic concentrations of towering glass edifices, heliports and tight green spaces powered by aeroponics, hydroponics, algae and the Danube.[11]

To my surprise, the majority of Liberland's numerous officials were not even at Hotel Lug. The justice minister (Kacper Zajac), the interior minister (Ondřej Příhonský), consultant and protocol adviser to the minister of foreign affairs (Vittorio Gifra), the special adviser for the Middle East (Olivier Donnet) and the First Lady (Vit's wife, Jana) were all absent. Even so, every third person held some kind of official post in the administration and took their role very seriously. Finance Minister Jan Purabek strode around looking solemn, in pressed trousers and polished shoes. Sven Sambunjuk, the representative of Liberland in Croatia, answered questions from interested parties in his dapper suit and tie. Everyone studiously called each other by their official titles: 'Ambassador, do you have a question?' 'Thank you minister, yes I do have a question,' etc. And officials always referred to Vit as 'Mr President', 'the president' or 'President Jedlička', never just 'Vit'.[12]

Vit's most important staff are the seventy representatives who lobby and campaign for official recognition all over the globe in their respective countries: Argentina, Brazil, Cyprus, the Canary Islands, Ecuador, Finland, Lebanon, the Netherlands, the United States, the United Kingdom and more. (There is even an unpublished twenty-page manual for representatives to follow.) Faisal Butt, the smartly dressed representative to Pakistan, spent much of the conference working on his phone. Faisal is a property developer based in the United Kingdom. He'd flown into Croatia on Air Liberland's privately chartered four-person flight from Prague. 'We are in talks with the Pakistan government, and hopefully within the next six months we should have a positive response,' he told me during one of the breaks, but he wouldn't give me any names. Straight after the conference, Faisal flew out to Pakistan for a three-month 'diplomatic offensive'.

Vit works extremely hard to create a believable fiction of a country. A few weeks after the conference, I visited Liberland's HQ, which was in Vit's home city of Prague, located in the diplomatic quarter of Vinohrady. Vit likes to say it's the former residency of the ambassador to Denmark. While technically correct, this grand building has been repurposed as a co-working space, and Vit and his assistant are just two of dozens of assorted start-ups and freelancers who rent tables and office space. It was full of young men and women wearing Apple headphones, zipping around drinking Nespressos from the industrial machine in the shared kitchen and staring into their laptops.

Vit works roughly sixteen hours a day in this office, primarily answering the hundreds of emails sent daily to president@liberland.org. I found him working on his latest plan to imagine Liberland closer to reality: to get people to live on the Swamp somehow. A settled population would aid his claim under the Montevideo Convention, and really put pressure on Croatia. A project to send in flag-planting drones was abandoned on learning that flying a drone in Serbia was illegal. He considered briefly having a music festival on the banks of the Danube, and getting hundreds of people in dinghies to invade simultaneously, but that didn't work out either. But he'd just bought a $30,000 boat, which in early 2017 he will sail down the Danube, leading a flotilla of houseboats, which will moor on the banks of Liberland. 'Technically neutral waters,' he said, chuckling as he showed me a map. 'So Croatia won't be able to stop us!' Forty Liberlanders have already expressed an interest.

Vit is a master of the art of leverage, and the official titles, the carefully designed flag and printed brochures, the constitution, the recently founded Liberland football team are all starting to pay off. Liberland currently receives around $20,000 in donations per month from over 2,000 donors, a decent number of whom are extremely rich. (Vit doesn't take a salary—he's just about sufficiently well-off not to need it—and so the donations cover Vit's travel costs, and events like this one year anniversary conference. All donations, along with Vit's spending, are available to view on their website.)

One of Liberland's largest donors is thirty-seven-year-old multimillionaire Roger Ver. Like Vit, Roger considers himself an anarcho-capitalist. He left the United States and renounced his citizenship a decade ago after being convicted of selling firecrackers on eBay, and subsequently made money in Silicon Valley start-up companies, and then became a very early investor in the cryptocurrency bitcoin. (Roger plans to be cryonically frozen by Alcor when he dies, like Zoltan.) He now lives in Tokyo running a bitcoin-based business and donates $10,000 a month to Liberland.[13] 'I know it's a long shot,' Roger told me via Skype, 'but the minute I'm assured the Croatian police aren't going to destroy any investment I make there, yeah, sign me up! I'll even consider moving there. And so would a lot of my friends.' Jet-setting around the world representing what appears to be a state in waiting, with glitzy brochures paid for by millionaire backers, Vit collects any crumbs of recognition—look who's shaken my hand—which he then uses in his next lobbying round. 'Twelve to fifteen MEPs have now expressed some support for Liberland,' he told me in Prague. 'So has the opposition party in Turkey, the Swiss Independence Party, the Norway Capitalist Party and the Finish Libertarian Party.' Vit will use all of this to convince other parties to recognise Liberland too. The Libertarian candidate for the 2016 US presidential election, Gary Johnson, said Liberland was 'wonderful' and that he would acknowledge Liberland officially if he won. (He didn't win. But he did finish third with a respectable 4.3 million votes—and was polling above 10 per cent in many states in the weeks before election day.)

But recognition can come in many forms, and Vit also uses objection to his advantage. As Vit's profile has grown, so has the interest from the Croatian government, which Vit skilfully turns into tacit acknowledgement that Liberland exists. Just before the lunch break I noticed that two suspicious, unsmiling men had been loitering only half-interested near the back of the room all morning. I asked around, but no one knew who they were. Damir later learned they were Croatian secret-service officers, here to keep an eye on us. As I walked outside to eat lunch I found Pavol, a Slovakian hacker, hunched over his laptop. 'Yep,' he said, excitedly. 'We're being bugged. I thought so. Probably the Croatian secret service.' He showed me his screen, which was a jumble of meaningless flashing dots and numbers. 'See? They've set up at least three telephone masts around the hotel,' he continued, pointing at different parts of Hotel Lug. 'There, there and, let me see, over there. All of our communication is being monitored.'

Come to think of it, the police did always seem to know where we were and what we were doing. On the way over I was stopped at Osijek airport by border police, who said they knew I was going to Gornja Siga, that I shouldn't and that I'd get arrested if I did. That was a little odd, because other EU passport holders sailed across the border. Everyone in Lug had a similar story. The half dozen Polish business students were held at the Hungary–Croatia border for three hours. When I got back to my hotel at the end of the first day, the receptionist told me the police had turned up and asked for a copy of my passport.

When we returned from the break, Vit mentioned that the Croatian police were taking an interest in our conference, which was proof that Liberland was real. He also formally thanked the police for protecting Liberland's borders by having closed the one road in.

There were also two suspicious men standing by Hotel Lug's front gate, wearing black suits, sunglasses, carrying walkie-talkies and looking on high alert.

'More spies?' I asked Damir.

'No, no!' Damir replied. 'That's Liberland security.' Expecting trouble, he'd hired them for the weekend. 'I didn't tell them to dress up like spies though! But this is a libertarian conference, so I can't tell them what to wear, can I?'

Where We're Going We Don't Need Roads

Liberland isn't the complete libertarian escape from the modern nation-state monopoly. With its official borders and elected representatives, it is still a nation state, albeit a radically slimmed-down version. All Vit's efforts are geared towards securing recognition from other nation states because in the end he wants Liberland to become a member of the club.

But for many libertarians, the really exciting action is online. In 1994 a retired physicist from California called Timothy May published *Cyphernomicon*, a manifesto for a small collection of radicals called 'cypherpunks' who were interested in combining digital cryptography and libertarian thinking. They saw that digital technology could potentially be used to undermine and even destroy the nation state entirely, replacing it with anarcho-capitalist societies online. (I discussed these groups in detail in my previous book, *The Dark Net*.) Internet use at the time was very small, and the technology they dreamt up wasn't quite up to the job. But over the last decade, as the world has gone digital, and as more of us worry about internet security and online privacy, there has been an explosion in all sorts of software that can help the libertarians: publicly available powerful encryption, censorship-free networks, anonymous Web browsers and digital currencies.

The truly radical vision is to use these technologies to create a nation without any physical existence at all. Cyberspace, after all, is infinite. There are as many *terrae nullius* as you can make. It's a space beyond the nation state and its borders and rules.[14] That's what Susanne Tarkowski Tempelhof, a champagne-drinking, forty-a-day polyamorous troublemaker, came to Hotel Lug to tell us about in the afternoon session. Liberland was just the latest stop in a hectic year of travelling, trying to sell her idea in Sweden, Brazil, the United Kingdom, France, Denmark, Ghana, Italy (to refugees), the Czech Republic, Finland, Estonia and Turkey. Susanne was joined by husband James Fennell, MBE, a very sharp former security contractor and aid worker in his fifties who'd turned anarchist after his experience in the 1994 Rwandan genocide. Working there for CARE International, he was informed that hundreds of Hutu had taken refuge up Bissesero Mountain and were surrounded by a Tutsi militia. Against his bosses' advice, James took all the money he had and persuaded a platoon of the French Foreign Legion to head up the mountain to protect them. (This is what he was later awarded his MBE for.) He learned that following orders wasn't always the right thing to do. 'Liberland is great,' Susanne told me when she arrived in Lug, hours later than everyone else. 'But it is re-creating the old model, with a border, an army, an assembly. What if Serbian or Croatian tanks roll in? I am building the world's first decentralised borderless voluntary nation, where no government can find you, tax you, or control you.' She calls this 'Bitnation'.

Susanne has a strange, unplaceable accent. Born in Sweden in 1983 to a Polish father and a French mother, she moved to France as a teenager, spent seven years working as a conflict-zone contractor for the US government in Afghanistan, Libya, Egypt and Washington DC, before moving to Brazil, and finally to Amsterdam where she dedicates her life to working on Bitnation. You could almost work out her life story from her accent. Basic vocabulary: Swedish accent. Swear words: French accent. Business words: American accent. All spoken in a husky voice due to chain-smoking and drinking. Susanne is also very unusual on account of her sex: according to one recent study, 94 per cent of libertarians in America are non-Hispanic whites, and over two-thirds are men.[15]

Unlike most libertarians, Susanne's world view was forged by a series of very personal experiences with anarchy and the state, which started all the way back in post-war Poland, where Susanne's grandfather, Jerzy Tempelhof, was working as an adviser to the minister of transport. Life as a Jew in post-war Soviet Poland got harder as Stalin became convinced that Jews were potentially a disloyal fifth column, and in the 1950s the family changed their name to Tarkowski, a more Polish-sounding name. When this was uncovered, Jerzy was accused of being a Zionist spy, and he and his family—including Susanne's father—applied for asylum in Sweden. It was finally granted but for a decade her father, who was a respected expert in immunology, was stateless.

Fast forward to 2009, and the peripatetic Susanne was working in Kabul, employing around 300 Pashtun to conduct research on their communities, which she was selling on to the US military.[16] When she hit a cash-flow problem, owing tens of thousands of dollars, thirty local Pashtun men turned up to her office and occupied it, threatening to kill her. Susanne, locked in her top-floor office, was desperately phoning friends and family back in Europe begging to borrow money, but no one would help her. The Pashtuns gave her two weeks to pay. The next day, local Afghanis with whom she worked, having heard what had happened, managed to cobble together $30,000, which they gave her. 'I realised that it was the state that had destroyed the bonds between people,' she told me, shortly after the Liberland conference. 'In Afghanistan, they saved my life. In the West, people rely on the state, because it provides everything for them.' Eternally grateful, she recalls leaving Afghanistan for the last time, and dozens of locals begged her to take them with her. Someone even tried to give Susanne their child to bring back to Europe. The experience pulled Susanne up short: borders are creating a geographic genocide, she thought. They're an affront to freedom. Afghanistan—and then a similar experience working in Libya with rebels fighting Gaddafi—turned her into a fully committed anarchist who thought state power was the root of most of the world's problems.[17]

In 2013 a former US military employee told her about bitcoin, and she immediately thought that it was a way to circumnavigate the state entirely. Bitcoin, which was invented in 2009, is digital cash, just string of numbers. Anyone can download a bitcoin wallet or QR code on to their computer or phone, buy bitcoins with traditional currency from a currency exchange and use them to buy or sell a growing number of products and services as easily as sending an email. Transactions are secure, fast and free, with no central authority controlling value or supply, and no middlemen taking a slice. You don't even have to give your real name to start up an account. Bitcoin wrestles control of the money supply away from the state. There is a cap on the total number of bitcoins that can ever be produced: 21 million. New bitcoins are not minted by any central authority. Instead, anyone who dedicates their computing power to verifying the transactions competes to earn a very small number of new bitcoins each time they do so (this is called 'mining'). As more bitcoins are created (approximately 14 million have been created so far), the remaining bitcoins require more computing power to mine.[*] The last bitcoin is expected to be mined around 2140.

It wasn't bitcoin itself that excited Susanne, but the way bitcoin stored information. It works because a copy of every transaction between users is stored on a public, chronologically ordered database, called the 'blockchain'.[18] A copy of that database is hosted on thousands of computers, and new transactions can only be added to that database once they've been verified by other computers that check them. The upshot is that it's possible to add new transactions to the blockchain, but not edit, change or delete old ones. It's like a magic spreadsheet: a massive, public, chronologically ordered, tamper-proof database that anyone can view and add to, but no one is in charge of it.

This relatively simple invention is revolutionary, since it might change the way information is stored (on multiple databases simultaneously), verified (by other people who use the system) and controlled (making centralised editing or control more difficult). Millions of dollars of investment

---

[*] Bitcoins can be divided into eight decimal places. The smallest non-divisible unit is known as a 'Satoshi'.

are pouring into blockchain, for business accounting, financial services, for proving ownership. There's Open Bazaar, a peer-to-peer marketplace that is impossible to shut down, hoping to out-compete Amazon with its cuts and its secretive algorithms, a decentralised Uber, decentralised file storage, a decentralised Web domain-name system. The most interesting of all is what technologists are doing with 'smart contracts'.[19] These are basically lines of code on a blockchain that execute instructions. The German company slock.it sells locks that are programmed to rent themselves out. When someone books a room, they pay for it in bitcoin (for example), and automatically receive a code that allows entry. When they check out, the lock can automatically order a cleaner, transfer payment to the cleaner and send leftover funds to the room owner. It's a whole, functioning company that doesn't exist, except as a computer programme.

Blockchains and smart contracts create problems as well as efficiencies. What if you forget your password code, or think you deserve a refund because the room wasn't as big as promised? And what happens if something incorrect or malicious is placed on one of these immutable databases?* Radical decentralisation is an excellent way to stop

---

* In 2015 a company called the DAO (decentralised autonomous organisation) was founded as an investor-directed capital fund, which exists only virtually, as a series of public smart contracts. Investors can buy shares in the DAO using Ethereum's (another blockchain) currency, which gives votes on investments. Anyone anywhere in the world can invest, it's all transparent, there is no board or employees at all, and shareholders receive any profits directly. One month after it was launched to great fanfare, hackers and/or investors managed to exploit a vulnerability by inserting some code that redirected shares into their personal wallets, allowing them to walk off with millions of dollars of investors' money. There was no way

the abuse of centralised power, but when things go wrong it's sometimes helpful having someone in charge.[20] Despite these problems, everyone at Hotel Lug was extremely excited by blockchains and their liberating, decentralising potential. (Vit told me blockchains would be 'absolutely vital' for Liberland's taxation and voting systems, and that bitcoin will be an official currency.)

The more Susanne looked into it, the more she became convinced it was a way to build a free-market anarchist state online, allowing citizens to meet, communicate, make agreements, resolve disputes, provide peer-to-peer security and social insurance and trade with each other in a way that could not be monitored or controlled. After travelling the world to research it further, in early 2014 she wrote a short paper announcing this new nation that would permit people to come together and voluntarily agree how to live: 'The arbitrarily drawn lines called borders, which were once supposed to provide stability, are now the direct cause of instability, due to their "one size fits all" design . . . [W]e need to replace the nation state model with a better, non-geographical and voluntary model: Bitnation.'[21] Unlike Liberland, everything is virtual. To become a 'Bitnation citizen' is extremely simple. In fact, I'm one of about 5,000 Bitnation citizens dotted all over the world. All I had to do was agree with the Bitnation constitution, which is a twelve-line poem, and sign up on the site.[22] I input my age, height and a photo, two witnesses watched and typed in

---

to change it, except to 'fork' the blockchain, which meant making a second copy without that malicious code in it. But that goes directly against the principle of an immutable, unchangeable, decentralised network. At the time of writing, this problem is still rumbling on, without any obvious solution.

their names, and that generated a 'World Citizenship ID'. A 'hash' of this ID (a unique string of numbers that can be used, in conjunction with a key, to re-create the original file) was then uploaded onto a blockchain, where it will now stay, unchanged, forever. Here's my QR code:

Several services are available to the Bitnation citizen. As I was travelling across Europe with Tommy Robinson and Pegida UK, campaigning against Angela Merkel's open stance toward refugees, Susanne was working on a project to help them. She realised most refugees had no ID, which meant they couldn't prove who they were or access any services. She started offering IDs to refugees, in the hope that countries would accept them (she even presented it to the United Nations, but little came of it). She also created a bitcoin credit card that could be automatically exchanged for legal tender at point of use. That meant refugees could have access to non-cash forms of money without opening a bank account. (At the time of writing a couple of hundred refugees have taken on Bitnation citizenship IDs and credit cards.) Her most successful product is probably a notary service, which allows people to register a document and upload a record of it onto the Bitnation blockchain, where it can be checked by others, but not tampered with. It has so far been used for recording freelance agreements, marriages, birth certificates, wills, land titles and even loans. (The Estonian government, sufficiently impressed

with this, now allows its 'e-citizens' to use Bitnation to no-
tarise important documents.)

Susanne doesn't believe in democracy. She thinks it's
just another form of collectivism, and doesn't guarantee
true liberty.[23] 'At school you're taught that democracy rests
on the consent of the governed,' she told me.[24] 'But that's
bullshit. Democracy is being forced to consent to rules
you don't agree with, and to pay taxes for things you don't
want! It's mob rule 101.' She's right about that: you cannot
get out of criminal law by explaining to a police officer that
you 'did not consent to it'. You cannot agree to receive no
services and pay no taxes. You have no opt-out. Central to
her thinking (and anarcho-capitalism generally, including
Liberland) is the 'non-aggression principle': the idea that
people should not be coerced in any way to do things they
do not voluntarily agree to (except in self-defence—for example, protecting your property).

I have been following Susanne around for several
months. I've met her at bitcoin or blockchain conferences
and events. I travelled with her and James after the Liberland conference for a couple of days. She hates being told
what to do. *Hates* it. She goes out of her way to break the
rules. When Susanne smokes a cigarette, which is nearly
every waking hour, it's done with pride, even a little ag-
gression. Yeah I'm knowingly smoking myself to an early
grave, and what are you going to do about *that*? At about
1 a.m. on the first night in Liberland, she and James paid
a local taxi driver a couple of euros to scour the area for
shops and bring them back some Marlboro Reds. Yeah?
And what the hell are you going to do about *that*?

When Susanne presented Bitnation to the conference—which she did while smoking—she explained that

the long-term aim of Bitnation, beyond the ID cards and notary services, is to provide a platform for people to come together with other free adults and live according to a set of laws and arbitration methods they've agreed and consented to amongst themselves. It is to create a nation based on the non-aggression principles. Bitnation allows you to take a system of law—modelled on common law, Sharia law or even a law code you've designed yourself—write it up as a private contract, put it on that unchangeable blockchain, and invite others to sign up and live by it, tying any digital assets to the agreements made. This is the outer reaches of libertarian thought: polycentric legal systems that live alongside each other and even compete with each other.

'I want to talk about my vision for a post–nation state,' she explained. 'I believe nation states are going away. The only thing we can do is make sure it happens in the right way. The future will either be a one-world government run by the United Nations, which will be a world of perpetual terror, or a world of millions of competing nations.'

Someone in the crowd asked what will happen when there are disputes between people, and no central authority to resolve it. Resolution (what I would call law) won't be through a court or legal system, she explained, but rather through paid arbitrators. But ideally, this wouldn't be necessary either, since everyone will have a reputation system that all other citizens could see, so they'll be incentivised to behave well. This was an idea explored by Charlie Brooker in a recent episode of *Black Mirror*, where, in a near future, people's social standing, employment prospects and even general happiness are all dependent on a single reputation score awarded by other citizens based on how they had behaved. It was a nightmarish dystopia, of course: a world of stressed, reputation-obsessed citizens terrified of speaking their mind in case it damaged their score. But for Susanne, nations would be forced to compete for citizens, who could change allegiance at any moment. Don't like your nation's criminal justice system, or the law on drugs? Move to another one. Don't think the health system is working? Start your own. Want to start a free-love commune in Southern Portugal with a sovereign system of law designed by the community? Here's the platform and technology: go for it. Far from creating an unworkable, dispute-riddled and fragmented mess of competing systems, all of which would be too small to get anything serious done, like build huge water infrastructure or electricity grids, Susanne thinks that this would inject some much needed competition into nations: resulting in 'more convenient, secure and cost-efficient governance services'.[25]

Looking for Liberland

Even though it's on the same side of the Danube as us, a mere twenty-minute drive from Lug, we'd have to cross a border to get to Liberland. Ever since the Croatian police shut the one road into Liberland in 2015, the only route is to drive over the Danube into Serbia, take a dirt road for forty-five minutes, scramble down a thickety bank and then travel back across the river by boat. Early on Sunday morning, around thirty of us boarded a large white double-decker bus that Damir had rented from a local company, and headed to the border. Vit would meet us on the other side at a nearby restaurant, and from there we'd all make our way to his boat.

First we had to get through passport control to exit Croatia, before crossing a hundred metres of no man's land to the Serbian border. Leaving Croatia was easy enough. But the Serbian police took a keen interest in the white double-decker carrying thirty political radicals inching towards them at the back of the twenty-vehicle queue and two stern border police were dispatched. No one likes border crossings. They're slow and annoying. But for Susanne, being forced to hand over a passport ('The state's way of controlling you,' she said) and let someone else decide if you can enter is a personal affront.

'Fucking pigs. Fascist pigs!' she muttered under her breath as the border police wandered over to our bus and climbed aboard. 'They are the people who put people on trains to Auschwitz!'

'Where are you going?' barked the officer. Fortunately, one of our crew was Paul Bradbury, an avuncular Brit and long-time Croatian resident who runs the English-language news website Total Croatia News. He was well versed in how to navigate the Balkans, and took control.

'We are going for lunch,' replied Paul, breezily, 'as we heard Serbian food is the best in the whole region, and there is a restaurant close by.'

'Yes it is!' said the police officer, who broke into a broad grin. 'And the restaurant has a new chef. His name is Vit Jedlička, from Liberland. Haha!'

We were on our way into Serbia. All except for one American, Adam, who foolishly decided to film all this as it was unfolding with his Go-Pro camera. The police hauled him off the bus, took him to a room for questioning, wiped the memory from his camera, and then let him go. He finally rejoined the bus, looking roughly the same colour as the vehicle itself.

After a short drive we arrived at the Solaris Restaurant, which was another rustic English-free zone, poised flush on the bank of the Danube. Vit's motorcade—three cars—rolled in and out stepped the president, smartly dressed in cream chinos, shirt and jacket, holding a bottle of Liberland Ale, his country's national beer. 'Welcome, welcome!' he said to everyone, smiling and shaking hands. Inside the restaurant, over a huge cauldron of fish stew, Vit made Damir, Rick Falkvinge and Susanne honorary Liberland citizens and ceremoniously handed out citizenship certificates, to applause. Susanne and Vit nipped out for a quick meeting to agree on a deal between their two fledgling nations: that citizens of one could freely access the services of the other.

Once all the formalities were over we headed to the riverbank where Vit's small boat was moored. When we finally arrived, after Susanne and husband James somehow found alcohol en route, and after getting lost with Damir, who'd somehow forgotten the way to his new country, our skipper, a twenty-year-old Austrian architecture student, welcomed us aboard an eight-seater boat moored to a rickety wooden post sticking out of the muddy riverbank.

Two Croatian police boats, both containing four officers, were floating in the middle of the 200-metre-wide Danube, directly between us and the seven-square-kilometre Swamp.

'I expected them. But it's good to see the Croatian police are guarding Liberland's borders,' said Vit. 'Thank you for protecting our borders!' he shouted, in their direction.

Liberland isn't much to look at. There's nothing save a couple of rubbly access roads and one solitary, abandoned building that Vit plans to use as the address for e-companies he's encouraging to set up there, or perhaps to house the assembly. It was about as different as possible from the futuristic tech paradise I'd been hearing about in Hotel Lug. But its lack of landmarks make it a more perfect canvas. For a few moments, we all stood on the shore, looking beyond the police boats, beyond the Swamp, beyond all reasonable prospects of success, and saw a world of freedom and prosperity, a hyper-modern city state of gleaming glass skyscrapers and 5 per cent flat tax and freedom of speech. Hong Kong, 1776 America, a futuristic bitcoin-powered paradise, right here in the middle of the Balkans.

'It's a beautiful beach, a Caribbean-style beach!' said Vit, looking out at what he calls 'the beloved homeland'. 'It's the place that can be the freest country in the world in a very short term . . . It will *always* be Liberland!'

We took it in turns to get on the boat. Six of the Polish business students, the Swedish vice consul and I excitedly climbed aboard, rocking as we lugged a six-foot-high yellow-and-black Liberland flag on board, which we lodged into one of the seats. The skipper fired up the engine and we headed south down the Danube, past the motionless police boats and their glaring crew. Fifty metres past them, we veered suddenly west towards the Swamp.

'We can make it!' shouted the Swedish vice consul.

'If we land this boat,' said the skipper, 'we'll get arrested for making an illegal border crossing.'

'Come on!' replied one of the Polish business students. 'Let's set foot on Liberland!'

I didn't really see the point of actually setting foot on the Swamp. Still, I thought to myself as we closed in on the freest country in the world, it *would* be interesting to see what those glaring police officers would do. What exactly would we be arrested for? According to the Croatian police, we would be crossing from Serbia into another bit of Serbia. Since April 2015 there have been more than fifty arrests of supporters who have attempted to enter Liberland. But the cases are often quietly dropped when they reach court because the Croatian government would have to admit Gornja Siga was in Croatia.[*][26]

But the moment we took a westward turn, one of the police boats steamed towards us at speed. We straightened up twenty metres from landfall, just as the police boat pulled up right alongside us, preventing us from getting any closer. Then it started u-turning violently, hoping to capsize our little boat, which was rocking uncontrollably.

'Haha! Come on!' shouted one of the Polish business students. 'You'll never sink us! Long live Liberland!'

For the next twenty minutes we both played this ridiculous charade. We made occasional half-hearted lurches towards the land, easily repelled by the police boat, which flanked us and periodically chopped up the water. We filmed them with our smartphones, and they filmed us with handheld video cameras. We waved at them with our hands and our flag, but they only glared back.

I had the feeling they had played this game a few times before.

---

[*] At the time of writing, the Croatian Supreme Court has judged that some of the arrests made were likely to be illegal, and ordered the lower courts to re-examine the charges, and delineate the border.

Finally, we limped back to Serbia, and the police boat returned to the middle of the river and turned the engine off again. That was the closest I was to get to the promised land.

All radicals are optimistic about their prospects of success; they have to be to keep going. But with the heady technological changes around us, none are more optimistic, more relentlessly upbeat or more ambitious than the people trying to forge out new spaces of freedom. Vit is planning on elections in 2017, full international recognition by 2020 and 30,000–50,000 citizens by 2025. He is convinced that at least one recognised country, possibly two, from Africa or Latin America will formally recognise Liberland in 2017. And before long, he's certain Croatia will accept that Liberland is no longer just in his head, but in everyone's. And what else is a nation state, in the end, except something in our heads? Susanne, meanwhile, thinks that blockchain and other technologies will lead to the collapse of governments within thirty years or so, and that Bitnation will be ready to provide an alternative when they do. She thinks it will come through first in places where nation states are already weak or non-existent. She and James are planning a world trip to propose Bitnation as an alternative to corrupt bureaucrats and inefficient governments, taking in favelas, shanty towns, conflict-ridden and lawless zones.

There are lots of practical problems. Both Vit and Susanne place a lot of trust in digital reputation systems to allow people who barely know each other to communicate and trade without a central authority: Amazon and eBay have demonstrated how well it can work. But even these systems require some kind of central authority to manage disputes, and behind them are formal legal systems that have evolved complicated codes to manage the problems reputation systems create: there are civil courts and trading-standards bodies to keep everyone honest. Buying books is one thing, but using a reputation system for every aspect of human life is less simple. Manipulation or gaming of the system would become more common, and far more serious. And how to deal with the millions of people who aren't techno-wizards and don't care as much about privacy, or aren't so rich that they could pay for private healthcare, education, security and sewage works? It's not surprising that libertarian philosophy tends to appeal most to those reasonably well off who can afford the luxury to dream about such things; and who'd be the most likely to succeed in a libertarian world. 'I don't want the poor to suffer,' said Vit, when I pushed him on this, 'but in Liberland *everyone* will be rich! It's a win-win for everyone.' This all sounds plausible in theory, but it's techno-optimism at its most extreme.

Ignore for a moment the many practical problems with these hopeful plans, because practical problems are often surmountable. There are more fundamental ones. Nation states, with their borders and their imperfect democracies, exist in some form to deal with the natural but often conflicting human impulse between living collectively and being the master of your own destiny.[27] History suggests that when there's no central authority to manage that tension, things often go badly wrong very quickly. Entering into agreements voluntarily is a very enticing prospect, especially when you are well educated and are reasonably well off. (Public spending in Susanne's home country of Sweden, where she was born and educated, has averaged 55 per cent between 1993 and 2015.[28]) There's a reason you don't get many libertarian movements in countries with weak and failing states: borders and functioning central governments provide security and stability. They allow a cohesive unit or group of people to live safely together according to their own culture and political beliefs, by raising and spending collectively raised finances to protect the nation, and pay for certain collectively agreed services. Without borders, it's hard to imagine a collective welfare state.[29] Nation states cause all sorts of problems. The absence of them would probably cause even more.

But both Vit and Susanne have spotted something important. The internet is a technology built on libertarian principles: censorship-free, decentralised and borderless. That technology—which was the preserve of a handful of academics and hobbyists just twenty-five years ago— is now ubiquitous, and it's putting the nation-state model under serious strain in all sorts of ways. Digital information can be shared at practically zero cost, an infinite number of times; it is very difficult to censor; and it does not easily recognise national borders. Thanks to modern communications, it's easier than ever for businesses and people to relocate anywhere, which is making it harder for governments to collect taxes. App technology like Uber and Deliveroo has led to a sudden and unexpected surge in a gig economy, which is estimated to cost the UK government £3.5 billion a year by 2020–1. There are already millions of people using bitcoin and blockchain technologies, and their number will continue to grow. The Net is also creating new affiliations and loyalties that aren't always national in nature: a growing number of people see themselves as 'global citizens', like Susanne.[30] The nation state evolved during a time of industrialisation, centralised 'command and control' bureaucracies and the growth of national loyalty. Modern technology tends in the opposite direction. Even borders themselves—the linchpin of the nation state—are being put under unprecedented pressure. If you are born in Saudi Arabia, then according to the United Nations Development Index you are in the 39th most developed country in the world. Born a few miles to the south, in neighbouring Yemen, and you're in the 160th.[31] It's a life lottery, and around the world people are less willing to accept it. People are on the move, driven by war, climate change, poverty or simply a desire to improve their lives.

Susanne's and Vit's claim that the nation state is no longer the best way of ordering society is worth consideration. To the people living under them, the collapse of Christendom, the Roman Empire, tribal living, city states and absolute monarchies all seemed utterly unthinkable too, until they happened. It's unlikely that the nation state will be around forever. It makes sense to start imagining what might replace it.

'Liberland stands for something,' Damir told me, just before I left Croatia. (He also asked me if I knew anyone in the United Kingdom who could help him market his new business idea, which is iodine-infused water.) 'It's the world's only libertarian state founded on principles of classical liberalism and freedom. I live in a part of Croatia where there is nothing. There are no jobs, no prospects, no real democracy and no real freedom. This is something worth fighting for.' Just ten kilometres down the road from him, past the police block, lies a seven-square-kilometre patch of no man's land. The product of borders, nation states, wars, misery and suffering. Every day, fourteen people leave Slavonja in search of a better life.

Epilogue
2016: An Ode

Every generation feels itself to be living in unprecedented times and facing unique challenges. But by any measure, 2016 was a peculiar year. It was the year the Overton window—that consensus that defines acceptable, 'normal' political ideas—noticeably moved. Although no one could say precisely where it moved to. Or if a brick had been thrown through it.

I began work on this book in 2014. By the time I finished over two years later, ideas that had seemed radical when I started were no longer quite so strange. In fact, being outside the mainstream had become a distinct advantage. In 2016 politicians—especially right-wing populists—found that pitching as a radical was a powerful asset. Donald Trump won a stunning victory in the US presidential election, promising to smash up the political establishment. The United Kingdom voted to leave the European Union, despite the overwhelming opposition of the political and business classes. In France, the far-right Front National became the second most popular party.

For many people, this was cause for celebration: the moment ordinary people 'took back' power from 'elites', the dawn of a new age of national and popular sovereignty. People who'd felt left behind for decades—and in many ways they had been—felt some semblance of political agency. But other, darker, forces were smuggled in with the surging anti-establishment zeitgeist. And amid the worrying growth in far-right demagoguery, Islamist violence and a background hum of economic hardship, analysts started looking for historical precedents. Most reached for the 1930s—naturally, since that after all is the only history most of us are taught in schools—and duly noted the similarities: a period of extreme economic difficulties, rising nationalism and the collapse of the moderate centre.

This account implies that right-wing populism—nationalism, xenophobia and anti-elitism—is irrevocably on the march. But there are many other types of radical ideas and movements also on the move. Trump surprised almost every seasoned Washington watcher, but so did openly socialist Bernie Sanders' close run for the Democratic Party candidacy. Jeremy Corbyn was also re-elected as leader of the UK Labour Party, promising democratic revolution and a strong left-wing agenda. In Spain the left-wing anti-austerity Podemos party, founded in January 2014 by a long-haired bearded professor, won 21 per cent of the vote in the year's national elections, effectively ending the two-party system. And some new movements and ideas couldn't be placed on the political spectrum at all. Beppe Grillo's Five Star Movement, only created in 2009, was leading in national polls the end of 2016, and had elected the first woman as mayor of Rome. Environmentalism, eco-villages, psychedelic movements and radical

libertarianism were all on the rise too. Some of them I suspect will outlast the current populist zeitgeist.

Therefore a better (and certainly more hopeful) analogy
is early nineteenth-century Europe. The period witnessed
what must have felt at the time like unprecedented change
and confusion: the onset of industrialisation, political revolution and counter-revolution, great leaps in science, the
first railways (which changed people's conception of 'the
nation'), war, state-building and mass urbanisation. A British prime minister was assassinated. Luddites smashed
machines, fearing that the power loom—that generation's
artificial intelligence—would cause mass unemployment.

The turmoil and instability shook up old assumptions as never before, stimulating a flowering of radical
ideas, some of which were stirrings of the modern world:
working-class consciousness, extended (albeit still limited) suffrage, Factory Acts, socialist theory, Robert Ow-
en's New Lanark, Catholic emancipation and utilitarian
dreams.* It was a time when people had outgrown the institutions of the day, but had not yet found new ones. A
time that was 'pregnant with change'.[1]

The Age of the Radical

There are two main reasons why radicals are important
now, why we need people shouting from the fringes that
we should aim at immortality, that nation states are done

---

* Appropriately enough, the term 'radical' was first used in the United
  Kingdom in a strictly political sense to describe loose political
  grouping that supported parliamentary reform and extended suffrage in the early nineteenth century.

for, that psychedelics can open a new window in our mind or that we must tear everything up and live in small sustainable eco-villages.

The first reason is that they might be right. 'Disobedience, in the eyes of anyone who has read history, is our original virtue' wrote Oscar Wilde. 'It is through disobedience and rebellion that progress has been made.' Radicalism is the source of new ideas, renewal and change. The list of outspoken radicals dismissed for being impractical or dangerous at the time, but whom modern society now extols, is extremely long: John Lilburne, John Stuart Mill, Rosa Parks, Thomas Paine, Emmeline Pankhurst, Harvey Milk, Martin Luther King, and on and on.

Ought we be so sure we've got it all figured out? That our way of living is the best one, and that alternatives could never work? It often takes outsiders to suggest that another world is possible. Even if they are not completely right—no single idea ever is—they are often half right. And we only know which half if radical ideas are allowed to flourish. The free-love commune Tamera might not be a plausible model for a complex post-industrial society, but water retention, energy autonomy and switched-off mobile phones are things we could all benefit from. Zoltan might be mostly interested in living forever, but his quixotic pursuit forces us to ponder the implications of technologies— AI and anti-ageing in particular—that are approaching quickly, and will have enormous ramifications. Susanne's madcap idea for a digital borderless nation is a moon shot: but her immutable blockchain-based records might help millions of people who currently live without adequate records of what they own.[2] (In 2016 the governments of Georgia and Honduras decided to develop their own versions of this.) If the Arctic ice sheet melts and sea levels rise significantly, future generations will look back at the environmental activists and conclude they were not the dangerous ones: the rest of us were.

The current Overton window of the centre-left has been reduced to a threadbare assortment of piecemeal policy change, reheated ideas and knee-jerk posturing, which, even combined, lacks anything close to a positive progressive vision. The center-right is being gravitationally pulled towards populist chest-beating and nativism, increasingly preferring a more closed world to an open one, which is at odds with most social and technological trends. Neither seems particularly inspiring, or in tune with the exciting possibilities and frightening challenges we face. But it's hard for most of us to see that because we're all stuck in a narrow ridge of thinking, unable to imagine anything too different from what we're used to. But radicals are not stuck, and that makes them a social and political petri dish. Their ideas are experiments in how to live differently. They ensure we have new ideas to draw on as our societies adapt, as they surely must, to the challenges of this century. And we need to tolerate, even encourage, a wide range of these experiments because we never know which ones we might need.

Radicals also open avenues that others might one day pursue, by injecting imagination, ambition and daring into politics. The Occupy movement of the last decade played a pivotal role in starting political conversations about corporate greed, wages, inequality and austerity (some of which Donald Trump has taken up). The 1968-ers did not turn France into a situationist/anarchist/Marxist state (thankfully), but many of its cultural arguments—over sexual liberation and feminism—transformed society in myriad positive ways. Sometimes new ideas are buried deeply by received opinion of the day but are later dug up when the time is right. The seventeenth-century Levellers proposed a set of utterly outrageous ideas by the standards of the day: rule by consent, extended suffrage, equality before the law and religious tolerance. They were 200 years too soon. But those ideas were always there somewhere in the background, ready for later generations to re-examine them.

Most people will probably go along with this reasonably inoffensive argument. They will agree that radicals play a useful role in society in stimulating new ideas. But they will usually find some sophisticated reason as to why this should not apply to ideas with which they strongly disagree. 'Yes, I agree we need radicals'—and I heard this often—'but not *those* radicals.' The natural impulse, especially when we are faced with uncertainty, is to retreat into the security of familiar ways of thinking. But radicals play an equally important role in a healthy democracy when they are mistaken, absurd and offensive. The second reason we need radicals is that they might be wrong.

Free societies and free citizens require constant challenge, since challenge stimulates. One of the (rarely discussed) reasons confidence in and support for parliamentary democracy is falling is complacency. Its unprecedented achievements of peace, prosperity and freedom aren't appreciated because they aren't threatened. We have forgotten an important truth: That no state of affairs is set in stone. They need to be fought for.

Tommy Robinson and Pegida-UK are necessary for the existence of its opposite. Their presence forces us to examine our ideas, work out what we believe, why we believe it and mobilise. If Pegida did not exist, the arguments against it—in this case in favour of multiculturalism, or an authentic British Islam—would lose their vitality and strength. Similarly, the existence of radical Islam, and the fundamental threat it poses to liberal democracy, gives life and meaning to the arguments in defence of individual liberty. Note how, for example, the most eloquent and passionate modern defenders of liberty are not to be found in the parliaments of Western democracies, but in places where it doesn't exist: in Russia, in Pakistan, in Iran. To realise the full dividend of radicalism requires more than just grudging acceptance. It is necessary to create a culture that embraces it. Freedom is a self-perpetuating public good: the more there is, the more it grows. The society that accepts groups like Pegida is also one in which Zoltan or Tamera can thrive, and vice versa. Liberals are bad at appreciating this obvious and essential point. Silencing, sneering or outlawing groups and ideas often seems justified in individual cases. But over time it accretes into a general culture of deadening conformity and risk aversion.

A liberal democracy with no radicals would atrophy and degenerate: Society would become ossified, gripped by a dreary and monotonous set of unchallengeable dogmas and received wisdoms that save people the trouble of thinking for themselves. This is precisely what has happened over the last thirty years. All the right words come out of the modern liberal's mouth—listening to the people, human rights, democratic values, tolerance, etc.—but the brain isn't properly engaged; it just auto-pilots through these platitudes.

Only through challenge can citizens become thoughtful and active. Perhaps 2016 was the year the liberal's 'progressive consensus' view of the world was displaced; but equally it could be the stimulus required for liberal thinking to regain some vigour after decades of hubris and idleness. It could be the chance for liberalism to become bold again, and to reach out to the millions it has left behind.

What makes liberal democracies uniquely powerful compared to fascist, totalitarian or theocratic regimes is not just the freedom they offer, it's also that they are never finished. They don't have an 'end goal' or a state of perfection. They are a constantly shifting set of ideas, conventions, wisdoms and institutions: one continuous journey of testing and hopefully improving the way we live together. They allow different ideas to coexist and vie with each other, which is why they are exceptionally good at avoiding violent revolution.[3] The US Constitution preamble aims for a 'more perfect union', rather than a perfect one. (Just try to imagine a 'perfect union': it would be either impossible or hellish.) Radical ideas are the engine in this never-ending endeavour, since they push and probe at society's boundaries.

How and why certain ideas shift from the fringes to the mainstream seems to rely on a mysterious, and quite unpredictable, combination of circumstance, individuals and events. There isn't really a precise formula. But some underlying conditions make it more likely that radical ideas find fertile ground. At present there is widespread discontent with and distrust of much of our current political, social and economic settlement: There are major unaddressed social challenges, which are likely to get worse. Rapid change, especially climatic, demographic and, above all, technological, is already placing great strain on institutions that govern our lives and will continue to do so. When those things are combined, just as they were in the early nineteenth century, radical new ideas are likely to catch on.

Even then it's difficult to say with any certainty which ideas or movements will succeed. Each of the groups in this book are taking a slightly different route. Zoltan, for example, cleverly used the media to get his message out. Beppe Grillo combined both grass-roots organising with shareable outrage and emotion, in a similar way to Donald Trump. Direct-action environmentalists, and perhaps Tamera, might need to wait until further catastrophic events lead people to their way of thinking. Liberland and Bitnation advocates believe the efficiency of their new nations will inevitably win out. The Psychedelic Society seems more focused on a gradual change: medical benefits combined with actual experiences might inch its ideas closer to the mainstream.

But radicals don't always need to win in order to influence mainstream thinking. Due to their energy and passion, they often exert a disproportionate influence and can move the political centre of gravity in their direction, sometimes very quickly. This is far easier if the centre is weak, lacks support and an absence of articulate defenders. The UK Independence Party, although it has only one elected member of parliament, has shifted UK politics in recent years. This is partly a result of its relentless campaigning of course, but in large part it's due to the apathy of the mainstream.

Liberal societies are inherently and necessarily unstable. And instability is risky. Everyone in this book, without exception, thought they had the answers, that those answers were pretty obvious, and that they were the good guys. They were all, like Yeats's famous line, 'full of passionate intensity'. That passion and certainty—necessary supplies to sustain life on the fringe—sometimes made them inflexible and puritanical. While in Prague to meet Vit, the president of Liberland, I had a long discussion with an anarcho-capitalist about the new country. 'What confuses me is this,' he said, looking perplexed. 'You seem to understand our arguments, but you said you're *not* an anarcho-capitalist? How is this possible?' I heard variations of this repeatedly. Radicals struggle with different views of the world, which means simply disagreeing isn't always possible: you don't understand, you're one of 'them'. That is why radical politics can tend toward polarisation. If you don't view your opponents as sincere or acting in good faith, then compromise, the essence of politics, is more difficult.

Radicals who promise easy answers without compromise will usually fail. That will bring more frustration, more dissatisfaction and yet more radicalism: a self-reinforcing spiral towards ever more extreme and illiberal thinking. Radical movements might one day find themselves getting elected, and moderate. Some might use their power humanely. But others might remove the conditions that allowed the existence of radical ideas in the first place. Our institutional bulwarks designed to defend against tyranny—representative democracy, separation of powers, human rights—are really just human inventions that can be dismantled far more quickly than they were raised (the reason our judges wear ridiculous headgear and follow peculiar arcane mores is to obscure that fact). They will say it is in the name of the common good, of course, a

label that comfortably justifies any type of oppressive behaviour. They might, like every demagogue of the present
and dictator of the past, find ever more scapegoats and enemies on which to blame their failure. Some will even, like
Robespierre, in the name of liberty, cut off any heads that
disagree. The argument over the limits of radicalism is an
endless and inevitable feature of any free society. As I see
it, the line is drawn at any effort—whether through law,
force or pressure—to remove the possibility of other ideas
and alternatives existing. Sometimes that takes the form
of banning ideas outright, but more often it's subtler, such
as undermining the checks and balances—a free media or
independent judiciary—that help ensure radical ideas are
given a hearing. Radicalism that, in the name of religion,
class struggle, offensiveness, the national interest or the
common good, kicks away the ladder for others to climb
is not healthy for a free society. That is the paradox of the
radical. Their energy, imagination and passion might save
us, but these very attributes might also lead to ruin and
desperation.

Yet for all this, radicals remain our best hope. The trends
that led us to these remarkable years show no sign of abat-
ing. If anything, they will intensify. What happens if, as
researchers from the University of Oxford predict, roughly
half of all US jobs are automated and taken over by computers by 2033? When everything in our house, our car
and our workplace is connected to the internet, all collected, stored and used by mega-companies based in California? Or if, as predicted by the United Nations, by 2050
the population hits 10 billion, half of them facing extreme

water shortages, and 250 million climate-change refugees are on the move looking for habitable places to live?⁴ If, as a growing number of scientists now believe, breakthroughs in gerontology mean life expectancy will significantly extend within a generation? Or when, within the next couple of decades, health services and pension plans become financially unsustainable, requiring dramatic tax increases, just as more and more people start using untraceable cryptocurrencies?⁵

And what if all these things happen at roughly the same time?

I don't have the answer. The radicals in this book might not either. But the more experiments in collective living, the more new ways of looking at problems, the more we encourage radical thinking, the greater our chances of improving the way we live together.

The one constant of history is that everything changes. We should not assume that liberal democracies are the natural order of things. For the last fifty years, they have been the most successful way of securing the maximum peace, prosperity, happiness, opportunity and freedom for the people who live under them. It's not certain they will remain so. If they fail, it won't be because of the existence of radical ideas, but rather their absence.

Acknowledgements

It seems a little unfair that only one name gets to go on the cover. But that's how it works.

The biggest thanks are to the people who took the time and risk to allow me to spend time with them. You might not agree with them, and some of them you may not like at all, but without their willingness to share, this book wouldn't exist. Zoltan Istvan and his assistant Roen, Lisa, Isla and Ava. The whole journalist crew on the Immortality Bus, especially Jeremiah and Dylan. Bio-hackers, notably Rich Lee. (Good luck with the LoveTron9000.) Tommy Robinson, Paul Weston and Anne Marie Waters let me tag along around Europe, and were all generous with their time. Along the way, I was also helped by Deano, Mike, Tom, Milan, Siggy, Martin, Lutz and Tania. The whole trip experience crowd in the Netherlands deserve a special thanks, as I now realise how weird it must have been to have a writer with you. Robin. Special thanks to the extra effort from Jake and Paolo, and above all Stephen Reid, who made it all happen. I've worked for several years on 'Prevent' in one way or another, and there are too many people to thank, but David Omand, Dilwar Hussein, Hifsa Iqbal, Matt Collins, Hanif Qadir, Rizwaan Sabir and the nameless Channel Panel all made that chapter work. Beppe Grillo took time out to meet me, and Ignazio Corrao allowed me to follow him around the European Union buildings in Brussels. But extra thanks are due to Marco Morosini and above all to Nicola Marini, without whom that chapter would not have been possible. From Tamera, many people were generous with their time but none more so than Monika and Maria. (Also thanks are due to Chris, whose work on British utopias is a remarkable resource). Everyone mentioned in that chapter is under pseudonym, but every conversation with all of them gave me something, especially Mario, Hannes, Jules and Laura. Everyone at the Earth First! moot, especially Simon and Indra. The whole Reclaim the Power team and everyone involved in the Ffos-y-fran action, especially Danni and Ellen. Tina, Julie and all the Nanas were incredibly friendly and helpful. I hope the activists from that chapter will understand it to be constructive criticism. The final chapter, out in Liberland and Bitnation: President Vit, the irrepressible Damir, Susanne and James. The whole crew at Paralelni Polis, including Smuggler, Frank, Pavol and everyone else I met along the way, including unicorns, ministers, representatives and the rest.

There are many others too, who must remain nameless.

Once again it has been a joy to work with Tom Avery at William Heinemann, who also edited my last book *The Dark Net*, and the rest of the team: David Milner was the copy-editor, Joanna Taylor and Nicky Nevin are the production team, Aled Lewis is the designer. Also my thanks to Najma Finlay and Gail Rebuck. For this US edition,

Katy O'Donnell, Katie Haigler and Kristina Fazzalaro from Nation Books all possess that rare combination of patience and professionalism, and I've enjoyed working with them very much. I'm grateful to my agent Caroline Michel who seems to understand precisely what I'm attempting to do even when I can't explain it very well, and the whole rest of the team at Peter Fraser & Dunlop who are always brilliant.

Several other people were interviewed for various chapters as experts or authorities, and many more connected me to the right people. (What you don't see from reading this book is how much time was spent finding the right people and following leads.) In no particular order: Hank Pelliser, Avi Roy, Richard Jones, Joel Busher, Nick Lowles, William Allchorn, Michael Fitzpatrick, Hannah Barnes, James Rucker, Robin Cahart Harris, Roland Griffiths, Bill Richards, John Higgs, Jamal, Jan Culik, David Anderson QC, Will Baldet, Rebecca Skellet, Tony Lee Martin, Shiraz Maher, Mathieu Munsch, Dave Page, Dilly Hussain, Hamza Tzortzis, Dirk Bruere, Duncan McDonnell, Federico Pistono, Alys, Amanda van Eck Duymaer van Twist, Jess Worth, John Jordan, Donal, Keegan Hanks, Tisha Brown, Alice Hooker-Stroud, the two miners, Jamie Peters, David and Hannah (not their real names), Ian Goldin, Roger Ver, William Knottenbelt, the happily married blockchain couple and Adam Ernest Kaleb.

Conversations, chapter reviews and general advice was kindly offered from friends and colleagues: David Goodhart, Jon Birdwell, Catrin Nye, Jake Chapman, AKJ, Josh Smith, Joe Miller, Joe Norman, Pablo, Aidan Griffin, Emlyn Timmons (a constant source of insight), Jon Hopkins, Ronan Harrington, Heather Grabbe, Padraig Reidy, Jamie Kelsey, Louis Reynolds, Roger Hallam, Jonathon

Porritt, the maven Vinay Gupta, Rick Falkvinge, Adam Pickering, Bill Thompson, Terry Brubaker (who also put me up in California) and Dr Jeremy Reffin. Carl Miller, my long-time collaborator at Demos, both reviewed chapters and worked double time to cover me. I think I'm due to return the favour shortly.

And to my family and friends who helped out in all sorts of ways: above all Lindsey, my mum, Dan, Spam, Phil (who read the whole draft) and my dad. Bob G. also read the whole thing. Pam put me up, and so did Tom and Morwenna. Noelle provided me with a perfect getaway for a five days while I was struggling with Chapter 2, and it really helped.

Hundreds of conversations with different people all helped me formulate my thinking. And so did all the faceless people with digital pseudonyms on Twitter or elsewhere who complained about me or my articles. Sometimes they had a point, so I suppose I should thank them too. Everyone at the orange shop, especially Hasan and J-Lo, who kept telling me who should and should not be appearing in this book.

My researchers and translators did a marvellous job, ensuring that I kept errors to a minimum. Jeremy Levett, Sam Bright, Francesca Arcostanzo, Friderike, Leah Selig Chauhan, Leo Sands and Sacha Hilhorst. Colleagues at Demos were forced, once again, to endure me being away for long periods of time. I say 'forced', even though they seemed to enjoy it greatly.

Reading back over this, I'm struck by just how many people I owe, and there are, I'm sure, others I've missed. I'm immensely grateful to everyone. I hope it does some justice to the subjects covered.

Notes

Prologue

1. Raj Chetty et al, 'The fading American Dream: trends in absolute income mobility since 1940', *National Bureau of Economic Research*, 2011.

2. Ibid.

3. Jeffrey M. Jones, 'Trust in U.S. judicial branch sinks to new low of 53%', Gallup, 2011, http://www.gallup.com/poll/185528/trust-judicial-branch-sinks-new-low.aspx; Jamie Bartlett, Jon Birdwell and Mark Littler, *The New Face of Digital Populism* (Demos, 2011), http://www.europarl.europa.eu/pdf/eurobarometre/2014/post/post_ee2014_sociodemographic_annex_en.pdf.

This is reflected in several data. Voting is the most visible and personal experience of engagement in politics. Voter turnout in the 2009 Bundestag elections was the lowest ever, at 70.8 per cent—but 80 per cent of sixty- to sixty-nine-year-olds voted, whereas only 59 per cent of twenty-one- to twenty-four-year-olds did. In France's 2014 European elections, 42 per cent of the total population turned out, but only 28 per cent of eighteen- to twenty-four-year-olds did so, against 51 per cent of the over-fifty-fives. Across the whole of the EU, voter turnout in the May 2014 European Parliament election was 51 per cent of over-fifty-fives, but only 28 per cent of eighteen- to twenty-four-year-olds. (A summary of these statistics is found in Jamie Bartlett, *E-Democracy in the EU* [Demos, 2015].)

By 2012, with membership falling all the time, 82 per cent of UK citizens said they 'tend not to trust' political parties. The trends are broadly similar across Europe, albeit at different rates. Only 2 per cent of voters in Germany and France are members of a mainstream political party. Ingrid van Biezen, Peter Mair and Thomas Poguntke, 'Going, going . . . gone? The decline of party membership in contemporary Europe', *European Journal of Political Research*, Vol 51:1, 2012, pp. 24–56.

In 1951, 4 million people were members of either the Conservative or Labour party. With some variation, the traditional big parties of Europe—centre-left and centre-right—have ruled European nations since the Second World War. Florian Hartleb, 'Anti-elitist cyber parties', *Journal of Public Affairs*, 2013.

However, there are occasional spikes in membership. The UK Labour party, which changed its rule for membership just before a leadership conference, enjoyed a surge in newzx membership. Francis Fukuyama, *Political Order and Political Delay* (Farrar, Straus and Giroux, 2011), p. 139.

4. David Bailey, 'The end of the European left? Social democracy, hope, disillusion, and Europe', Near Futures Online 1, 2016, http://nearfuturesonline.org/the-end-of-the-european-left-social-democracy-hope-disillusion-and-europe/; Asbjørn Wahl and Roy Pedersen, 'The Norwegian national election: Europe's most leftist government defeated by right-wing coalition', Global Research, 2013, http://www.globalresearch.ca/the-norwegian-national-election-europes-most-leftist-government-defeated-by-right-wing-coalition/5350919.

5. Ludwigshafen, Piraeus and Valletta, 'Rose thou art sick: The centre-left is in sharp decline across Europe', *Economist,* 2 April 2016, http://www.economist.com/news/briefing/21695887-centre-left-sharp-decline-across-europe-rose-thou-art-sick; 'UK European election results: Vote 2014', BBC, 2014, http://www.bbc.co.uk/news/events/vote2014/eu-uk-results; Philip Bump, 'In a polarizing 2016, moderate voters are on the decline', *Washington Post*, 24 February 2016, https://www.washingtonpost.com/news/the-fix/wp/2016/02/24/in-a-polarizing-2016-moderate-voters-are-on-the-decline/.

In the most recent US election cycle, fewer voters described themselves as 'moderates' than in 2012, 2008 and 2004. '7 things to know about polarization in America', Pew Research Center, June 2014, http://www.pewresearch.org/fact-tank/2014/06/12/7-things-to-know-about-polarization-in-america/; 'Political polarization in the American republic', People Press, 6 December 2012, p. 6, http://www.people-press.org/2014/06/12/political-polarization-in-the-american-public/.

Chapter 1

1. 'Available datasets', The Transparency Project, http://www.the transparencyproject.org/Availabledataset.htm.

2. In his 1929 essay, British Marxist scientist Desmond Bernal argued that 'men will not be content to manufacture life; they will want to improve on it', predicting that one day humanity might even become 'completely etherealised.' Nick Bostrom suggests that transhumanism can be traced to the rational humanism of the eighteenth century. Benjamin Franklin is said to have mused, 'I wish it were possible . . . to invent a method of embalming drowned persons, in such a manner that they might be recalled to life at any period, however distant; for having a very ardent desire to see and observe the state of America a hundred years hence, I should prefer to an ordinary death, being immersed with a few friends in a cask of Madeira, until that time, then to be recalled to life by the solar warmth of my dear country! But . . . in all probability, we live in a century too little advanced, and too near the infancy of science, to see such an art brought in our time to its perfection.' Marvin Minsky, '2007: What are you optimistic about?', Edge, n.d., https://www.edge.org/response-detail/11934.

3. He's also trying to live by what he has invented and described as 'the three laws of transhumanism', as described in his book: '1) A transhumanist must safeguard one's own existence above all else; 2) A transhumanist must strive to achieve omnipotence as expediently as possible—so long as one's actions do not conflict with the First Law; 3) A transhumanist must safeguard value in the universe—so long as one's actions do not conflict with the First and Second Laws.'

4. Zoltan Istvan, 'Should a transhumanist run for US president?', *Huffington Post*, 2014, http://www.huffingtonpost.com/zoltan-istvan/should-a-transhumanist-be_b_5949688.html.

5. Zoltan has also arranged for a scientist transhumanist to turn up to say farewell: Maria Konovalenka, a PhD candidate at USC in her midtwenties who specialises in stem-cell research. She serves as Zoltan's longevity adviser.

6. This is Grindfest number 1. Confusingly, this is the second—the first was Grindfest 0, held in March 2015.

7. Debra Kelly, '10 things you should know about biohacking', Listverse, 2015, http://listverse.com/2015/05/20/10-things-you-should-know-about-biohacking/.

8. Since then, Warwick has been using his own body to experiment with different ways of blending biology and technology: biohacking. Ben Popper, 'Cyborg America: Inside the strange new world

of basement body hackers', The Verge, 2012, http://www.theverge
.com/2012/8/8/3177438/cyborg-america-biohackers-grinders-body
-hackers; The Engineer, 'Cyborg pioneer Prof Kevin Warwick', 2011,
http://www.theengineer.co.uk/cyborg-pioneer-prof-kevin-warwick/.

9. 'DIY bio', https://diybio.org/; 'DIY bio', Facebook page, https://www
.facebook.com/pages/DIYbio/133382700033412?fref=ts.

10. One group of grinders came together to found Grindhouse Wet-
ware, a Pennsylvania-based association founded by Tim Cannon. In
October 2013 Cannon had an operation to install one of the first-ever
computer-chip implants that can receive and record biometrical data.
Your fingertips have lots of nerve endings jammed into one area and
they are really sensitive to stimuli. Magnets twitch or move in the presence of magnetic fields, and when you implant one in your finger you
can really start to feel different magnetic fields around you. So it is like
a sixth sense.

11. His chip was bought from a website, dangerousthings.com, which
was launched by the bio-hacker Amal Graafstrain in 2013.

12. There are many academic challenges to this research, including the replicability of the studies. Gratsiela Toneva, 'Anti-aging study
sees much-needed affirmation', IFL Science, http://www.iflscience
.com/health-and-medicine/anti-aging-study-sees-much-needed
-affirmation; Puellakas, 'Anti-aging formula slated to begin human
trials', IFL Science, http://www.iflscience.com/health-and-medicine
/anti-aging-formula-slated-begin-human-trials.

13. Heidi Ledford, 'Ageing: Much ado about ageing', Nature,
2010, http://www.nature.com/news/2010/100324/full/464480a.html
#B2; David Stipp, 'Beyond Resveratrol: The anti-aging NAD fad', Sci-
entific American, 2015, http://blogs.scientificamerican.com/guest-blog
/beyond-resveratrol-the-anti-aging-nad-fad/.

14. The world's most famous longevity researcher is probably the
US-based British scientist Aubrey de Grey, who is the Transhumanist Party's anti-ageing adviser. He founded and runs the Strategies for
Engineered Negligible Senescence research foundation, which spends
around $5 million per year trying to cure age-related disease. De
Grey believes that the first person to live to 1,000 may be alive now,
and might already be over fifty. De Grey divides the scientific community. Some complain that his work is based on a desired outcome
rather than a detached observation of the biological evidence. But he
is also respected by academics. In 2005 the MIT Technology Review
offered a $20,000 prize to any molecular biologist who could prove to
a panel of independent judges that de Grey's theory of rejuvenating

biotechnology was 'so wrong that it was unworthy of learned debate.' No one has yet claimed the prize. Ricky Piper, '10 things we learned from Liz Parrish's Reddit AMA', Life Mag, 2015, http://lifemag.org /article/10-things-we-learned-from-liz-parrish-s-reddit-ama.

15. Of the nineteen tech entrepreneurs or investor billionaires who have signed the Giving Pledge to donate half their wealth, at least half are financing healthcare and medical research.

Ben Popper, 'Understanding Calico: Larry Page, Google Ventures, and the quest for immortality', The Verge, 2013, http://www.the verge.com/2013/9/19/4748594/understanding-calico-larry-page-google -ventures-and-the-quest-for.

16. Peter Thiel, co-founder of PayPal, donated $3.5 million to the forerunner of de Grey's SENS research centre, called the Methuselah Foundation. Ariana Eunjung Cha, 'The tech titans latest project: Defy death', *Washington Post*, 2015, http://www.washingtonpost.com/sf /national/2015/04/04/tech-titans-latest-project-defy-death/.

17. In order to minimise cell degeneration, this needs to happen as soon after death as possible. Alcor maintains a watch list of members in failing health. When an individual appears to be nearing his/her final days, the company sends a 'standby team' to literally stand by the person's bed until they die, so that the preservation process can begin immediately. 'Alcor membership statistics', Alcor Life Extension Foundation, http://www.alcor.org/AboutAlcor/membershipstats.html; Rose Eveleth, 'For $200,000, this lab will swap your body's blood for antifreeze', *Atlantic*, 2014, http://www.theatlantic.com/technology/archive/2014/08 /for-200000-this-lab-will-swap-your-bodys-blood-for-antifreeze/379074/.

18. 'About us', Cryonics Institute, http://www.cryonics.org/about-us/.

19. Ibid.; 'Frozen body: Can we return from the dead?', BBC, 2013, http://www.bbc.co.uk/science/0/23695785; Michael Hendricks, 'The false science of cryonics', *MIT Technology Review*, 2015, https://www .technologyreview.com/s/541311/the-false-science-of-cryonics/.

20. Anders Sandberg and Nick Bostrom, 'Whole brain emulation: A road map', Technical Report #2008-3, Future of Humanity Institute, Oxford University, 2008, http://www.fhi.ox.ac.uk/brain-emulation-road map-report.pdf.

21. In 2013, a research group from MIT prompted the Obama administration to launch the Brain Research through Advancing Innovative Neurotechnologies (BRAIN) Initiative, which sponsors researchers to map the brain's neurons. A similar initiative is taking place in Europe, called the Human Brain Project, which aims to create super-computer simulations to show everything we know about how the human brain operates.

22. Maddie Stone, 'What happens when we upload our minds?', *Vice*, 2015,http://motherboard.vice.com/read/what-happens-when-we-upload-our-minds; Tanya Lewis, 'The singularity is near: Mind uploading by 2045', Live Science, 2013, http://www.livescience.com/37499-immortality-by-2045-conference.html.

23. Susan Schneider, 'The philosophy of "her"', *New York Times*' Opinionator blog, 2014, http://opinionator.blogs.nytimes.com/2014/03/02/the-philosophy-of-her/?_php=true&_type=blogs&_r=1.

24. Richard Jones, *Against Transhumanism* (self-published e-book: 2016), p. 10, http://www.softmachines.org/wordpress/wp-content/uploads/2016/01/Against_Transhumanism_1.0.pdf.

25. Ibid.

26. For a general reader, one of the best accounts of this phenomena is in Erik Davis, *Techgnosis* (North Atlantic Books, 2015). And a more academic analysis is in Fred Turner, *From Counterculture to Cyberculture* (University of Chicago Press, 2006).

27. B. A. Robinson, 'U.S. polling data: Beliefs about life after death', Ontario Consultants on Religious Tolerance, updated in 2015, http://www.religioustolerance.org/polls-about-life-after-death.htm.

28. '"Nones" on the rise', Pew Research Center, 2012, http://www.pewforum.org/2012/10/09/nones-on-the-rise/; 'America's changing religious landscape', Pew Research Center, 2015, www.pewforum.org/2015/05/12/americas-changing-religious-landscape/.

29. Peter Holley, 'Bill Gates on dangers of artificial intelligence: "I don't understand why some people are not concerned"', *Washington Post*, 2015, https://www.washingtonpost.com/news/the-switch/wp/2015/01/28/bill-gates-on-dangers-of-artificial-intelligence-dont-understand-why-some-people-arc-not-concerned/; Peter Holley, 'Stephen Hawking just got an artificial intelligence upgrade, but still thinks AI could bring an end to mankind', *Washington Post*, 2014, https://www.washingtonpost.com/news/speaking-of-science/wp/2014/12/02/stephen-hawking-just-got-an-artificial-intelligence-upgrade-but-still-thinks-it-could-bring-an-end-to-mankind/; Derek Thompson, 'A world without work', *Atlantic,* 2015, http://www.theatlantic.com/magazine/archive/2015/07/world-without-work/395294/; Andrew Keen, *The Internet Is Not the Answer* (Atlantic, 2015); Brian Resnick, 'Why Stephen Hawking is more afraid of capitalism than robots', Vox.com, 2016, http://www.vox.com/2016/2/27/11119804/stephen-hawking-robots; Matthew Yglesias, 'The automation myth', Vox.com, 2015, http://www.vox.com/2015/7/27/9038829/automation-myth.

30. Cha, 'Tech titans' latest project'.

31. George Annas, Lori Andrews and Rosario Isasi, 'Protecting the endangered human: toward an international treaty prohibiting cloning and inheritable alterations', *American Journal of Law and Medicine*, 28:151, 2002.

32. Oddly, after I got back from the trip Jeremiah emailed me with a story about Roen he'd found online. Back in 2003 Roen and his older brother had run away from home and were found by the police camping in the forest near Vancouver. They told the media they were born and raised in the wilderness. There had been quite a lot of media interest in the 'wild boys', as they were dubbed, until the truth emerged and they returned to California.

33. Daniela Cutelas, 'Life extension, overpopulation and the right to life: against lethal ethics', *Journal of Medical Ethics*, 2008, http://www.ncbi.nlm.nih.gov/pubmed/18757626.

34. According to some estimates, Hillary Clinton had raised nearly $100 million towards her campaign, much of which was from Democratic Party committees. Republican Jeb Bush—who quit the presidential race in February 2016—had raised over $125 million.

35. 'Ballot access for presidential candidates', Ballotpedia.com, https://ballotpedia.org/Ballot_access_for_presidential_candidates#Requirements_for_independents.

36. At the time of writing, there are two independent senators (including Bernie Sanders who ran for president—but as a Democrat). Most successful independents are/were affiliated with or previously belonged to one of the main parties, and many who gained prominence were either elected by the parties before going independent, or initially built their renown with a party machine behind them before splitting off. Andrew Buncombe, 'Revealed: The US presidential candidates who have raised the most money', *Independent*, 2015, http://www.independent.co.uk/news/world/americas/us-elections/revealed-the-us-presidential-candidates-who-have-revealed-the-most-money-a6706552.html; '2016 presidential race', OpenSecrets.org, http://www.opensecrets.org/pres16/; 'The 2012 money race: Compare the candidates', *New York Times*, http://elections.nytimes.com/2012/campaign-finance.

37. At the time of writing, the petition had ninety-one signatures. 'Transhumanists disavow Zoltan Istvan candidacy for US presidency', IPetition, http://www.ipetitions.com/petition/transhumanists-disavow-zoltan-istvan-candidacy.

38. 'I did go to the FEC as best as I can, I am fighting some battles. We are a PAC. It's not something that's too legitimate yet. I got to be honest to start a party costs 200k, it takes five states with parties and five people running to run for office. It's a pain in the butt.'

Chapter 2

1. In German: Patriotische Europäer Gegen die Islamisierung des Abendlandes.

2. There are several Prague Declarations, most famously the 2008 Declaration on European Conscience and Communism, which committed countries to condemn and educate about the crimes of Communism.

3. Matthew Goodwin, *Right Response: Understanding and Countering Populist Extremism in Europe* (Chatham House, 2011), https://www .chathamhouse.org/publications/papers/view/178301#sthash.2eyEr1AY.dpuf.

4. Also in Bulgaria, Finland, France, Hungary, Latvia, Slovakia, Sweden and Switzerland, as well as the European Parliament.

5. The spark appears to have been violent street clashes in Hamburg and Celle between supporters of the Kurdish PKK and Islamist extremists that took place around that time.

6. 'Economic forecasts', European Commission, 2015, http://ec .europa.eu/economy_finance/eu/forecasts/2015_autumn/box1_en.pdf; Jim Brusden, 'EU forecasts growth dividend from projected 3m migrant influx', *Financial Times*, 5 November 2015 http://www.ft.com/cms/s/0 /d4a39baa-83bd-11e5-8095-ed1a37d1e096.html.

7. Agence France-Presse, 'Angela Merkel issues New Year's warning over right-wing Pegida group', *Guardian*, 30 December 2014, http:// www.theguardian.com/world/2014/dec/30/angela-merkel-criticises -pegida-far-right-group-germany.

8. Alison Smail, 'In German city rich with history and tragedy, tide rises against immigration', *New York Times*, 7 December 2014, http:// www.nytimes.com/2014/12/08/world/in-german-city-rich-with-history -and-tragedy-tide-rises-against-immigration.html.

9. *Religionmonitor verstehen was verbindet* (Bertelsmann Stichtung, 2015), http://www.bertelsmann-stiftung.de/fileadmin/files/Projekte/51 _Religionsmonitor/Zusammenfassung_der_Sonderauswertung.pdf; 'DeutschevermutenNeonazisundbesorgteBürgerhinterPEGIDA',Presse-portal, 11 December 2014, http://www.finanznachrichten.de/nachrichten -2014-12/32268552-umfrage-deutsche-vermuten-neonazis-und-besorgte -buerger-hinter-pegida-003.htm (accessed 11 February 2015); 'Anti-Islam-Proteste: Jeder Zweite sympathisiert mit Pegida', Die Zeit, 15 December 2014, http://www.zeit.de/politik/deutschland/2014-12/islam-pegida -fluechtlinge-deutschland-umfrage (retrieved 11 February 2015).

10. The threat nationally from Islamist terrorism had in fact receded in 2009, the year the EDL formed, but tensions in Luton had not. Maria Sobolewska, 'Religious extremism in Britain and British Muslims:

Threatened citizenship and the role of religion', in Roger Eatwell and Matthew Goodwin (eds.), *The New Extremism in 21st Century Britain* (Routledge, 2010).

11. Britskelisty, 'Facebook has taken down a page operated by a major Czech anti-Muslim and anti-refugee group', 1 November 2016, http://blisty.cz/art/80622.html#sthash.kn3ZEtof.dpuf.

12. The Czech Republic is the most sceptical of all EU countries about immigration from outside the EU: 81 per cent say they don't like it (compared to 57 per cent in Denmark, 55 per cent in the UK and 54 per cent in Germany). 'Public opinion in the European Union', *Standard Eurobarometer 83* (2015), http://ec.europa.eu/public_opinion/archives/eb/eb83/eb83_publ_en.pdf.

13. I cannot confirm this figure. At the time, official figures were that around 8,000 migrants per day were arriving into Europe, so it seems unlikely that 5,000 were arriving in Germany. However, it was certainly a very large number, and there was (and is) a lot of uncertainty.

14. Hilary Aked, 'Sharia Watch UK and the evolution of Anne Marie Waters', Institute of Race Relations, 21 January 2015, http://www.irr.org.uk/news/sharia-watch-uk-and-the-metamorphosis-of-anne-marie-waters/.

15. TellMAMA, 'Liberty GB—An insight into the "group"', 14 January 2014, http://tellmamauk.org/liberty-gb/.

16. Matthew Collins, 'Lennen announced his Pegida team', Hope Not Hate, 4 January 2016, http://www.hopenothate.org.uk/blog/insider/pegida-already-smells-stale-4684; Matthew Scott, 'Paul Weston is a racist but that doesn't mean he shouldn't be prosecuted', Barrister Blogger, 1 May 2014, http://barristerblogger.com/2014/05/01/paul-weston-racist-prosecuted/#more-744.

17. Pegida-UK, 'Pegida UK leadership announcement', YouTube video, 5 January 2016, https://www.youtube.com/watch?v=F9zTQRFerII.

18. The movement started out as Pegida-Denmark but then changed the name to For Frihed (For Freedom). Nicolai Sennels, a controversial Danish psychologist who has written a book arguing Muslims and non-Muslims have psychological differences, set up Pegida-Denmark in 2015, but asked Tania to take over soon after because he was too busy to run it. Tania only got involved in politics recently. 'I've been monitoring the small, incremental steps that Islam has been making into Danish culture, and I don't like it,' she told me, on arrival.

19. This translates as Antifascist Action, and there are also notorious branches in Sweden, the Netherland and Germany. It also exists in the United Kingdom but is not as big.

20. William Alchorn, 'When anti-Islamic protest comes to town: Political responses to the English defence league' (unpublished PhD thesis, 2016).

21. Julian Borger, 'German police arrest 211 after far-right riot in Leipzeig', *Guardian*, 12 January 2016, http://www.theguardian.com /world/2016/jan/12/german-police-arrest-211-after-far-right-riot-in-leipzig.

22. Richard *Griffiths, An Intelligent Person's Guide to Fascism* (Duckworth, 2000).

23. Helena Smith, 'Neo-fascist Greek party takes third place in wave of voter fury', *Guardian*, 21 September 2015, https://www .theguardian.com/world/2015/sep/21/neo-fascist-greek-party-election -golden-dawn-third-place.

24. The Göttinger Institut für Demokratieforschung finds that the majority of German Pegida supporters are positive about the notion of democracy, with only 19 per cent being unhappy or very unhappy with it.

25. Kate Connolly, 'Estimated 15,000 people join 'pinstriped Nazis' on march in Dresden', *Guardian*, 15 December 2014, https://www.the guardian.com/world/2014/dec/15/dresden-police-pegida-germany-far -right; 'Anti-Muslim movement rattles Germany', *Der Spiegel*, 21 December 2014, http://www.spiegel.de/international/germany/anti-muslim -pegida-movement-rattles-germany-a-1009245-2.html.

In December 2014, 15,000 Pegida supporters marched through Dresden, Germany. Two football-hooligan organisations participated in the demonstration: Faust des Ostens ('Fist of the East') and Hooligans Elbflorenz ('Florence of the Elbe Hooligans'). They were also accompanied by members of the far-right National Democratic Party (NPD). Hans Pfeifer, 'PEGIDA, neo-Nazis, and organized rage', *Deutsche Welle*, 25 January 2015, http://www.dw.com/en/pegida-neo-nazis-and-organized -rage/a-18212964; Alex Derasier, 'Capturing Europe's immigration tension on the streets', *GJ Global Journalist*, 3 March 2016, http://global journalist.org/2016/03/capturing-europes-immigration-tension/.

26. Asa Bennet, 'How patriotic are British Muslims? Much more than you think, actually', *Telegraph*, 17 November 2015, http://www.telegraph .co.uk/news/religion/12000042/How-patriotic-are-British-Muslims -Much-more-than-you-think-actually.html.

27. This is not unique to Pegida. According to Murray Edelman's *Constructing the Political Spectacle* (University of Chicago Press, 1988), it is by linguistically evoking values, symbols and myths that political actors strategically reframe issues, events and phenomena by fitting them into a narrative compatible with an audience's ideology. David Barrett, 'British Muslims becoming a nation within a nation, Trevor

Phillips warns', *Telegraph*, 4 October 2016, http://www.telegraph.co.uk /news/2016/04/10/uk-muslim-ghettoes-warning/.

28. Miqdaad Versi, 'It's time the media treated Muslims fairly', *Guardian*, 23 September 2015, http://www.theguardian.com/commentis free/2015/sep/23/media-muslims-study.

The most flagrant example in local years being the *Sun*'s claim that one in five British Muslims sympathise with ISIS, which was highly misleading. The *Sun* was forced to apologise for that. Pamela Duncan, 'Does the *Sun*'s claim about UK Muslims' sympathy for jihadis stack up?', *Guardian*, 23 November 2015, http://www.theguardian .com/media/reality-check/2015/nov/23/does-the-suns-claim-about -uk-muslims-sympathy-for-jihadis-stack-up.

For an example of trust in mainstream media versus internet sources, see Jamie Bartlett, Jonathan Birdwell and Mark Littler, *The New Face of Digital Populism* (Demos, 2011) and Jamie Bartlett and Mark Littler, *Inside the EDL* (Demos, 2011).

29. Joel Busher, 'Understanding the English Defence League: Living on the front line of a "clash of civilisations"', London School of Economics and Political Science blog, 2 December 2015, http://blogs.lse .ac.uk/politicsandpolicy/understanding-the-english-defence-league-life -on-the-front-line-of-an-imagined-clash-of-civilisations/; also see *Responding to Populist Rhetoric: A Guide* (Counterpoint, 2015), http:// counterpoint.uk.com/wp-content/uploads/2015/01/Responding-to -Populist-Rhetoric-A-Guide.pdf.

30. Joel Busher, *The Making of Anti-Muslim Protest: Grassroots Activism in the English Defence League* (Routledge, 2015).

31. Ben Goldacre, *Bad Science* (Fourth Estate, 2008).

32. 'Muslims "give most to charity," ahead of Christians, Jews and Atheists, poll finds', *Huffington Post*, 21 July 2013, http://www .huffingtonpost.co.uk/2013/07/21/muslims-give-most_n_3630830 .html; Kate Razall, 'Muslim women "stopped from becoming Labour councilors"', BBC, 5 February 2016, http://www.bbc.co.uk/news /uk-politics-35504185.

33. Kate Brady, 'PEGIDA founder Lutz Bachmann found guilty of inciting hatred', *Deutsche Welle*, 3 May 2016, http://www.dw.com/en /pegida-founder-lutz-bachmann-found-guilty-of-inciting-hatred/a -19232497.

34. Baron Bodissey, 'Tommy Robinson on Sadiq Khan', Gates of Vienna, 13 May 2016, http://gatesofvienna.net/2016/05/tommy-robinson -on-sadiq-khan/.

35. Audrey Allegretti, 'Tommy Robinson's "Sadiq Khan's Wife" tweet sees Pegida leader well and truly caught out', *Huffington Post*, 9 May 2016, http://www.huffingtonpost.co.uk/entry/tommy-robinson-gets -caught-confusing-london-muslim-mayor-sadiq-khans-wife-with-hijab -wearing-woman_uk_57304f39e4b0e6da49a6772c.

36. In an article on his website, Paul called the three (British) teen-age girls from Bethnal Green who left the UK to join ISIS 'Muslim girls domiciled in the UK'. Paul Weston, 'Allah's little whelpers', 31 March 2015, http://www.libertygb.org.uk/news/allahs-little-whelpers.

37. In 2007 Paul predicted that there would be a civil war between Islam and Europe by 2025 because by that year the ratio of white Euro-pean males to Muslim males would be 5:1—enough to spark major con-flagration. ('Europeans wouldn't just sit back and let their culture and history become Islamicised,' he said.) He has also written that a civil war between Muslims and non-Muslims is inevitable by 2025 because of demographic trends and suggested to me that, to avoid this unwel-come clash, we might have to 'start sending people back'—although who, and where to exactly, is never clear.

38. Stoking anti-immigration or anti-Islamic feeling—suggesting they're all terrorists or sex offenders—creates an atmosphere that con-tributes to anti-immigration crime, which, in Germany at least, is up this year. Kate Connolly, 'Germany braces for rise in anti-immigrant attacks', *Guardian*, 22 October 2015, http://www.theguardian.com /world/2015/oct/22/germany-braces-for-rise-in-anti-immigrant-attacks.

The UK police also recorded 816 Islamophobic offences in Lon-don alone—up 70 per cent in 2015. Some of that is down to Muslims being more willing to report crime, but not all of it. Press Association, 'Hate crimes against Muslims soar in London', *Guardian,* 7 Septem-ber 2015, http://www.theguardian.com/world/2015/sep/07/hate-crimes -against-muslims-soar-london-islamophobia.

39. Vikram Dodd, 'Soldier jailed for making nail bomb avoids terror charge', *Guardian*, 28 November 2014, http://www.theguardian.com/uk -news/2014/nov/28/soldier-jailed-nailbomb-ryan-mcgee-manchester-bomb.

40. David Millward, 'White working class is becoming a dying breed in the East End borough of Newham according to BBC documentary', *Telegraph*, 15 May 2016, http://www.telegraph.co.uk/news/2016/05/15 /white-working-class-is-becoming-a-dying-breed-in-the-east-end-bo/. See David Goodhart, *The British Dream* (Atlantic, 2013), pp. 246–57, for a discussion of these trends.

41. Dr Steve Garner, 'White working-class neighbourhoods: Common themes and policy suggestions', Joseph Rowntree Foundation, November 2011, https://www.jrf.org.uk/file/39033/download?token=9V _tLkpn; Alexander Ward, 'Report finds that Britain's wages are the most unequal in Europe', *Independent*, 2011, http://www.independent .co.uk/news/uk/politics/report-finds-that-britains-wages-are-the-most -unequal-in-europe-10259077.html; Hilary Osborne, 'Generation rent: The housing ladder starts to collapse for the under-40s', *Guardian*, 22 July 2015, http://www.theguardian.com/money/2015/jul/22/pwc -report-generation-rent-to-grow-over-next-decade; Sam Bright, '5 infographs that will change how you think about American politics', Backbench, 19 January 2016, http://www.bbench.co.uk/#!5-infographs -that-will-change-how-you-think-about-American-politics/crhk/569e19 010cf2ca1e5ff607ce.

In the United States, while GDP increased by $6.5 trillion between 1989 and 2012, real median income fell by $700. Between 2008 and 2014, the real wage of the median British worker (the middle earner in the nation) fell by approximately 10 per cent. Stephen Machin, 'Real wages and living standards: the latest UK evidence', London School of Economics and Political Science blog, 6 April 2015, http://blogs .lse.ac.uk/politicsandpolicy/real-wages-and-living-standards-the-latest -uk-evidence/; 'Compare your job to the national average in your job', This Is Money, 28 January 2013, http://www.thisismoney.co.uk/money /article-2269520/Best-paid-jobs-2012-Official-figures-national-average -UK-salaries-400-occupations.html.

42. Nadia Khomami, 'White British pupils least likely to go to university, says research', *Guardian*, 11 November 2015, http://www .theguardian.com/education/2015/nov/11/white-british-pupils-least-likely -to-go-to-university-report; Geoff Evans and James Tilley, 'The new class war', IPPR, 30 March 2015, http://www.ippr.org/juncture/the -new-class-war-excluding-the-working-class-in-21st-century-britain.

According to the pollsters YouGov, young white men have the worst reputation of any social or ethnic group. We think they are generally rude, unintelligent and impolite. Peter Kellner, 'Introducing the most derided ethnic group in Britain', YouGov, 14 December 2015, https:// yougov.co.uk/news/2015/12/14/young-white-men-most-derided/.

43. In a reverse version of this story, told from the side of a young Muslim growing up around the same time, see Maajid Nawaz, *Radical* (WH Allen, 2012).

44. 'Suspect charged with 1995 murder', BBC, 17 February 2007, http://news.bbc.co.uk/1/hi/england/beds/bucks/herts/3497127.stm.

45. OxfordUnion, 'Tommy Robinson—Main speech', YouTube video, 16 March 2015, https://www.youtube.com/watch?v=_YQ94jFg_4A.

In the following years, al-Muhajiroon would be tied to several convicted terrorists and was eventually outlawed in January 2010.

46. The single most common background of Labour MPs in the 2015 parliament is defined as 'political organisers'. One in four Labour MPs is essentially a professional politician—advisers, activists, organisers, campaigners. In 1979, 16 per cent of MPs were drawn from 'manual professions'; by 2015 it was just 3 per cent. Lukas Audickas, 'Social background of MPs 1979–2015', Briefing Paper CBP 7483, House of Commons Library, 25 January 2016, http://researchbriefings.files.parliament.uk/documents/CBP-7483/CBP-7483.pdf.

47. According to Robert Garner and Richard Kelly in their book *British Political Parties Today* (Manchester University Press, 1998), the single most notable feature of voting since the 1960s has been a working-class desertion of the Labour Party. The London borough of Newham, a traditionally white working-class area that once provided workers for London's docks, saw 70,000 immigrants arrive in the last three decades. Now three in four are non-white.

48. On 10 May 2015, Tommy appeared on a local BBC Radio debate with Martin Cottingham, a Christian working for Islamic Relief. Islamic Relief had recently paid for adverts to be put up on London buses during Ramadan. 'Subhana Allah' they read, meaning 'praise be to God.' The idea was to encourage Muslims to give more to charity, and publicise the fact that Muslims give a lot of money to humanitarian causes.

On the radio, Martin said Islam is a religion of peace. 'One of the scriptures we're inspired by is a verse from the Qu'ran which says "if you have taken the life of one person, it's as if you've taken the lives of all mankind."'

Tommy responded: 'Martin, how dare you as a Christian come on the radio and use the verse 5:32, which is what you just said, which in the Qu'ran it says "if you kill one man you've killed all of humanity." Why not put it in context and read the very next verse? Which says "unless they have caused mischief in the land, then they can be executed, and have their hands and feet cut off, and exiled from the land." Martin, tell me about the very next verse, verse 5:33. Open the Qu'ran, read out what you just said, if you kill one man, you kill the whole of humanity, and read the very next verse.'

'Tommy I'm not going to get into a detailed conversation with you about every verse in the Qu'ran.' said Martin. 'You're cherry-picking verses.'

'No,' Tommy cut in, '*you* picked out a line. You're a disgrace Martin.'

49. The first important essay setting out this trend was David Goodhart, 'Discomfort of Strangers', *Guardian*, 24 February 2004, http://www.theguardian.com/politics/2004/feb/24/race.eu; 'The Brexit index', Populus, May 2016, http://www.populus.co.uk/2016/05/brexit -index-whos-remain-leave-supporters/; 'EU referendum "How did you vote" poll', Lord Ashcroft Polls, June 2016, http://lordashcroftpolls.com /wp-content/uploads/2016/06/How-the-UK-voted-Full-tables-1.pdf; 'Public opinion in the European Union', *Standard Eurobarometer 83*.

A YouGov survey in 2014 found that different social classes have different attitudes towards immigration: 62 per cent of those defined as 'working class' agreed with the statement that 'immigration into Britain should be stopped completely for the next few years', in contrast, 44 per cent of those defined as 'middle class' agreed with the statement. 'Prospect survey results', YouGov, January 2014, http://d25d2506sfb94s .cloudfront.net/cumulus_uploads/document/kqc6uojxq7/Prospect _Results_Social_Class_140129_website.pdf.

In a 2015 report into why the Labour Party lost the general election that year, Jon Cruddas suggested the party was now really only appealing to those who are at home in 'metropolitan modernity', who 'value openness, creativity, self-fulfilment and self-determination'. 'Public opinion in the European Union', *Eurobarometer 83*.

50. Jonathan Walker, 'Jeremy Corbyn joins opposition to Pegida-UK's Birmingham march', *Birmingham Mail*, 4 February 2016, http:// www.birminghammail.co.uk/news/midlands-news/jeremy-corbyn -joins-opposition-pegida-10835496.

51. Hilary Pilkington, *Loud and Proud: Passion and Politics in the English Defence League* (Manchester University Press, 2016); also see the excellent work from the academic Joel Busher, who spent sixteen months with the EDL, Joel Busher, 'Understanding the English Defence League', London School of Economics and Political Science blog, 2 December 2015, http://blogs.lse.ac.uk/politicsandpolicy/understanding -the-english-defence-league-life-on-the-front-line-of-an-imagined-clash -of-civilisations/.

52. Lars is a journalist and author who founded the Free Speech Society and a newspaper called *Dispatch International*—both of which are known to be very critical of Islam. He was convicted (and then

acquitted on appeal) in 2011 for hate speech against Islam. Ingrid is a distinguished senior fellow of the US-based Gatestone Institute, a noted counter-jihadist website.

53. It is extremely difficult to accurately document all Tommy's dealings with the police. But from what I can piece together, he was arrested in February 2010 at Luton airport on suspicion of criminal damage at a Sheffield hotel and a racially aggravated incident involving a receptionist. The police raided his house and confiscated his computer. He was acquitted, and the Independent Police Complaint Committee found that the police had a signed statement by the hotel manager that it wasn't Tommy all along. Later that year, he was charged with assaulting a police officer when he jumped over a barrier to stop a 'Muslims Against Crusades' rally burning poppies. The case was dropped when video footage revealed he did not assault an officer, only for him to be re-arrested for the same incident under a section 4 public order offence. In 2013 he was arrested while doing a charity walk through Tower Hamlets for obstructing a police officer. He was acquitted again. On 27 November 2012 Tommy was arrested and charged with mortgage fraud. Three years earlier the police started to investigate Tommy for money laundering and froze his assets as they scoured his personal accounts, as well as those of his plumbing business and his wife's tanning salon, for evidence of misconduct. They found something. Some years earlier, Tommy had lent his wife's brother £20,000 for a deposit on a house, who then exaggerated his earnings to secure the mortgage. He bought the house, and six months later sold it for £30,000 profit, paying back Tommy the £20,000 he'd borrowed. Although Tommy did not personally benefit from the transaction, he was sentenced to eighteen months in prison and fined £125,000 (the total value of the property). Although Tommy denies it, Judge Andrew Bright described Robinson as the instigator of the frauds, having introduced others to a fraudulent mortgage broker. He went to prison in January 2014. At the time of writing, Tommy is seeking to have that overturned. While inside, Tommy claims he was approached by someone from a unit called the Metropolitan Investigation Bureau (MIB), who said they could get his fine reduced if he agreed to be their man on the inside. (The MIB did indeed exist as a fairly secretive police department. See in particular the National Archives on the Duggan Inquiry and Robert Milne's recent book *Forensic Intelligence* (CRC Press, 2013).) Tommy said no. Tommy was out six months later on licence (even though his conviction related to a

mortgage-fraud case, the terms of his licence included a restriction on all political activity). Six weeks later he was arrested again on a burglary charge while driving in the North of the United Kingdom. He claims he was driven to a distant police station, strip-searched, drug tested and then released without charge. He says the MIB got back in touch saying they could help him, and that he refused. Then, a few days later, he was told his mortgage-fraud fine was going to be increased to over £300,000. Again the MIB showed up, saying they could make it disappear. He refused again, and when it came to court, the judge did not increase the fine. The day after the press conference to announce Pegida-UK's launch, the police brought a racially aggravated common-assault charge against Tommy, even though he'd been told that case had been dropped. Tommy's QC successfully argued the trial could not continue, because the Crown Prosecution Service (who'd originally told Tommy's lawyers they wouldn't bring charges) had failed to disclose vital evidence. All this is documented in his book *Enemy of the State* (The Press News Ltd, 2015), although I tried to independently verify all the claims made.

I have a copy of the email in which the police say, on 1 October 2015, 'no further action' is being taken against him. Further information is here: 'Right-winger charged with assault at Muslim poppy-burning protest', *Evening Standard*, 2011, http://www.standard.co.uk/news/right -winger-charged-with-assault-at-muslim-poppy-burning-protest -6535648.html; Alan Lake, 'The persecution of Tommy Robinson— Collected articles', 4 Freedoms, 19 January 2014, http://4freedoms.com /group/uk/forum/topics/the-persecution-of-tommy-robinson-collected -articles; English Defence League, 'Tommy Robinson has been re- arrested', 2 January 2011, http://theenglishdefenceleagueextra.blogspot .co.uk/2011/03/tommy-robinson-has-been-re-arrested.html; 'Public Order Act 1986', The National Archive, http://www.legislation.gov.uk /ukpga/1986/64/section/4; Beds, Herts and Bucks, 'Tommy Robinson, former EDL leader, jailed for fraud', BBC, 23 January 2014, http://www .bbc.co.uk/news/uk-england-25862838; Steven Hopkins, 'Tommy Rob- inson claims police tried to blackmail him into spying on Britain First's Paul Golding', *Huffington Post*, 5 December 2015, http://www.huffington post.co.uk/2015/12/05/tommy-robinson-claims-pol_n_8726770.html; Paul Right, 'Watch Tommy Robinson's prison brawl following "threats from Muslim extremists"', *International Business Times*, 4 May 2016, http://www.ibtimes.co.uk/watch-tommy-robinsons-prison-brawl -following-threats-muslim-extremists-1558162; Paul Right, 'Tommy Rob-

inson', *International Business Times*, 6 January 2016, http://www.ibtimes
.co.uk/tommy-robinson-pegida-uk-figurehead-be-charged-assault-days
-after-launch-anti-islam-group-1536415.

54. The song 'Imagine' by John Lennon was played with the lyrics
'Imagine there's no Islam'. Georgina Connery, 'Reclaim Australia Rally
drowns out counter protesters', *The Canberra Times*, 6 February 2016,
http://www.canberratimes.com.au/act-news/reclaim-australia-rally
-drowns-out-counter-protesters-20160206-gmnezn.html.

55. 'Anti-Islam movement PEGIDA stages protests across Europe',
Reuters, 6 February 2016, http://www.reuters.com/article/us-europe
-migrants-protests-germany-idUSKCN0VF0P4.

56. Ibid.

57. Dan Griffin, 'RTÉ to file complaint after cameraman is injured in
protest', *Irish Times*, 7 February 2016, http://www.irishtimes.com/news
/ireland/irish-news/rt%C3%A9-to-file-complaint-after-cameraman-is
-injured-in-protest-1.2525530; Olivia Kelleher, 'Identity Ireland disappointed with political response to attack', *Irish Times*, 9 February 2016,
http://www.irishtimes.com/news/politics/identity-ireland-disappointed
-with-political-response-to-attack-1.2528311.

58. '20 arrests as tensions rise at Amsterdam Pegida rally', *Dutch
News*, 20 February 2016, http://www.dutchnews.nl/news/archives
/2016/02/20-arrests-as-tensions-rise-at-amsterdam-pegida-rally/.

59. 'Austria sees first "anti-Islamisation' Pegida march," *Channel 4 News*, 3 February 2015, http://www.channel4.com/news/austria
-pegida-anti-islamisation-march-protest-anti.

60. Joe Mulhall, 'Pegida UK', Hope Not Hate Ltd, http://www.hope
nothate.org.uk/features/pegida/; Zuzana Botíková, 'Pro-Pegida protest
in Bratislava ends as farce', RTVS, 2 August 2016, http://enrsi.rtvs.sk
/articles/news/99733/pro-pegida-protest-in-bratislava-ends-as-farce.

61. Mulhall, 'Pegida UK'.

Chapter 3

1. John Higgs, *I Have America Surrounded: The Life of Timothy Leary*
(Barricade Books, 2006).

2. I came with a BBC producer, Hannah Barnes, for a radio documentary that was broadcast on Radio 4 in April 2016. She didn't take
anything either.

3. Home Office, '2015 Crime Survey for England and Wales'; Ashik
Siddique, 'Psychedelic drug use in United States as common now as in

1960s generation', Medical Daily, 23 April 2013, http://www.medicaldaily
.com/psychedelic-drug-use-united-states-common-now-1960s-generation
-245218.

Evidence of celebrity use is widely documented, for example:
Claudio, '10 famous people you didn't know took LSD', *Richest*,
16 June 2016, http://www.therichest.com/rich-list/most-influential
/10-famous-people-you-didnt-know-used-lsd/?view=all.

4. In 2010 Professor David Nutt, director of the Neuro-psychophar-
macology Unit at Imperial College London (who was fired from his
position as chair of the government's advisory council on the misuse
of drugs in 2009 after saying riding horses was more dangerous than
ectasy), ranked the twenty most commonly used drugs in order of the
harm they cause for society and for users. Alcohol came top with seventy-two points, followed by heroin with fifty-five. Psilocybin scored six
points; LSD, seven.

5. The significance of users' mindsets and the setting in which the
drugs are taken has been discussed among those who study psychedelics in great detail. For a thorough overview, see William A. Richards,
Sacred Knowledge: Psychedelics and Religious Experiences (Columbia
University Press, 2016).

6. Jay Stevens, *Storming Heaven: LSD and the American Dream*
(Grove Press, 1987).

7. Higgs, op. cit.

8. Stevens, op. cit., Chapter 1. See also Myron J. Stolaroff, *The Secret
Chief Revealed* (MAPS, 2005).

9. In 1953 Humphry Osmond, an English psychiatrist, introduced
Huxley to mescaline, an experience he chronicled in *The Doors of Perception* in 1954. (Osmond coined the word 'psychedelic', which means
'mind-manifesting', in a 1957 letter to Huxley.) Huxley is on record saying the people who would benefit most from these drugs were professors, 'or almost anybody with fixed ideas and a great certainty'. Huxley
proposed a research project involving the 'administration of LSD to terminal cancer cases, in the hope that it would make dying a more spiritual, less strictly physiological process'. He had his wife administer LSD
to him while on his deathbed.

10. Aldous Huxley, *The Doors of Perception* (Vintage Books, 1954).

11. Michael Pollan, 'Trip Treatment', *New Yorker,* September 2015.

12. Kevin Franciotti, 'Mind altering drug could offer life free of heroin', *New Scientist*, August 2013; 'LSD assisted psychotherapy', MAPS;
Benedict Carey, 'LSD, reconsidered for therapy', *New York Times*, 3

March 2014; Arran Frood 'Ayahuasca psychedelics tested for depression', *Scientific American* 8 April 2015; Pablo Noguiera, 'Ayahuasca: A possible cure for depression and alcoholism', *Vice*, 25 December 2015; Thomas Brown, 'Observational study of the long-term efficacy of ibogaine--assisted treatment in participants with opiate addiction', MAPS, October 2012; Dave Dean, 'Can MDMA cure PTSD?', *Vice*, 27 April 2013; 'The safety and efficacy of ±3,4-methylenedioxymethamphetamine-assisted psychotherapy in subjects with chronic, treatment-resistant post-traumatic stress disorder: the first randomized controlled pilot study', *Journal of Psychopharmacology*, vol. 25, no. 4, April 2011, 439–52. (MAPS [the Multidisciplinary Association for Psychedelic Studies] has good summaries of much of the current research.)

13. Some psychologists believe that there are five main 'domains': openness, conscientiousness, extroversion, agreeableness and neuroticism. Each person's personality is composed of where they sit on a scale of them; these traits are vital in forming your political views—not because you're hardwired to be left wing or right wing, but because where you sit on these scales makes you more or less likely to react in certain ways to key political questions. Openness, for example, is associated with being more liberal, more likely to support racial tolerance and environmentalism. In short, people with high openness scores are more likely to be left wing. Most psychologists believe that these foundational traits—which are part inherited part nurtured—are more or less fixed by the age of about thirty. Sean N. Boileau, *Openness to Experience, Agreeableness, and Gay Male Intimate Partner Preference Across Racial Lines* (ProQuest LLC, 2008); Melinda Wenner, 'Political preferences in half genetic', *Live Science*, 24 May 2007. See also Steven Pinker, *The Blank Slate: The Modern Denial of Human Nature* (Allen Lane, 2002).

14. Katherine A. MacLean, Matthew W. Johnson and Roland R. Griffiths, 'Mystical experiences occasioned by the hallucinogen psilocybin lead to increases in the personality domain of openness', *Journal of Psychopharmacology*, November 2011; Maia Szalavitz, 'Magic Mushrooms Trigger Lasting Personality Change', *Time*, October 2011; Scott McGreal, 'Psilocybin and personality', *Psychology Today*, September 2012.

15. Most of the current studies are what's called 'phase 1', where the drugs are given to small groups of volunteers. Roland Griffiths hopes to get permission to do the first phase 2 test, which would be trying it on a limited number of patients. If that goes well, a phase 3 study would

follow, where researchers show what the drug does (including the side effects) on a very large group of people, typically numbering between 200 and 5,000. That usually costs between £500 million to £1 billion and takes up to eight years. And because of all the screening, the patient care and the regulation, this type of research is slower and more expensive than for other drugs. Even if all these hurdles were overcome, psychedelics would also have to be re-categorised from Schedule 1 (meaning no medicinal use) to Schedule 2 (some medicinal use). No drug has even been re-categorised into a looser schedule in the UK. Interestingly, the UN has no established protocol for rescheduling drugs. The UK schedules are simply mimics of the UN schedules.

16. An example of this 'cosmic care' is the Zendo Project. The Psychedelic Society's website stresses that they do not engage in illegal activity. 'Don't get involved to illegally buy or sell substances.'

17. This is how the definition given by www.scienceandnonduality. com puts it.

18. Tony Parson, 'The open secret', n.d., www.theopensecret.com (accessed August 2016).

19. Stevens, op. cit., p. 150.

20. In the Netherlands, the mushroom form of psilocybin is illegal, but the truffle form is legal and available from several shops and online stores. Mushrooms were banned in 2008 (dried form) and 2009 (fresh form).

21. One clinical psychologist who I showed this chapter to said he thought I might be 'underplaying the discussion about the dangers of making psychedelics freely available'. Another, a professor of systems thinking and author of several pamphlets about drug policy, said 'I think you make too much of the dangers of psychedelics.'

22. Huxley, op. cit. Huxley described having seen 'what Adam had seen on the morning of creation—miracle, moment by moment, of naked existence'. Sir Geoffrey Vickers, a well-known British lawyer, British Army colonel and Victoria Cross winner and then systems theorist described his psychedelic experience as follows: 'This leaf and I, its participant, had drawn the miles-wide landscape into an attentive, breathless synthesis, focused here on this inch-long form . . . and for some timeless space there was no movement, no sound and no distinction or identifying of parts in all that had been united. For there was no "I" that gazed. No tiniest fraction of me stood aside to watch me watching. I and what I watched were on; and through that tiny gateway I became one with what was boundless.'

23. I owe this insight to Jake Chapman.

24. Kate Wighton, 'The brain on LSD revealed: First scans show how the drug affects the brain', Imperial College London, News, 11 April 2016.

25. Michael Pollan, 'Trip treatment'.

26. Ibid.

27. From the Psychedelic Society's website: 'Group applications for our psychedelic experience weekends are now open. You specify the size of your group, your preferred dates and your motivations. If your application is accepted we will then work together to find a suitable venue (in the Netherlands), select experienced facilitators and fine-tune the timetable. The weekends are a great way for groups to have safe, legal and affordable psychedelic experiences in a setting that maximises the potential for mystical / spiritual experience. Apply today!'

28. The breaking down of formal religious institutions creates some legal tensions. Peyote is a powerful psychedelic and has been used in Native American Indian spiritual and religious ceremonies since long before the arrival of White Europeans. But it is now listed as a Schedule 1 controlled substance. An exception was made in the 1994 American Religious Freedom Act Amendments, for 'bone fide religious ceremonies'. But, argue its advocates, if Native American Indians can take them for spiritual purposes, why not others if they are doing it with a spiritual purpose in mind?

29. From the Psychedelic Society's website: 'The year is 2023. You walk into the pharmacy and head towards the "psychoactive substances" section. On the top shelf, there are pharmaceutically pure psychedelics including DMT, mescaline and LSD, all available legally, and at afford-able prices. On the shelf below, dried magic mushrooms of many varieties. You pick up a pack of DMT and head to the checkout, where the pharmacist checks your age and asks you a series of questions to ensure you understand how to use the substance safely. As you head out of the shop, you bump into a colleague from work, who's just bought some 2-CB. She explains how she's felt calmer and kinder since she stopped drinking and started using psychedelics. The Psychedelic Society is working to make this dream a reality.'

30. For an example see Rick Strassman et al., *Inner Paths to Outer Space: Journeys to Alien Worlds Through Psychedelics and Other Spiritual Technologies* (Park Street Press, 2008). For a more sceptical look, see 'Are entities and plant spirits real? A skeptic's guide to tripping', *Psychedelic Frontier*, April 2014.

31. Natalie Valios, 'Prince's trust: One in ten young people feel life is meaningless', *Community Care*, 5 January 2009.

There is much research on the incident and cost of depression and other mental health conditions. Paul E. Greenberg et al., 'The economic burden of adults with major depressive disorder in the United States (2005 and 2010)', *Journal of Clinical Psychiatry*, 76(2):155–62, 2015.

32. '"Nones" on the rise', Pew Research Center, 9 October 2012.

33. Michael King et al., 'Religion, spirituality and mental health: results from a national study of English households', *British Journal of Psychiatry*, January 2013, 202(1): 68–73.

34. Stevens, op. cit.; Higgs, op. cit., p. 160; Diana Trilling, *We Must March My Darlings* (Harcourt, 1977), p. 16.

Chapter 4

1. Dominic Casciani, 'An extremist in the family', BBC News, November 2016.

2. Dick Pountain and David Robins, *Cool Rules* (Reaktion Books, 2000), p. 177.

3. Back in 2007 al-Qaeda's Global Islamic Media Front (GIMF) released their own encryption software called Asrar al-Mujahedeen. This was the first purpose-made Islamist encryption software, primarily used for email communications. It has since been updated many times, and now contains additional functions for text messages posted on bulletin boards and promoted in jihadist magazines. Tor (the anonymity network), anonymous browsers and anonymity best practice are frequently discussed by terrorists on forums and websites, and not only by Islamic extremists. Manuel R. Torres Soriano, 'The vulnerabilities of online terrorism', *Studies in Conflict and Terrorism*, vol. 35, no. 4 (March 2012). Extract from Anders Breivik's manifesto available at https://public intelligence.net/wp-content/uploads/2011/07/AndersBehringBreivik Manifesto_Page_0012.jpg (accessed 5 September 2014).

4. Andrew Gilligan, 'Hizb ut-Tahrir is not a gateway to terrorism, claims Whitehall report', *Daily Telegraph*, 25 July 2010, http://www .telegraph.co.uk/journalists/andrew-gilligan/7908262/Hizb-ut-Tahrir-is -not-a-gateway-to-terrorism-claims-Whitehall-report.html (accessed 29 November 2016); Vikram Dodd, 'Suicide bomber's family "kept plan secret"', *Guardian*, 27 April 2004, https://www.theguardian.com/uk/2004 /apr/27/terrorism.israel (accessed 29 November 2016).

There were some grounds to be concerned since some people affiliated with Hizb ut-Tahrir had left the group and moved on to terrorist activity. Most infamously in 2003 British national Omar Sharif, a would-be suicide bomber, was radicalised partly by Hizb activists at his London university. Sharif travelled to Israel with another British man, Asif Hanif, to partake in a suicide-bombing mission, but his bomb failed to detonate and he was found dead twelve days later in a river. David Leigh, 'Background: Hizb ut-Tahrir', *Guardian*, 22 July 2005, https://www.theguardian.com/media/2005/jul/22/pressandpublishing (accessed 29 November 2016). A 2002 leaflet produced and distributed by Hizb ut-Tahrir included a line from the Qu'ran that was used to threaten Jews, stating 'Kill them wherever you find them and turn them out from where they have turned you out.'

5. 'Muslims "must root out extremism"', BBC News, 4 July 2006, http://news.bbc.co.uk/1/hi/5144438.stm (accessed 29 November 2016).

6. In 2016, for example, the Quilliam Foundation, an anti-extremism think tank, wrote that Prevent-style work should be integrated into the following areas: education, criminal justice, faith, charities, the internet and health. These are all places, says the report, 'where there are risks of exposure to extremist ideologies or which could support counter -extremism work'. This is roughly every single aspect of modern life.

7. Home Office, 'Preventing violent extremism—communities and local government committee', 30 March 2010, http://www.publications .parliament.uk/pa/cm200910/cmselect/cmcomloc/65/6504.htm#n13 (accessed 29 November 2016). It was further complicated by the fact it was jointly run by the Home Office and Department of Communities and Local Government.

8. Jamie Bartlett and Jonathan Birdwell, *From Suspects to Citizens* (Demos, 2010); Shiraz Maher, *Choosing our friends wisely* (Policy Exchange, 2009).

9. Secretary of State for the Home Department, 'Prevent strategy', Crown, Secretary of State for the Home Department, June 2011, https:// www.gov.uk/government/uploads/system/uploads/attachment_data /file/97976/prevent-strategy-review.pdf p6; Joana Dawson, 'Counter-extremism policy', Briefing Paper No. 7238, House of Commons Library, 19 May 2016, http://researchbriefings.files.parliament.uk/documents /CBP-7238/CBP-7238.pdf.

People get themselves wound up into all sorts of linguistic contortions over these words. What radicalisation is, whether extremism is the same as terrorism. According to the 2011 Prevent Strategy: 'Government policy regarding groups who may be associated with extremism (notably policy regarding Ministerial or official engagement) will also be coordinated by DCLG. But the line between extremism and terrorism is not always precise. As we have said in the first part of this document, terrorist groups very often draw on extremist ideas developed by extremist organisations. Some people who become members of terrorist groups have previously been members of extremist organisations and have been radicalised by them. Others (though not all) pass through an extremist phase. The relationship between terrorism and extremism is therefore complicated and directly relevant to the aim and objectives of Prevent. It will not always be possible or desirable to draw clear lines between policies in each of these areas. But the lines can be clearer than they have been hitherto. That will also bring greater clarity to the *Prevent* strategy.' (HM Government 2011b, 24–5, paragraphs 6.3–6.6.) This doesn't really add any greater clarity at all, quite the reverse. It now covers extremism, which is an even more difficult phrase. Here's another example: 'We note that previous Prevent documents used the phrase "violent extremism." The review found that the term is ambiguous and has caused some confusion in the past, most notably by giving the impression that the scope of Prevent is very wide indeed and includes a range of activity far beyond counter-terrorism. We avoid using the phrase here, although we recognise that programmes comparable to Prevent are being run in other countries under the banner of preventing or countering violent extremism.' (HM Government 2011b, 25, paragraph 6.7.)

10. 'Driving away the shadows', *Economist*, 20 August 2016, http://www.economist.com/news/britain/21705307-early-intervention-prevent-terrorism-tough-get-right-britain-does-not-do-bad; Home Office, *Prevent: Training Catalogue* (HMSO, 2016), p. 6, https://www.gov.uk/government/uploads/system/uploads/attachment_data/file/503973/Prevent_Training_catalogue_-_March_2016.pdf (accessed 30 October 2016); Simon Hooper, 'Prevent courses on sale to schools deemed "poor quality" by UK government', Middle East Eye, 7 September 2016, http://www.middleeasteye.net/news/uk-prevent-training-catalogue-schools-1706962311> (accessed 30 October 2016).

11. David Anderson, 'Supplementary evidence submitted by David Anderson QC', 29 January 2016, http://data.parliament.uk/writtenevidence/committeeevidence.svc/evidencedocument/home-affairs

-committee/countering-extremism/written/27920.pdf (accessed 30 October, 2016). Section 202(2) of the Education Reform Act 1988 places an obligation on universities to 'have regard [in the exercise of their functions] to the need to ensure that academic staff have the freedom within the law to question and test received wisdom, and to put forward new ideas and controversial or unpopular opinions, without placing themselves in jeopardy of losing their jobs or privileges they may have at their institutions'. This duty is replicated in the governance documents of many higher-education institutions. Home Office, *Prevent Duty Guidance: for higher-education institutions in England and Wales* (HMSO, 2015), https://www.gov.uk/government/uploads/system/uploads/attachment _data/file/445916/Prevent_Duty_Guidance_For_Higher_Education __England__Wales_.pdf (accessed 30 October 2016).

12. Open Society Justice Initiative, *Eroding Trust* (Open Society Foundation, 2016), https://www.opensocietyfoundations.org/sites/default /files/eroding-trust-20161017_0.pdf. The United Nations has a 'plan of action' for preventing violence extremism, and so does the Organization for Security and Cooperation in Europe and the EU; Erin Marie Saltman and Melanie Smith, 'Till martyrdom do us part', Institute for Strategic Dialogue, 2015, http://icsr.info/wp-content/uploads/2015/06/Till _Martyrdom_Do_Us_Part_Gender_and_the_ISIS_Phenomenon.pdf.

13. 'Legislative scrutiny: Counter-extremism Bill, HC647', Joint Committee on Human Rights testimony, 9 March 2016, http://data.parliament .uk/writtenevidence/committeeevidence.svc/evidencedocument /human-rights-committee/countering-extremism/oral/30366.html.

14. See, for example, Katherine E. Brown and Tania Saeed, 'Radicalization and counter-radicalization at British universities: Muslim encounters and alternatives', *Ethnic and Racial Studies*, 38:11, 1952–68, DOI: 10.1080/01419870.2014.911343 (2015).

15. Open Society Justice Initiative, *Eroding Trust*.

16. If we polled people from Kent (where I'm from) every other week about whether they felt 'Kentish' or 'British' and whether they'd be prepared to defend Kent in the event of a French invasion, and published the results with headlines like '32 per cent of Kentish People Don't Feel Loyal to Britain', before long there would be a Kentish Independence Movement. It would be full of people who'd never even thought about Kent before. If you put a magnifying glass to a group of people, give them a label and then keep asking them about it, it will inevitably create an 'us' and 'them' feeling for all concerned.

17. Louis Reynolds and Ralph Scott, *Digital Citizenship* (Demos, 2016).

18. The 'Prevent Professional Concerns' programme in Scotland.

19. Josh Halliday, 'Almost 4,000 people referred to UK deradicalisation scheme last year', *Guardian*, 20 March 2016, https://www.theguardian.com/uk-news/2016/mar/20/almost-4000-people-were-referred-to-uk-deradicalisation-scheme-channel-last-year (accessed 30 October 2016). This is an increase from 1,681 in 2014, and just five in 2006–7 when the programme began. 'Freedom of information request reference number: 00026/16', National Police Chiefs' Council, 7 March 2016, http://www.npcc.police.uk/Publication/NPCC%20FOI/CT/02616Channel Referrals.pdf; Vikram Dodd, 'Muslim Council of Britain to set up alternative counter-terror scheme', *Guardian*, 19 October 2016, https://www.theguardian.com/uk-news/2016/oct/19/muslim-council-britain-set-up-alternative-counter-terror-scheme (accessed 1 November 2016); NPCC, National Channel referral figures, http://www.npcc.police.uk/FreedomofInformation/NationalChannelReferralFigures.aspx (accessed 1 November 2016).

20. Arund Kundnani, *A Decade Lost* (Claystone, 2015), http://mabonline.net/wp-content/uploads/2015/01/Claystone-rethinking-radicalisation.pdf. The Royal Canadian Mounted Police provide a good definition of radicalisation: the process by which 'individuals are introduced to an overtly ideological message and belief system that encourages movement from moderate, mainstream beliefs towards extreme views'. For the UK government it's 'the process by which a person comes to support terrorism and extremist ideologies associated with terrorist groups'. For example, Moghaddam's model entails that personal feelings of injustice and oppression are key to the initial stages of radicalisation into violence. Conversely, the NYPD model clearly states that radicalisation is not triggered by oppression, suffering or desperation. More fundamentally, stage models outline clear phases, in line with the psychological literature that stresses the importance of a tipping point marking the decision to move from language to action. However, this contradicts Marc Sageman's claim that radicalisation into violence is not a linear progressive process at all, but rather emerges once several factors are present.

21. Jamie Bartlett, Jonathan Birdwell and Michael King, *The Edge of Violence* (Demos, 2010) for a review of the literature. (The lack of definitive answers has made it prone to political interpretation: right-wing

analysts tend to think ideology is the major factor, while left-wing analysts place greater stress on social conditions or injustices.)

22. Simon Cottee, 'The pre-terrorists among us', 27 October
2015, http://www.theatlantic.com/international/archive/2015/10
/counterterrorism-prevention-britain-isis/412603/.

23. Pountain and Robins, op. cit., p. 177; Sara Khan, *The Battle for British Islam* (Saqi Books, 2016), Chapter 1; C. J. Werlemen,
'IS taps into a mass culture of violence', Middle East Eye, 8 November 2015, http://www.middleeasteye.net/columns/how-isis-taps-our
-new-appetite-violence-1185583344.

Islamic State is just drawing on a long history of this. The Toronto
18—a group convicted of planning a terrorist attack in Canada in
2006—used to train at Washago. They used a '9 mm semi-automatic
pistol; an air rifle; paint-ball guns and engaged in jihadist discussions,
military-style marches'. One radical reported someone trying to recruit
him by telling him they were off 'to the forest with a 9 mm to fire off
a couple of shots'. A Parisian sermon from 2002 promised similar excitement: *'Le Jihad, c'est mieux que les vacances à Los Angeles. C'est
l'aventure. On mange, on découvre le paysage. En plus, on aide nos frères.'*
('Jihad, it's better than holidays in Los Angeles. It's an adventure. One
eats, one discovers the countryside. And one helps brothers.') Charlie Winter, 'Documenting the virtual "Caliphate"', Quilliam Foundation, October 2015, http://www.quilliamfoundation.org/wp/wp-content
/uploads/2015/10/FINAL-documenting-the-virtual-caliphate.pdf (accessed 18 November 2016); Charlie Winter, 'The Virtual "Caliphate":
Understanding Islamic State's Propaganda Strategy', Quilliam Foundation, July 2015, https://www.quilliamfoundation.org/wp/wp-content
/uploads/publications/free/the-virtual-caliphate-understanding-islamic
-states-propaganda-strategy.pdf (accessed 18 November, 2016).

24. Terrorists typically draw on a narrow band of thinkers, and four
names frequently appear: Ibn Taymiyya, Sayyid Qutb, Muhammed Ibn
Wahhab, Abu Muhammad Al-Maqdisi and Abdullah Azzam; Lizzie
Dearden, 'Isis: Islam is "not the strongest factor" behind foreign fighters joining extremist groups in Syria and Iraq—report', *Independent*,
16 November 2016, http://www.independent.co.uk/news/world/europe
/isis-foreign-fighters-british-european-western-dying-radicalised-islam
-not-strongest-factor-cultural-a7421711.html (accessed 19 November 2016).

25. Khan, op. cit.; Alan Travis, 'MI5 reports challenges views on terrorism in Britain', *Guardian*, 20 August 2008, https://www.theguardian

.com/uk/2008/aug/20/uksecurity.terrorism1.

In January 2014 two British men left the UK and went to Syria to join an al-Qaeda affiliate group. Before leaving they had bought *Islam for Dummies*.

26. He wouldn't tell me how many people had been through a government programme and still gone to Syria. He probably doesn't know, but it must be some. In October 2015 a fourteen-year-old from Blackburn who had been referred to Channel was jailed for life for plotting to behead Australian police officers.

27. Peter Neumann, in Homa Khaleeli, '"You worry they could take your kids": Is the Prevent strategy demonising Muslim schoolchildren?', *Guardian*, 23 September 2015, https://www.theguardian.com/uk-news/2015/sep/23/prevent-counter-terrorism-strategy-schools-demonising-muslim-children (accessed 30 October 2016).

28. Khan, op. cit. See Henrietta McMicking, 'Cage: Important human rights group or apologists for terror?', BBC News, 27 February 2015, http://www.bbc.co.uk/news/uk-31657333; Douglas Murray and Robin Simcox, 'The evidence shows that Cage is a pro-terrorist group', *Daily Telegraph*, 21 July 2014, http://www.telegraph.co.uk/news/uknews/law-and-order/10981050/The-evidence-shows-that-Cage-is-a-pro-terrorist-group.html; Asim Qureshi, 'The "Science" of Pre-Crime: The Secret "Radicalisation" Study Underpinning Prevent', *Cage Advocacy*, 2016, https://cage.ngo/wp-content/uploads/2016/09/CAGE-Science-Pre-Crime-Report.pdf; http://www.telegraph.co.uk/news/uknews/terrorism-in-the-uk/11442602/Cage-the-extremists-peddling-lies-to-British-Muslims-to-turn-them-into-supporters-of-terror.html.

29. Khan, op. cit.

30. PreventWatch UK, 'I live in a "terrorist house": police speak to Muslim boy, 10, over spelling error', Twitter Post, 20 January 2016, https://twitter.com/preventwatchuk/status/689724686930984964; 'The "terrorist house" case', Prevent Watch UK, February 2016, http://www.preventwatch.org/terrorist-house-case/; 'Legalising Islamophobia is a growing international trend', CAGE, 27 October 2016, https://cage.ngo/article/legalising-islamophobia-is-a-growing-international-trend/; *Preventing Education? Human Rights and UK Counter-Terrorism Policy in Schools* (Rights Watch [UK], July 2016), http://rwuk.org/wp-content/uploads/2016/07/preventing-education-final-to-print-3.compressed-1.pdf (accessed 10 November 2016).

31. Advanced search conducted using www.idiscover.lib.cam.ac.uk database of academic books and articles.

32. Home Office, 'Revised Prevent duty guidance for England and Wales' (HMSO, 2015), p. 3, https://www.gov.uk/government/uploads /system/uploads/attachment_data/file/445977/3799_Revised_Prevent _Duty_Guidance__England_Wales_V2-Interactive.pdf (accessed 30 October 2016).

33. Google Scholar search for 'radicalisation, or de-radicalisation', https:// scholar.google.co.uk/scholar?as_q=&as_epq=&as_oq=radicalisation %2C+de-radicalisation+&as_eq=&as_occt=any&as_sauthors=&as _publication=&as_ylo=2015&as_yhi=2015&btnG=&hl=en&as_sdt=0%2C5.

Chapter 5

1. Dario Fo, Beppe Grillo and Gianroberto Casaleggio, *Il Grillo canta sempre al tramonto* (Chiarelettere Srl., 2013).

2. Paul Taggart, *Populism* (Open University Press, 2000).

3. For example, in the Netherlands, anti-Islam politician Geert Wilders (leading in the Dutch opinion polls at the time of writing) claims 'citizens no longer feel represented by their national governments and parliaments'. Geert Wilders, 'Let the Dutch vote on immigration policy', *New York Times*, 19 November 2015, http://www.nytimes .com/2015/11/20/opinion/geert-wilders-the-dutch-deserve-to-vote-on -immigration-policy.html.

Capitalist Donald Trump wants to 'declare independence from the elites'. Arch-socialist and Democrat candidate Bernie Sanders, thinks Americans are 'sick and tired of establishment politics and economics'. Daniel Marans, 'Sanders calls out MSNBC's corporate ownership—in Interview on MSNBC', *Huffington Post*, 7 May 2016, http://www.huffingtonpost.com/entry/bernie-sanders-asks-who -owns-msnbc_us_572e3d0fe4b0bc9cb0471df1.

4. Ingrid van Biezen, Peter Mair and Thomas Poguntke, 'Going, going ... gone? The decline of party membership in contemporary Europe', *European Journal of Political Research* 51:1 (2012), pp. 24–56. By 2012, with membership falling all the time, 82 per cent of UK citizens said they 'tend not to trust' political parties. The trends are broadly similar across Europe, albeit at different rates. Only 2 per cent of voters in Germany and France are members of a mainstream political party; Florian Hartleb, 'Anti-elitist cyber parties', *Journal of public affairs*, 2013. In 1951, 4 million people were members of either the Conservative or Labour parties. Also see Francis Fukuyama, *Political Order and Political Delay* (Profile, 2014), p. 139; Douglas Carswell, *The End of Politics and*

the Birth of iDemocracy (Biteback, 2012), pp. 77–8; Cas Mudde, 'The populist Zeitgeist', *Government and Opposition*, 39(4), 2004, pp. 542–63.

5. Jeffrey M. Jones, 'Trust in U.S. judicial branch sinks to new low of 53%', Gallup, 18 September 2015, http://www.gallup.com/poll/185528 /trust-judicial-branch-sinks-new-low.aspx; Jamie Bartlett, Jonathan Birdwell and Mark Littler, *The New Face of Digital Populism* (Demos, 2011); *Post-election survey 2014* (Public Opinion Monitoring Unit, October 2014), http://www.europarl.europa.eu/pdf/eurobarometre/2014 /post/post_ee2014_sociodemographic_annex_en.pdf; Aktuelle Mitteilungen, 'Bundestagswahl 2017: Wahlberechtigte nach Ländern', 7 February 2017, http://www.bundeswahlleiter.de/en/bundestagswahlen /BTW_BUND_09/presse/77_Repr_WStat.html. This is reflected in several data. Voting is the most visible and personal experience of engagement in politics. Voter turnout in the 2009 Bundestag elections was the lowest ever, at 70.8 per cent—but 80 per cent of sixty- to sixty-nine -year-olds voted, whereas only 59 per cent of twenty-one- to twenty -four-year-olds did. In France's 2014 European elections, 42 per cent of the total population turned out, but only 28 per cent of eighteen- to twenty-four-year-olds did so, against 51 per cent of the over-fifty-fives. Across the whole of the EU, voter turnout in the May 2014 European Parliament election was 51 per cent of over-fifty-fives, but only 28 per cent of eighteen- to twenty-four-year-olds.

6. Jan A. G. M. van Dijk, 'Digital democracy: Vision and reality' in Ig Snellen, Marcel Thaens and Wim van de Donk (eds.), *Public Administration in the Information Age: Revisited* (IOS Press, 2013). Also see Evgeny Morozov, *To Save Everything, Click Here* (Allen Lane, 2013), pp. 124–39 for discussion of cyber-utopianism in relation to networks and flat hierarchies. Also see Richard Barbrook and Andy Cameron, 'The Californian ideology', *Mute*, September 1995, and Richard Barbrook, *Media Freedom: The Contradictions of Communications in the Age of Modernity* (Pluto Press, 1995), p. 14 for an early critique.

7. James Politi, 'Lunch with the *FT*: Beppe Grillo', *Financial Times*, July 2015, http://www.ft.com/cms/s/2/55d3242a-2bb2-11e5-8613 -e7aedbb7bdb7.html (accessed 9 August 2016).

8. Shortly before then, in autumn 2004, Grillo had uploaded several of his articles on to the website of the magazine *Internationale*, for whom he used to write occasionally. Once the blog was set up, this ended.

9. Politi, 'Lunch with the *FT*: Beppe Grillo'; Filippo Tronconi (ed.), *Beppe Grillo's Five Star Movement: Organisation, Communication and Ideology* (Ashgate, 2015), p. 17; www.beppegrillo.it archive.

10. The first groups were established in Milan, Rome and Naples, and then Vicenza, Salerno, Turin, Florence, Bologna and La Spezia. See, for example, the lack of grass-roots activity in Berlusconi's party, the PdL, discussed in Duncan McDonnell, 'Silvio Berlusconi's personal parties: from Forza Italia to the Popolo della Libertà', *Political Studies* 61, 2013.

11. Beppe Grillo, '8 settembre 2007: nelle città d'Italia, Guarda la mappa, V-Day', Beppe Grillo.it, www2.beppegrillo.it/vaffanculoday/; www.youtube.com/watch?v=Cw2ZSMy6wi8#t=4m40s (accessed 14 December 2012).

350,000 signatures were collected for a bill to be presented by the general public, proposing that: a) no Italian citizen who has been found guilty at any one of the three levels of justice envisaged by the Italian legal system can stand for Parliament; b) no Italian citizen can be elected to Parliament for more than two terms (valid retroactively); c) parliamentary candidates must be voted into office by preference voting.

12. The video of Grillo's appearance on stage in Bologna is at: Fragole Mature, *V-DAY—Beppe Grillo spettacolo completo*, 21 August 2013, https://www.youtube.com/watch?v=6KXc82LOJEc (accessed 14 February 2017).

13. This one was slightly different, calling for new powers in respect of freedom of information, a referendum removing public subsidies for newspapers and making it easier to get permission for new publications.

14. Eugenio Scalfari, 'L'invasione barbarica di Grillo', *La Republicca*, 12 September 2007, http://www.repubblica.it/2007/08/sezioni/cronaca /grillo-v-day/invasione-grillo/invasione-grillo.html (accessed 9 August 2016).

15. Some activists called for no participation in electoral politics, some suggested using civic lists and others supported cooperation with existing parties (in particular, the Italia dei Valori party). In a few cases candidates standing for Italia dei Valori were also supported by Grillo.

16. Beppe Grillo, 'Comunicato politico numero venticinque', 9 September 2009, www.beppegrillo.it/2009/09/comunicato_politico_numero _venticinque.html (accessed 9 August 2016); Beppe Grillo, 'Regolamento', Movimento Beppegrillo.it, 10 December 2009, www.beppegrillo .it/iniziative/movimentocinquestelle/Regolamento-Movimento-5-Stelle .pdf (accessed 14 December 2012).

17. There are a number of areas not covered in the document. Little is said about foreign policy, immigration, civil unions, public finances or the EU. On 6 November 2012, Grillo wrote on his blog that 'the decision whether to remain in the euro should be taken by Italian citizens via a

referendum. I believe that Italy cannot afford the luxury of being in the euro, but it should be the Italians who decide this and not a group of oligarchs or Beppe Grillo.'

18. He was convicted of manslaughter in 1981 after a car he was driving crashed, killing his three passengers—a mother and father and their nine-year-old boy. They were close friends of Beppe's.

19. Compared to unelected candidates, MPs were more involved in Meetups (70 per cent versus 40 per cent) and half of them (34 per cent) held positions of responsibility in such groups (founder, organiser, co-organiser, assistant organiser). Local Meetups would then organise local assemblies—face-to-face meetings. See 'The Movimento 5 Stelle and the Web' in Tronconi (ed.), op. cit.

20. Members of the movements are those who complete their registration/affiliation to the M5S by signing into the website, certifying their identity and uploading a valid ID document. To run, one needs to enter a CV and some formal documentation here: http://www.beppegrillo .it/movimento/regole_politiche_2013.php#candidati).

21. Beppe's way of talking about these subjects seems to have been particularly important. In a similar way, Donald Trump's word use when discussing subjects other politicians appeared reluctant to bring up was significant. See for example: Stacey Liberatore, 'Donald Trump's language could win him the presidency', MailOnline, 21 March 2016, http://www.dailymail.co.uk/sciencetech/article-3502925/Donald -Trump-s-language-win-presidency-Candidates-use-emotional-words -votes-times-crisis.html#ixzz4Br9rMAYL (accessed 9 August 2016).

22. Gian Antonio Stella and Sergio Rizzo, *La Casta: così i politici italiani sono diventati intoccabili* (ebook, Rizzoli, 2010). Data on trends in Italian trust in politics is available in various Eurobarometer studies and the Global Corruption Barometer.

23. Beppe Grillo meetup groups, http://beppegrillo.meetup.com (accessed 14 December 2012). See 'Top Italia: Generale', BlogItalia, 30 November 2012, www.blogitalia.it/classifica/ (accessed 14 December 2012), and 'beppegrillo.it: il blog di beppe Grillo', Alexa, n.d., www.alexa.com /siteinfo/beppegrillo.it (accessed 14 December 2012).

24. As a result, during the forty-five-day official 2013 campaign period, the Five Star Movement was discussed for only forty-one minutes in the main newscasts and political talk shows of the principal television networks, as opposed to two hours and twenty-two minutes for Berlusconi's Popolo della Libertà.

25. Tronconi (ed.), op. cit., p. 143.

26. The party forced anyone over forty to be automatically moved onto the Senate lists, where there is an age minimum of forty to be elected.

27. 'Movimento 5 Stelle, i nuovi parlamentari: ecco nomi e storie degli eletti', *Oggi*, 26 February 2013, http://www.oggi.it/attualita /notizie/2013/02/26/movimento-5-stelle-i-nuovi-parlamentari-ecco -nomi-e-storie-degli-eletti/ (accessed 9 August 2016).

28. Tronconi (ed.), op. cit., pp. 3, 166. Its internal organisation is also different. The central party has a Directive Committee—essentially the leadership group for the parliamentary group—which is rotated and elected (five in total). The group lasts a year, and each member has three months in charge. The Assembly is attended by all Five Star deputies and senators. They meet once a month to elect the Directive Committee, decide political lines and sort out the finances. It's all live streamed online too.

29. Unusual among European democracies, the Italian Parliament reserves seats for the considerable number of Italians living overseas: twelve in the Chamber and six in the Senate. But under Italian electoral law new parties need 1,000 notarised signatures from citizens who live in the relevant electoral district before they are allowed to present candidates on the ballot paper. The European Meetup spent one month shuttling Italians into consulates in London, Amsterdam, Barcelona and elsewhere to collect signatures so Five Star could present candidates for those overseas seats.

30. At local Meetups, for example, although technically leaderless, invariably certain characters by weight of experience or authority have more powers than others. Power, instead of being acknowledged, is hidden beneath rituals and liturgies. Whoever holds the password for the Meetup group, for example, usually gets to decide when the group meets.

31. Piero Ignazi, 'La doppia anima dei Cinque Stelle', *La Repubblica*, 7 February 2016. For papers and reports on the supporters and voters for the Five Star Movement, see Luigi Ceccarini, Ilvo Diamanti and Marc Lazar, 'End of an era: The disintegration of the Italian party system' in Anna Bosco and Duncan McDonnell (eds.), *Italian Politics: From Berlusconi to Monti* (Berghahn Books, 2013); Fabio Bordignon and Luigi Ceccarini, '5 Stelle, un autobus in movimento', *Il Mulino* 5 (2012), pp. 812–13; Tronconi (ed.), op. cit., p. 186; Jamie Bartlett, Caterina Froio, Mark Littler and Duncan McDonnell, *New Political Actors in Europe: Beppe Grillo and the M5S* (Demos, 2013); Bordignon and Ceccarini, '5 Stelle, un autobus in movimento'. When voters of Five Star are asked

to place themselves on a one to five left–right scale they average some-where in the middle. But that obscures the fact it's an average of people from the left and people from the right.

32. Ignazio Corroa, 'Italian M5S 5-Star Movement debut in Europe', YouTube video, https://www.youtube.com/watch?v=i65HY6PCqqo.

33. Here is an example of the amendments he made to the 'Opin-ion on Report Transparency Accountability and Integrity in EU Insti-tutions' report the week I was there. From this: 'Calls for an overall improvement in the prevention of, and the fight against, corruption in the public sector through better public access to documents and more stringent rules on conflicts of interest and transparency registers, with a view to developing a coherent global approach to these issues.' To this: 'Calls for an overall improvement in the prevention of, and the fight against, corruption in the public sector through a holistic approach, commencing with better public access to documents and more strin-gent rules on conflicts of interest, support for investigative journalism and for anti-corruption watchdogs, the introduction or strengthen-ing of transparency registers, the provision of sufficient resources for law-enforcement measures and through improved co-operation among Member States as well as with relevant third countries.' Committee on Budgetary Control, 'Transparency, accountability and integrity in the EU institution: Amendments 1–14', PE560.864 - 2015/2041(INI) European Parliament, 11 September 2015, http://itcointergroup.eu /file/2015/04/20151109-ITCO-Amendments-CONT-Opinion-on-Report -Transparency-Accountability-and-Integrity-in-EU-institutions.pdf.

34. Tronconi (ed.), op. cit., pp. 123–4. In the 2013 elections the Demo-cratic Party won the elections, but due to the fact that the previous elec-toral law wasn't majority-assuring in the Senate, they had enough seats in the Parliament but not in the Senate, which made them unable to form a one-party government. As a consequence, they were seeking possible coalitions with other parties, and Five Star was the closest one. Five Star refused to make a coalition, and the Democratic Party formed a coalition with right-wing parties such as the NCD, a party which resulted from the scission of the previous Berlusconi party Popolo della Libertà.

35. Full list is: Fabio Castaldo 4th, Ignazio Corrao 5th, Marco Valli 6th, Marco Zanni 33rd, Laura Agea 34th, Eleonora Evi 35th, Isabella Adinolfi 42nd, Piernicola Pedicini 45th, Dario Tamburrano 55th, Ti-ziana Beghin 60th, Rosa D'Amato 81st, Marco Affronte 109th, Laura Ferrara 119th, Marco Zullo 123rd, Daniela Aiuto 160th, David Borrelli 175th, and Guillia Moi 372nd. Moi is rumoured to not get along very well with the other MEPs.

36. Douglas Rushkoff, 'The new nationalism of Brexit and Trump is the product of the digital age', *Fastcoexist*, 7 July 2016.

37. Gaby Hinsliff, 'Trash talk: How Twitter is shaping the new politics', *Guardian*, 31 July 2016, https://www.theguardian.com/technology /2016/jul/31/trash-talk-how-twitter-is-shaping-the-new-politics?CMP =share_btn_tw.

38. Rene Pfitzner, Antonios Garas and Frank Schweitzer, 'Emotional divergence influences information spreading in Twitter', Association for the Advancement of Artificial Intelligence, 2012, https://www.sg.ethz .ch/media/publication_files/manuscript_AAAI_2012.pdf.

39. Francesco Bailo, 'Between anti-elite populism and policy. A textual analysis of the relation between Beppe Grillo's posts and his commenters', University of Sydney paper, September 2015, https://ecpr.eu /Filestore/PaperProposal/2683fd50-c329-43da-87b5-8578e32d794a.pdf (preliminary draft).

40. Jason le Mierre, 'Did the media help Donald Trump win? $5 billion in free advertising given to president-elect', *International Business Times*, 9 November, 2016, http://www.ibtimes.com/did-media-help-donald -trump-win-5-billion-free-advertising-given-president-elect-2444115.

41. See 'MoVimento 5 stelle, ma quale democrazia? Le regionali mettono in crisi le liste di Grillo', *Yes, political!*, 28 December 2009. The first media to report that was *Wired*, followed by *Corriere della Sera* and *La Repubblica*. Rousseau is not only the new platform on which to vote, but a coordinating point for all the movement's activities; it allows several actions, and some of them still have to be activated. It is a closed system, accessible only to registered members, who are identified and then can act on the basis of their identity. As Casaleggio explained, 'it will be possible for one to vote for Milan's municipal candidate if he is resident in Milan, or to intervene on a regional law in Lombardia if he is resident in Lombardia'. Thus, this system inherits the regional peculiarity of Meetup. For the moment, there are sections on: 'vote' (when a vote is ongoing), 'laws' (EU, Parliament, Regions), and 'Shield' and 'Fundraising' are active. It's too early to know if and how this might change the dynamics of the movement.

42. Jonathan Freedland, 'Post-truth politicians such as Donald Trump and Boris Johnson are no laughing matter', *Guardian*, 13 May 2016.

43. Art Swift, 'Americans' trust in mass media sinks to new low', Gallup, 14 September 2016, http://www.gallup.com/poll/195542/americans -trust-mass-media-sinks-new-low.aspx.

44. According to *Corriere della Sera*, Pittarello is seen as 'the custodian of Casaleggio's agenda', and one of the very few people who has the blog's password. He is often with Grillo at shows. See also Paola Alagia, 'Movimento 5 stelle: Beppe Grillo e il suo cerchio magico', *Lettera* 43, 6 March 2014.

45. Tronconi (ed.), op. cit., pp. 33–4. In addition to the staff, there is also a Gruppo Comunicazione ('Communication Group'), which supports the parliamentary group—especially in its relationship with the outside media. Beppe has the freedom to choose who's in that group too.

46. Carlo Tecce, 'Ecco perché Casaleggio scelse Grillo', *Il fatto quotidiano*, 26 March 2013. In an interview with the journalist Carlo Tecce, Enrico Sasson, a long-term associate of Casaleggio's, said 'Grillo knew nothing about the internet when it was proposed to him.'

47. Tronconi (ed.), op. cit., pp. 18, 117–18.

48. Andrea Guerrieri, an Italian blogger, has developed a system (available at nocensura.eusoft.net) that periodically crawls Grillo's blog to keep track of comment removals. Salvatore Merlo, 'L'affaire Casaleggio', *Il Foglio*, 20 February 2016.

49. Paolo Alagia, 'Movimento 5 stelle: Beppe Grillo e il suo cerchio magico', *Lettera* 43, 6 March 2014, http://www.lettera43.it/politica/movimento -5-stelle-beppe-grillo-e-il-suo-cerchio-magico_43675124001.htm.

50. The law on civil partnership, without the stepchild adoptions, was approved by Parliament with 372 votes in favour, 51 against and 99 abstained (they needed to take stepchild adoption out in order to reach the majority without M5S deputies). M5S deputies didn't vote, they abstained. 'Unioni civili, ok definitivo della Camera: approvata la legge. Renzi: giorno di festa', Il Sole 24 Ore, 11 May 2016, http://www .ilsole24ore.com/art/notizie/2016-05-11/unioni-civili-rush-finale —fiducia-e-voto-oggi-camera-renzi-giorno-festa—123438.shtml?uuid =ADouvaF&refresh_ce=1.

51. See the following for specific cases, including Valentino Tavolazzi; the three senators controversially expelled via a vote on the blog; and Federico Pizzarotti, Parma mayor. For the case of the senators, the original vote is available on Beppe's blog (archive, February 2014). 'M5S, Orellana si dimette da senator: per Grillo siamo pedine', *Internazionale*, 26 February 2014; Michele Pierri, 'Vi racconto la dittatura a 5 stelle di Casaleggio. Parla Orellana', *Formiche*, 1 February 2014; Giovanni Bucchi, 'Perche dico addio al Movimento 5 Stelle. Parla Paolo Becchi', *Formiche*, 5 January 2016; 'Federico Pizzarotti publica le mail e attacca il direttorio e Luigi Di Maio: "Irresponsabili"', *Huffington Post*, 14 May 2015.

52. Tom Postmes and Suzanne Brunsting, 'Collective action in the age of the internet: mass communication and online mobilization', *Social Science Computer Review*, vol. 20, no. 3 (2002); Manuel Castells, 'The mobile civil society: social movements, political power and communication networks' in Manuel Castells et al., *Mobile Communication and Society: A Global Perspective* (MIT Press, 2007); Hansard Society, *2013 Audit of Political Engagement*; Gerry Stoker, 'Building a new politics?' in Peter Taylor-Gooby (ed.), *New Paradigms in Public Policy* (OUP/British Academy, 2014). Stoker points out that most citizens do not care to engage in politics on a regular basis—so the last reform that would interest them is more participation. Hansard research found that only 29 per cent of British voters think that having more of a say would bring about a significant improvement in the political system.

53. Carswell, *The End of Politics and the Birth of iDemocracy*, op. cit.; 'Revealing misconceptions: Young people's new approach to politics', European Parliament, April 2015; *Eurobarometer 81* (2014); see Carl Miller, *The Rise of Digital Politics* (Demos, 2016) for a good discussion of these trends.

54. For a discussion of the Web primaries, see Tronconi (ed.), op. cit., pp. 137–9. The issue of how good digital tools are at engaging voters is a much-debated subject. It can best be defined, at present, as disappointing but showing potential. Take, for example, the much-vaunted European Citizens' Initiative (ECI), which was introduced by the Lisbon Treaty in 2009. If 1 million citizens from at least four EU countries sign a petition inviting the European Commission to bring forward proposals in an area where it has the power to do so, the commission is obliged to examine it. However, only one proposal has so far reached this stage—partly because of how cumbersome it is to collect and verify signatures, and because most petitions have been on subjects outside the commission's competence. Further discussion is in Jaron Lanier, *Who Owns the Future* (Simon & Schuster, 2013), p. 199. On the role of political parties, a good historical view is offered by Francis Fukuyama in his excellent *Political Order and Political Delay*, p. 139. Fukuyama argued that political parties still play a vital role in allowing collective action on the part of like-minded people, aggregating disparate social interests around a common platform, articulated positions and politics and creating 'a stability of expectations'.

55. All the Meetups are listed on the website: http://www.meetup.com/topics/beppegrillo/.

56. For a full discussion of this, see Morozov, op. cit., Chapter 4.

57. One example has been the amount of abuse women receive, including political representatives. See for example, 'Labour leadership: Female MPs urge Corbyn to tackle abuse', *BBC News*, 22 July 2016.

58. Bernard Crick, *In Defence of Politics* (Weidenfeld & Nicolson, 1962).

59. Voting record in US Congress 1947–2012 from *Vital Statistics on Congress* (Brookings Institute, 2017).

60. See Hannah Arendt, *On Revolution* (Viking Press, 1963).

61. One example in particular for English readers is Nicholas Farrell, 'Beppe Grillo: Italy's New Mussolini', *Spectator*, March 2013.

Chapter 6

1. In the literature on this subject there is some disagreement about the exact title of places like Tamera: intentional communities, communes, communal experiments, utopian communities, model villages, alternative societies are all used. Common features usually include an unusually high degree of social interaction and a common social, political and spiritual vision; along with collective sharing or responsibility and resources. Perhaps more important is the conscious desire to live in a way that's different to 'out there'.

2. Dieter Duhm, *The Sacred Matrix* (SYNergie, 2001), p. 24. See also Dieter Duhm, *Terra Nova* (Verlag Meiga, English edition 2015), Chapter 8.

3. There was a small reduction for Portuguese visitors, and some visitors stayed longer than five days.

4. Leila Dregger, 'Project meiga: How it all began', 1 December 2001, http://www.jugglerpress.com/jockm/zegghistory.html.

5. Astrid Uldum Fabrin, 'Free love and save the world' (dissertation at Lunds University).

6. The Tamerians are a little secretive about how the forum actually works. However, a detailed description of forums at ZEGG—also inspired by Dieter Duhm—is available online, and explains how facilitators are vital, and run the session. They last around ninety minutes, during which someone (the 'actor') will sit in the middle and talk about what's on their mind, who they'd like to sleep with, who's upset them and so on. Only the facilitator can intervene, perhaps to interrupt, guide, probe, or even suggest they perform something in order to break a thought pattern. Once finished, others then go into the centre and 'mirror' back, saying what they feel in response. The whole idea is to

inculcate a radical honesty and transparency. 'It is there that we reveal our patterns in power and decision-making, where we lay bare what is happening in our love lives, where we bring to awareness our real intentions, where both the light and the dark get their due', writes Dolores Richter in 'What is the ZEGG Forum?', available at http://www.nfnc.org/index.php/info-old/document_library/what_is_the_zegg_forum/. (Less often, there are 'plenary' forums—usually twice a week in Tamera—where everyone in the community takes part, but usually forums just involve relevant people.)

7. Iris Kunze and Flor Avelino, 'Social Innovation and the Global Ecovillage Network. Research Report', TRANSIT, 2015.

8. Duhm, *Sacred Matrix*, p. 271.

9. Dieter Duhm, *Terra Nova*, Chapter 6. In 2012 rats invaded Tamera, and no one knew what to do. So they started to pray, conducted 'dream research', meditated, and even built a rat home. At some point the rats eventually left, which the Tamerians credited to their spiritual efforts, which created 'a field of friendship in relation to them'.

10. 'The tyranny of free sexuality. AAO, Muehl-Commune, Friedrichshof', *Austrian texts for social criticism*, pp. 57, 63; Duhm, *Sacred Matrix*, pp. 112–13.

11. See David Leopold, 'Socialism and Utopia', *Journal of Political Ideologies* 12, 2007, 219–37. Although most fictional accounts of utopia present a picture of harmony (More's *Utopia*, William Morris's *News from Nowhere*), most historical accounts suggest tensions, disagreements and squabbling are common. (Before 1848, the dominant strain of socialist thought was utopian; Saint-Simon, Fourier and Owen published treatises detailing their imagined egalitarian paradises. Marxism lambasted this approach; Marx and Engels realised that paradise was useless without a roadmap of how to get there, and so they developed their theory of dialectical materialism and class consciousness. Since Marx, revolution has replaced utopianism as the focus of socialists' energy.

12. Jim Arnold, 'Owenstown' in Chris Coates, James Dennis and Jonathan How (eds.), *Diggers and Dreamers* (D&D Publications, 2015), p. 11. In a similar way to Dieter, Owen hoped that people would 'unlearn many, almost all indeed, of the bad habits which the present defective arrangement of society have forced upon them: then, to give only habits and dispositions to the rising generation and thus withdraw those circumstances from society which separate man from man.'

13. From a pamphlet about the Genesis Project that circulated at the time, in the late 1970s: 'The community which we are in the process

of creating will be a rural one, with all the land and material that we need for producing our own food and energy . . . [I]t will be simple but comfortable. In some ways it will be very sophisticated, its members and those passing through it will find in it outstanding opportunities for self-development and spiritual growth.' Timothy Miller, *The 60s Communes: Hippies and Beyond* (Syracuse University Press, 1999), p. xix.

14. Dylan Evans, *The Utopia Experiment* (Picador, 2015).

15. Kunze and Avelino, op. cit.; Grace Media, 'Tamera—Solar Village testfield 2011', YouTube video, 12 July 2011, https://www.youtube.com /watch?v=duuk_r—lqU.

16. Stirling engines turn any form of heat into mechanical energy. Although very efficient, especially if they use heat energy left over from other processes, such as the solar greenhouse, the problem is they can never be as small as an internal combustion engine, as used in most cars. Stirling engines are a drum of air. In this case half the air is heated with the vegetable oil pipes, which expands the air, moving a piston. The piston's movement shifts the hot air into the cold half of the drum and the process starts again: and the piston's motion creates electricity (1.5 kW) and mechanical output (1.7 kW) which is good for lighting, machinery, water pumps, air compressors and more.

17. 'Tamera water retention landscape to restore the water cycle and reduce vulnerability to droughts,' European Climate Adaptation Platform, 2015, http://climate-adapt.eea.europa.eu/metadata/case-studies /tamera-water-retention-landscape-to-restore-the-water-cycle-and -reduce-vulnerability-to-droughts.

18. Dieter thinks that our modern woes can be traced back to 8,000 years ago, when man left tribal life and turned to agriculture and sedentary existence. This shift created new social relations, notably norms of privacy, ownership and patriarchy. Dieter thinks that before this 'Great Separation' man lived in highly developed cultures that had access to 'higher cosmic knowledge' than we do today and that were connected to creation in an entirely different way. But according to author Steven Pinker, the shift from hunter-gatherer tribes to agricultural civilisation resulted in a fivefold *decrease* in rates of violent death. Rates of violence have been on the decline ever since, albeit with spikes. In current hunter-gatherer communities, homicide rates dwarf rates in Europe and North America.

19. Duhm, *Sacred Matrix*, p. 37. Also Duhm, *Terra Nova*: 'It works according to different laws than the material body. If we succeed in introducing the right information into the spirit body, our entire organism would change instantly.'

20. Duhm, *Terra Nova*, Chapter 8; Duhm, *Sacred Matrix*, pp. 25, 36; Fabrin, op. cit. Dieter has something called a holographic view of the world: the information in a single particle contains the information of the entire universe, something he calls the 'overall information'.

21. 'If we are fully opened to the control pulses of our body, if we listened to its voice with increasingly precise sensors, we would certainly live in complete physical power and health' writes Dieter in *The Decision, Part* 2 (only available through Tamera), bullet point 122. Also see *Sacred Matrix*, pp. 176–7.

22. A decent discussion on the difficulties of explaining modern science is available here: Chad Orzel, 'Malcolm Gladwell Is Deepak Chopra', ScienceBlogs, 11 October 2013, http://scienceblogs.com/principles /2013/10/11/malcolm-gladwell-is-deepak-chopra/; Duhm, *Sacred Matrix*, p. 256.

23. Long before New Ageism become popularised in the 1960s, theosophy more generally was a popular movement, and with several influential women, which was quite unusual at the time, including Madame Blavatsky and Annie Besant, and Alice Bailey.

24. Dan Sperber, 'The Guru Effect', Springer Science + Business Media, 6 March 2010; Harry G. Frankfurt, *On Bullshit* (Princeton University Press, 2005).

25. Joel Kramer and Diana Alstad, authors of *The Guru Papers* (Frog Books, 1993), call this 'the hidden and more pervasive mechanism of authoritarian control'.

26. Bullet point 24: 'There is infinite power in the universe. You are one aspect of this power. You are a manifestation of this power because you are a manifestation of God.'
    Bullet point 39: 'I am here and want to pave a way for you to walk with me. If you understand this step of trust, it will constantly become easier.'

27. Kunze and Avelino, op. cit.

28. Ibid., p. 81.

29. 'A crisis of masculinity: men are struggling to cope with life', *Telegraph*, 19 November 2014 http://www.telegraph.co.uk/men/thinking -man/11238596/A-crisis-of-masculinity-men-are-struggling-to-cope -with-life.html.

30. 'Number of unhappy relationships in the UK doubles', Stowe Family Law LLP, 26 September 2016, http://www.marilynstowe .co.uk/2016/09/26/number-of-unhappy-relationships-in-uk-doubles/.

31. 'Marriage and Divorce', American Psychological Association, http://www.apa.org/topics/divorce/; 'How common are sexually inactive

marriages?', *Relationships in America* (The Austin Institute for the Study of Family and Culture, 2014), http://relationshipsinamerica.com /relationships-and-sex/how-common-are-sexually-inactive-marriages.

32. See, for example, Rosabeth Moss Kanter, *Commitment and Community: Communes and Utopias in Sociological Perspective* (Harvard University Press, 1972); and Philip Abrams and Andrew McCulloch with Sheila Abrams and Pat Gore, *Communes, Sociology and Society* (Cambridge University Press, 1976).

33. Timothy Miler, 'Intentional Communities: The Evolution of Enacted Utopianism' in Eileen Barker (ed.), *Revisionism and Diversification in New Religious Movements* (Routledge, 2014).

34. Roger Hallam, 'Let's Talk About Power' in Coates, Dennis and How (eds.), op. cit., p. 64.

35. A series of articles in the left-wing German newspaper Taz concluded that it was neither a cult nor a sex camp. See, for example, Von Gerd Nowakowski, 'Salvation through free love', *Taz*, 30 July 1993, http://www.taz.de/1/archiv/?dig=1993/07/30/a0173; Von Kirsten Küppers, 'Free love and soy sausages', *Taz*, 8 August 1988, 'http://www.taz.de/1 /archiv/?dig=1998/08/08/a0179; Von Florian Hohne, 'The village of love possibilities?', *Taz*, 24 July 2004, http://www.taz.de/!722874/.

One research group concluded that ZEGG is not a cult but 'a cross between a reactionary substitute for religion and the New Age version of Club Méditerrané'. That's a fairly decent description of Tamera too. See 'Zeggsismus' *Nadir*, 19 June 1997 https://www.nadir.org/nadir/archiv /Antifaschismus/Organisationen/zegg/brosch_rosa/zegg_all.html.

36. Natalie Valios, 'Prince's Trust: One in ten young people feel life is meaningless', Community Care, 5 January 2009, http://www.community care.co.uk/2009/01/05/princes-trust-one-in-ten-young-people-feel-life -is-meaningless/; William Davies, *The Happiness Industry* (Verso, 2015); Jo Griffin, *The Lonely Society?* (Mental Health Foundation, 2010), p. 21, http://www.mentalhealth.org.uk/sites/default/files/the_lonely _society_report.pdf; Monika A. Bauer, James E. B. Wilkie, Jung K. Kim and Galen V. Bodenhausen, 'Cuing Consumerism: Situational Materialism Undermines Personal and Social Well-Being', *Psychological Science*, March 2012, http://www.archpsychological.com/blog/wp-content /uploads/2012/05/luxury-items-depress-n-isolate.pdf; Kanter, op. cit.; Kramer and Alstad, op. cit.

37. See William Powers, *Hamlet's BlackBerry* (HarperCollins, 2010); Joseph Schumpeter, 'Too much information: How to cope with data overload', *Economist*, 30 June 2011; 'Self harm, suicide and risk: helping

people who self-harm', Royal College of Psychiatrists College Report CR158, June 2010, http://www.rcpsych.ac.uk/files/pdfversion/cr158.pdf.

38. Monika Alleweldt, 'The healing biotopes plan: A plan for the healing of humankind and the earth', https://www.tamera.org/basic -thoughts/the-healing-biotopes-plan/.

Chapter 7

1. 'Climate change 2013: The physical science basis', Intergovernmental Panel on Climate Change, Cambridge University, 2013, http://www .ipcc.ch/report/ar5/wg1/.

2. In 2014 the Intergovernmental Panel on Climate Change released its Fifth Assessment Report, a sort of summary of the scientific consensus on the subject, written collectively by more than 800 authors. It concluded that it's 95 to 100 per cent likely that temperatures are rising, and it's us humans doing it. While that will result in some benefits in some areas, overall the net effects will be strongly negative, with significant costs associated: 'Continued emission of greenhouse gases will cause further warming and long-lasting changes in all components of the climate system, increasing the likelihood of severe, pervasive and irreversible impacts for people and ecosystems.'

3. 'Top UNHCR official warns about displacement from climate change', UNHCR, December 2008, http://www.unhcr.org/493e9bd94 .html; Justin Gillis, 'U.N. climate panel endorses ceiling on global emissions', New York Times, 27 September 2013, http://www.nytimes .com/2013/09/28/science/global-climate-change-report.html?_r=0. Thomas Stocker, the co-chair of the Intergovernmental Panel on Climate Change, called climate change the greatest challenge of our time.

4. Cited in Steve Hilton, More Human (WH Allen, 2015), pp. 360–2.

5. 'Divestment commitments', Fossil Free, September 2016, http://go fossilfree.org/commitments/; 'Global trends in renewable energy investment 2016', Frankfurt School FS-UNEP Collaborating Centre for Climate & Sustainable Energy Finance (2016), p. 12, http://fs-unep-centre.org /sites/default/files/publications/globaltrendsinrenewableenergyinvestment 2016lowres_0.pdf; 'Record fall in global coal consumption driven by low oil price', Daily Telegraph, 8 June 2016, http://www.telegraph.co.uk /business/2016/06/08/record-fall-in-global-coal-consumption-driven-by -low-oil-price/; 'Aggregate effect of the intended nationally determined contribution: an update', United Nations Framework Convention on

Climate Change, 2 May 2016, http://unfccc.int/resource/docs/2016/cop22 /eng/o2.pdf.

6. 'Global mean sea data level', GSFC, 2016, Global Mean Sea Level Trend from Integrated Multi-Mission Ocean Altimeters TOPEX/ Poseidon Jason-1 and OSTM/HDR Jason-2 Version 3, http://climate.nasa .gov/vital-signs/sea-level/ (dataset accessed 15 October 2016); Dr Pieter Tans, NOAA/ESRL, 'Trends in atmospheric carbon dioxide', Earth System Research Laboratory, NOAA, http://www.esrl.noaa.gov/gmd/ccgg /trends/data.html (dataset accessed 15 October 2016); 'Global land-ocean temperature index', NASA's Goddard Institute for Space Studies, http://climate.nasa.go.v/vital-signs/global-temperature/.

7. In 2005 G8 leaders were meeting in Scotland to discuss international development and global warming. Fed up with the traditional anti-globalisation protests—typically street marches—a group of anarchist groups and environmental activists decided to try something different. They set up a huge 'eco-village' near the G8 meeting: a functioning, self-sufficient, anarchic community. This morphed into Climate Camp. Between 2006 and 2010 around a dozen similar camps were created to accompany direct-action protests, in the United Kingdom and beyond. But even this was drawing on older strands. The 'neighbourhood' system was partly from earlier anti-G8 movements, inspired themselves by Argentinian uprisings in 2001 where decisions were made by 'barrios'. Affinity groups go back to anarchists in the Spanish Civil War and from the 1920s Makhnovite movement in the Ukraine. A good general overview of the Climate Camps written by those involved in setting them up is Raphael Schlembach, 'How do radical climate movements negotiate their environmental and their social agendas? A study of debates within the Camp for Climate Action', *Critical Social Policy*, vol 31, no 2, 16 February 2011, http://journals.sagepub.com /doi/abs/10.1177/0261018310395922; 'Criticism without critique: A climate camp reader' shift magazine / dysophia production', January 2010, https://dysophia.files.wordpress.com/2010/01/cca_reader.pdf.

8. John Vidal, 'Twyford Down's Dongas return 20 years after M3 protest', *Guardian*, 28 September 2012, http://www.theguardian.com /world/2012/sep/28/twyford-down-20years-m3-protest.

9. A good example of this in action: 'Drawing a line in the sand: The movement victory at Ende Gelande opens up the road of disobedience for Paris', The Laboratory of Insurrectionary Imagination, 31 August 2015, https://labofii.wordpress.com/2015/08/23/drawing-a-line-in-the

-sand-the-movement-victory-at-ende-gelande-opens-up-the-road-of
-disobedience-for-paris/.

10. Dorceta E. Taylor, 'The state of diversity in environmental orga-
nizations', Green 2.0, 2014, http://vaipl.org/wp-content/uploads/2014/10
/ExecutiveSummary-Diverse-Green.pdf; 'Toward a new ecological majority', Environics, 2006, http://stonehousesummit.com/sites/default
/files/papers/American Environics - Earthjustice Roadmap to an Ecological Majority.pdf; Tom Bawden, 'Green movement must escape
its 'white, middle-class ghetto', says Friends of the Earth chief Craig
Bennett', *Independent*, 4 July 2015, http://www.independent.co.uk
/environment/green-movement-must-escape-its-white-middle-class
-ghetto-says-friends-of-the-earth-chief-craig-10366564.html. For further
literature on the subject, see Frederick H. Buttel and William L. Flinn,
'Social class and mass environmental beliefs: A reconsideration', University of Wisconsin, 1976. Although old, when this work came out it
was widely cited and continues to be so today. It argues that education
levels almost entirely determine attitudes towards the environment.
Emily Enderle (ed.), *Diversity and the Future of the Environmental
Movement* (Yale University Press, 2007), is a series of articles—mainly
by people of colour in the US environmental movement—highlighting
the movement's lack of racial diversity. 'Working together: A call for
inclusive conservation', *Nature* 515, 7525, 5 November 2014. There are
240 signatories to this article, bemoaning the lack of women working
in conservation science. John-Henry Harter, *New Social Movements,
Class, and the Environment* (Cambridge Scholars, 2011). This case study
of Greenpeace Canada explores (in Chapter 2) the movement's dominance by the professional managerial class.

11. 'Practical protest techniques', Activist Legal Project, http://www
.activistlegalproject.org.uk/practicalprotest.pdf.

12. The day after the terrorist attacks in Paris in November 2015, I
went to Central St Martin's art school in north London to take part in
a 'Red Lines Art Action Build Workshop', which had been put on by a
veteran activist called Jamie Kelsey, a fast-talking Londoner who writes
for the magazine *New Internationalist*. The workshop was to teach activists two techniques: 'subvertising' (creating fake adverts and putting
them up in bus shelters) and how to build inflatable cobblestones. Fifty
or so people, mostly young students from St Martin's, were there for
six hours, learning new techniques that they might employ in Paris or
here in London where a demonstration was still planned for 29 November. The artist Arta Van Baden from the group 'tools for action' had

designed the inflatable cobblestones: 1.5 metre-squared silver inflatable cobblestones, made of foil with a single red line through the middle. Velcro-ing these cubes together made a long single red line. The idea was that they could be deployed at demonstrations to symbolise the 'red line' and frustrate the police. They can be put up in a couple of minutes, and serve as a barrier between protesters and the police, which might give the protesters the chance to get away. Activists already in Paris beamed in via Skype from their flat to teach us how to unfurl them, how to inflate them and how to stick them together. This is a lot harder than it sounds.

13. A sign of the times: In 2006 inventor Howard Stapleton, based in Merthyr Tydfil, developed the technology that has given rise to the recent mosquito tone or 'teen buzz', which produces high-pitch sounds only heard by teenagers and is played all night to stop them hanging around in train stations. The Romantic writer Thomas Carlyle visited Merthyr in 1850, writing that it was filled with such 'unguided, hard-worked, fierce, and miserable-looking sons of Adam I never saw before. Ah me! It is like a vision of Hell, and will never leave me, that of these poor creatures broiling, all in sweat and dirt, amid their furnaces, pits, and rolling mills.'

14. 'Supply and consumption of coal', 'Chapter Two: Solid fuels and derived gases', in the Digest of United Kingdom Energy Statistics (DUKES), Department for Business, Energy & Industrial Strategy, https://www.gov.uk/government/statistics/solid-fuels-and-derived-gases -chapter-2-digest-of-united-kingdom-energy-statistics-dukes.

15. Astra Taylor, 'Against activism', *Baffler* 30, 2016, https://thebaffler .com/salvos/against-activism.

16. 'Hydraulic fracturing accounts for about half of current U.S. crude oil production', U.S. Energy Information Administration, 15 March 2016, http://www.eia.gov/todayinenergy/detail.php?id=25372; 'Frequently asked questions: How much shale gas is produced in the United States', Energy Information Administration, 13 February 2017, http://www.eia.gov/tools/faqs/faq.cfm?id=907&t=8.

17. Estimates as to the volume of available gas has varied, although it is certainly billions of cubic feet, and the Institute of Directors has suggested the industry could create 74,000 jobs, although this is highly speculative (and disputed). The Royal Society and Royal Academy of Engineering has reviewed the risks, and concluded that, although they exist, they can be effectively managed. *Public Health England* concluded in 2014 that potential risks to public health from exposure to shale gas

emissions was low, as long as it was all well regulated. The study determined that the risk to public health posed by fracking stemmed mostly from poor operational practices. It argued that mining-induced earthquakes can be controlled by trained operators, and that most incidents of water contamination in the United States were caused by unsatisfactory well construction and cementing, rather than by the fracking process itself. Jeanne Delebarre, Elena Ares and Louise Smith, 'Shale gas and fracking', Briefing Paper Number 6073, Commons Library, 4 January 2017, http://researchbriefings.files.parliament.uk/documents/SN06073/SN06073.pdf.

18. 'High volume fracturing in NYS', Department of Environmental Conservation, New York State, 29 June 2015, http://www.dec.ny.gov/energy/75370.html.

19. Dominic C. DiGiulio and Robert B. Jackson, 'Impact to underground sources of drinking water and domestic wells from production well stimulation and completion practices in the Pavillion, Wyoming, field', *Environmental Science Technology* 50(8), March 2016, pp. 4524–36.

20. One survey conducted by the Balcombe Parish Council in 2012 found that 82 per cent of residents wanted the Council to oppose fracking. Rodney Saunders, 'Balcombe residents against fracking?', Balcombe Parish Council, 17 August 2013, https://balcombeparishcouncil.com/2013/08/17/balcombe-residents-against-fracking/.

A door-to-door poll conducted in 2013 found that 85 per cent of Balcombe households surveyed were against fracking, with only 6 per cent in favour: 'Balcombe survey claims massive opposition to fracking', *Mid Sussex Times*, 6 August 2013, http://www.midsussextimes.co.uk/news/balcombe-survey-claims-massive-opposition-to-fracking-1-5358034.

21. Erving Goffman, *Frame Analysis: An Essay on the Organization of Experience* (Harvard University Press, 1974). See also Dan Kahan and Donald Braman, 'Cultural cognition and public policy', *Yale Law and Policy Review* 24(1), 2006, pp. 151, 158–9; William A. Gamson, 'The social psychology of collective action', in Aldon D. Morris and Carol McClurg Mueller (eds.), *Frontiers in Social Movement Theory* (Yale University Press, 1992), pp. 53–76.

22. 'Birds of a feather: Homophily in social networks', *Annual Review of Sociology*, vol. 27, 2001, pp. 415–44; Thomas Schelling, 'Models of segregation 1969' and 'Dynamic models of segregation 1971', *Micromotives and Macrobehavior* (WW Norton, 1978). In one famous study, the economist Thomas Schelling investigated racial segregation in Chicago. He

found that even very small preferences can result in enormous cumulative results. If people wanted at least one of their neighbours to be the same race as them, fairly soon people start moving around to make themselves more content, and soon enough neighbourhoods can end up surprisingly segregated along racial lines.

23. William Jordan, 'Public opposition to fracking grows', YouGov, 19 May 2015, https://yougov.co.uk/news/2015/05/19/opposition-fracking -britain-grows/; Press Association, 'UK public support for fracking falls to lowest level', *Guardian*, 27 October 2016, https://www.theguardian. com/environment/2016/oct/27/uk-public-support-for-fracking-falls -to-lowest-level; 'Opposition to fracking mounts in the US', Gallup, 30 March 2016, http://www.gallup.com/poll/190355/opposition-fracking -mounts.aspx.

24. Press Association, 'Coal electricity generation falls to record UK low this spring', *Guardian*, 29 September 2016, https://www.theguardian .com/environment/2016/sep/29/coal-electricity-generation-falls-to-record -uk-low-this-spring.

25. *Renewables 2016 Global Status Report*, REN21 Secretariat, 2016, http://www.ren21.net/wp-content/uploads/2016/06/GSR_2016_Full _Report_REN21.pdf.

26. 'International energy outlook 2016', *US Energy Information Administration*, 11 May 2016, https://www.eia.gov/forecasts/ieo/coal.cfm.

27. Francesca Polletta and James M. Jasper, 'Collective identity and social movements', *Annual Review of Sociology*, vol. 27, 2001, p. 295.

28. Aric McBay, Lierre Keith and Derrick Jensen, *Deep Green Resistance* (Seven Stories Press, 2011), p. 239.

Chapter 8

1. The Badinter Commission, set up to resolve this dispute, ended up settling on the Danube, but that assigned ten times more historically Croatian land to Serbia than historically Serbian land to Croatia.

2. Daniel Nolan, 'Liberland: Hundreds of thousands apply to live in world's newest "country"', *Guardian*, 24 April, 2015, http://www .theguardian.com/world/2015/apr/24/liberland-hundreds-of-thousands -apply-to-live-in-worlds-newest-country.

3. 'The consolidation of large nation-states, 1859–1871', in R. R. Palmer, Joel Colton and Lloyd Kramer, *A History of Europe in the Modern World* (McGraw-Hill College, 2013), http://www.mheducation.com

/content/dam/mhe/mhhe-product-pages/social-sciences/history/western
-civilization-european-history/Palmer_Sample_Chapter_13.pdf.

4. 'End of nations: Is there an alternative to countries?', *New Scientist*, 3 September 2014, https://www.newscientist.com/article/mg22329850-600 -end-of-nations-is-there-an-alternative-to-countries/.

5. Matt Carr, 'Beyond the border', *History Today*, vol. 63, no. 1, January 2013, http://www.historytoday.com/matt-carr/beyond-border.

6. Vit says the president of Liberland is just a temporary title until the country is recognised, at which point there will be elections (which he says he won't run for, but I doubt it). When Vit first announced Liberland, nearly half a million applied for citizenship by emailing the official account. So they started the process again and asked people to fill in an online form. Only people who could justify their support for libertarianism were accepted—around 100,000 have filled in this form.

7. James Crawford, *The Creation of States in International Law* (Oxford University Press, 2006).

8. John O'Brien, *International Law* (Cavendish, 2001), p. 185.

9. Gabriel Rossman, 'Extremely loud and incredibly close (but still so far): Assessing Liberland's claim of statehood', *Chicago Journal of International Law*, vol. 17, no. 1, 2016, http://chicagounbound.uchicago .edu/cjil/vol17/iss1/10.

10. Crawford, op. cit.; Jessica L. Noto, 'Creating a modern Atlantis: Recognizing submerging states and their people', *Buffalo Law Review*, vol. 62, 2014, pp. 747, 754.

11. The winners, announced a couple of months later, were Raw-NYC Architects, who won 10,000 merits with 'Liberland: An algae-powered sustainable micro-nation of innovators'. Buildings would be stacked like a pancake, so as people arrive it will increasingly resemble a Tetris screen of scrambled blocks on top of each other. Each layer used algae urban farming for food and power.

12. Paul Bradbury from the website Total Croatia News, sitting next to me all morning, said it was one of the most peculiar things he'd ever seen and wrote an article about it all called 'Liberland conference: Reflections on a weekend in Alice in LiberWonderLand'.

13. He gives a lot of money to various libertarian causes, including offering US senator Bernie Sanders $100,000 to debate with him about socialism versus libertarianism. More controversially he donates money to a fund set up to help Ross Ulbricht, the man who founded the notorious darknet market, the Silk Road.

14. Back in the 1990s Timothy May imagined a world where virtual regions called 'cybersteads', protected by powerful encryption, could be created online, leaving individuals free to make consensual economic arrangements among themselves with no state at all—a world of on-line communities of interest interacting directly with each other, as the 'meat world' of mediocre, inefficient governments watched helplessly on the side. Around the same time, cyberlibertarian (and former Grateful Dead lyricist) John Perry Barlow declared the 'Independence of Cyber-space', announcing to the real world that 'your legal concepts of prop-erty, expression, identity, movement, and context do not apply to us . . . our identities have no bodies, so, unlike you, we cannot obtain order by physical coercion'. Barlow believed that the lack of censorship and the anonymity that the Net seemed to offer would foster a freer, more open society, where tyrannous governments had no power. Barlow's essay has become better known, but Timothy May's work is in fact far more insightful. Cybersteads already exist in a way, in places like Second Life, World of Warcraft, Eve and Utherverse, where hundreds of thou-sands of people meet, spend time and money and create meaningful and functioning communities of interest. In 2014 thousands took part in the 'Bloodbath of B-R5RB' in the online universe of Eve, in which 11 trillion InterStellar Kredits' worth of in-game assets were destroyed, with a real-world value of $300,000.

15. Daniel Cox, Juhem Navarro-Rivera and Robert P. Jones, '2013 value survey: In search of Libertarians in America', PRRI, 29 October 2013, http://www.prri.org/research/2013-american-values-survey/.

16. In 2009 the *Daily Mail* reported that a British attaché to Afghan-istan had been 'sent home' after an affair with 'a sultry Swedish PR': Susanne Tempelhof. 'Diplomatic sources in Kabul said Ms Tempelhof has been seen regularly on the arm of Col Diggins at expat parties in the Afghan capital and in the bar of the British embassy.' She told me she was living with him.

17. In Libya, rather than chaos without a central government, she says she found that people had managed to construct their own functioning community where people seemed to look out for each other. (I imagine there was a strong sense of community because people do tend to band together when in a crisis, and work out ways of getting things done. I'm not sure most of Libya's citizens would agree it was an anarchic para-dise.) Since the civil war, economic growth has tumbled and inflation has skyrocketed. Four-fifths of Libyan nursing staff left the country, 20

per cent of their hospitals closed, and another 60 per cent are inaccessible. Enrolment in schools declined dramatically, and half of Benghazi schools need to be rebuilt. Perhaps a better example for Susanne would be Somalia. Between 1991 and 2012 it lacked an official government, but some indicators suggest that things actually improved in the country over this period. And there is some evidence that a generous welfare system does have some detrimental effects. Susanne's home country of Sweden has the highest proportion of people living alone, and one of the highest consumption levels of antidepressants in the world. But that's probably because it's cold, dark and antidepressants are widely available. William Danvers, 'Next steps in Libya: Economic and government stabilization in the face of political and security challenges', Center for American Progress, July 2016, https://cdn.americanprogress .org/wp-content/uploads/2016/07/26074652/2LibyaStabilization-report.pdf; Peter Leeson, 'Better off stateless', *Journal of Comparative Economics*, http://www.peterleeson.com/Better_Off_Stateless.pdf; http://www.bbc .co.uk/news/world-africa-14094503; 'Health at a glance: Europe 2012', OECD, 16 November 2012; Eric Klinenberg, 'I want to be alone: The rise and rise of solo living', *Guardian*, 30 March 2012, https://www.the guardian.com/lifeandstyle/2012/mar/30/the-rise-of-solo-living; 'Learning anarchism through revolution', *Anarchast*, episode 97, https://www.you tube.com/watch?v=jKxDKopR4cU.

18. I have included a slightly more technical description here. Every time someone sends a bitcoin as payment, a record of the transaction is timestamped to the microsecond, and stored in something called a 'blockchain' (each block representing about ten minutes' worth of transactions). The blocks are ordered chronologically, and each includes a digital signature (a 'hash') of the previous block, which administers the ordering and guarantees that a new block can join the chain only if it starts from where the preceding one finishes. A copy of the blockchain—which is basically a record of every single transaction ever made—is kept by everyone who has installed the bitcoin software. To ensure everything is running as it should, the blockchain is constantly verified by the computers of certain key users who compete to crack a mathematical puzzle that allows them to officially verify the blocks are all in order (and in exchange they get to mint a small number of new bitcoins). Obviously that's a lot of information (there are thousands of new transactions added every day to the bitcoin blockchain). To manage that, a standard algorithm is run over a file, and that reduces the file to

a sixty-four-character code, called a hash—which cannot be backward-computed (i.e., you cannot take the hash and work out what was in the original file. Some algorithms work like this: it's like cracking an egg, much easier than uncracking it). That hash is put, along with some other data, into the header of the proposed block. This header then becomes the basis for an exacting mathematical puzzle that involves using the hash function yet again. This puzzle can only be solved by trial and error. Across the network, miners grind through trillions and trillions of possibilities looking for the answer. When a miner finally comes up with a solution, other nodes quickly check it (that's the one-way street again: solving is hard but checking is easy), and each node that confirms the solution updates the blockchain accordingly. The hash of the header becomes the new block's identifying string, and that block is now part of the ledger. All the payments in that block are then confirmed. That hash is then included in the transaction list, which adds a timestamp. Make a change anywhere, though—even back in one of the earliest blocks—and that changed block's header will come out different. This means that so will the next block's, and all the subsequent ones. The ledger will no longer match the latest block's identifier, and will be rejected. The upshot is that, at any point, every computer who uses bitcoin knows exactly how many bitcoins everyone else has, so they cannot be copied or spent twice. For the first time, ownership over a digital asset can be transferred but never duplicated—and all without the assistance of a centrally controlled ledger.

19. Amir Taaki created original programming for using blockchain technology to create a decentralised online market. I followed him in my previous book, *The Dark Net*.

20. There is, at the time of writing, a major divide in the bitcoin community between those who want to make the system more efficient by executing more transactions per block, which requires a major redesign, and those who reject the idea as being too centralised. The blocks of transactions would need to get very large indeed, otherwise they will start queuing up. Because the designer and creator of bitcoin, Satoshi Nakamoto, decided to cap the size of a block at one megabyte, or about 1,400 transactions, it can handle only around seven transactions per second, compared to the 1,736 a second Visa handles in America. Blocks could be made bigger, but bigger blocks would take longer to propagate through the network, worsening the risks of forking. Many people assume bitcoin to be completely decentralised, but if a miner, or a group

of miners, controlled over half the computing power that works on verifying the transaction, it could feasibly force a change on the blockchain
transaction list however it wished, create a fork of the blockchain, and
all the other computers would start to work on the new version (the protocol is written so that all computers work from the longest blockchain).
In bitcoin, a few large pools can register most of the new bitcoin blocks,
which could push them to the 51 per cent threshold for mining power:
which could result in a takeover. Indeed, in 2014 one mining rig took
over 51 per cent of bitcoin's hashing power for twelve straight hours.
One of bitcoin's goals was to be a free system, independent of anyone's
control. With small pools, no one has this kind of control. There is also
an environmental problem. With no other way to establish whether
miners are bona fide, the bitcoin architecture forces them to do a lot
of hard computing; this 'proof of work', without which there can be no
reward, insures that all concerned have skin in the game. But it adds
up to a lot of otherwise pointless computing. According to blockchain.
info, the network's miners are now trying 450,000 trillion solutions per
second. And every calculation takes energy.

21. You can buy crypto-equity in Bitnation, as it runs a bit like a company, making a profit on the services it offers. During a crowd-sale in
2015, some members of the Bitnation team quit, saying Susanne may
have been breaking (US) law by offering crypto-equity without clear
structures. Susanne thinks, however, they didn't really understand the
point of Bitnation. 'I made it very clear . . . our purpose is to replace all
legacy state structures. There was no doubt [we would be ignoring nation states]. That's the whole point.'

22. 'We are Bitnation / We are the Birth of a New Virtual Nation / We
are a Future for Our World and Humanity / We are Sentinels, Universal
and Inalienable / We are Creativity and Visionary / We are Rights and
Freedoms / We are Tolerant and Accepting / We are Polity and Entity /
We are Privacy and Security / We are Openness and Transparency / We
are a Dream and a Reality / We are Bitnation.'

23. Debora MacKenzie, 'End of nations: Is there an alternative to countries?', *New Scientist*, 3 September 2014, https://www
.newscientist.com/article/mg22329850-600-end-of-nations-is-there
-an-alternative-to-countries/.

24. Ilya Somin, 'Why real-world governments don't have the consent of the governed—and why it matters', *Washington Post*, 27 January 2016, https://www.washingtonpost.com/news/volokh-conspiracy/wp

/2016/01/27/why-real-world-governments-dont-have-the-consent-of-the
-governed-and-why-it-matters/.

25. 'Bitnation governance 2.0', Bitnation, https://docs.google.com
/document/d/16HDB9AABa5rTOVFJj_8VLdOxgMguovLLAMvia
TkZ1q4/edit.

26. The Croatian courts have tried to charge Liberland citizens four
times, but Liberland lawyers appealed and won three times. In fact the
appeal court ordered the lower courts to rule on the exact location of
the Croatian border. In one of the cases, the judge ruled that 'it is in-
disputable that all defendants were caught in the territory of Serbia':
the official statement issued by the Serbian Ministry of Foreign Affairs
states unequivocally that the land in question is not and never has been
a part of Serbia.

27. The most famous and influential libertarian philosopher of the
last century, Robert Nozick, thought anarcho-capitalist society would
invariably result in the emergence of a monopolistic private defence and
judicial system that was more efficient than the others, and that everyone would eventually sign up to it: in short, a small state.

28. 'Sweden government spending to GDP: 1993–2017', Trading
Economics, http://www.tradingeconomics.com/sweden/government
-spending-to-gdp.

29. 'Democracy in America', *Economist*, May 2015; John Gray, 'Coming anarchy', *New Statesman*, November 2015.

30. Naomi Grimley, 'Identity 2016: "Global citizenship" rising, poll
suggests', BBC News, 28 April 2016, http://www.bbc.co.uk/news/world
-36139904.

31. 'Saudi Arabia: Human development indicators', Human Development Reports, United Nations Development Programme, http://hdr
.undp.org/en/countries/profiles/SAU; 'Yemen: Human development indicators', Human Development Reports, United Nations Development
Programme, http://hdr.undp.org/en/countries/profiles/YEM.

Epilogue

1. For an account of the period, see Richard Reeves, *John Stuart Mill:
Victorian Firebrand* (Grove Atlantic, 2007), p. 75.

2. Michael Casey, 'Could the blockchain empower the poor and
unlock global growth?', Techonomy, 7 March 2016, http://techonomy
.com/2016/03/blockchain-global-growth/.

3. Jack A. Goldstone, 'Causes of Revolution: The Role of Youth and other Social Factors', Fragile States, http://www.fragilestates.org /2012/11/25/causes-of-revolution-the-role-of-youth-and-other-social -factors/; Jack A. Goldstone, 'Youth Bulges and the Social Conditions of Rebellion', World Politics Review, 20 November 2012, http://www.world politicsreview.com/articles/12507/youth-bulges-and-the-social-conditions -of-rebellion. There are various conditions that precede violent revolution, at least in recent years. They usually include a closed state that doesn't allow popular control, some kind of crisis (fiscal distress, sustained inflation and so on), elite divisions and tensions. It's usually accompanied by rapid educational expansion, and popular grievances aligned with mobilisation networks.

4. Steve Connor, 'Lack of fresh water could hit half the world's population by 2050', Independent, 24 May 2013, http://www.independent .co.uk/news/science/lack-of-fresh-water-could-hit-half-the-world-s -population-by-2050-8631613.html.

5. Heather Stewart and Diane Taylor, 'NHS plans closures and radical cuts to combat growing deficit in health budget', Guardian, 26 August 2016, https://www.theguardian.com/society/2016/aug/26/nhs-plans -radical-cuts-to-fight-growing-deficit-in-health-budget; Dan Hyde, 'Pensioners are £9 a week better off than those in work', Daily Telegraph, 20 October 2015, http://www.telegraph.co.uk/finance/personalfinance /pensions/11944141/Pensioners-are-9-a-week-better-off-than-those-in -work.html.

Index

Pelle Sjödén

Jamie Bartlett is the director of the Centre for the Analysis of Social Media at Demos and a technology columnist for the *Telegraph*. His first book, *The Dark Net*, was longlisted for the Orwell Prize, nominated for the Debut Political Book of the Year and the Transmission Prize, and was named a best book of the year by NPR and the *Washington Post, New Statesman, Independent,* and *Flavorwire*. He has appeared on NPR and has written for *Salon, Spectator, New York Times, Guardian,* and *Aeon*.

NATION
BOOKS

The Nation Institute

Founded in 2000, **Nation Books** has become a leading voice in American independent publishing. The imprint's mission is to tell stories that inform and empower just as they inspire or entertain readers. We publish award-winning and bestselling journalists, thought leaders, whistle-blowers, and truthtellers, and we are also committed to seeking out a new generation of emerging writers, particularly voices from under-represented communities and writers from diverse backgrounds. As a publisher with a focused list, we work closely with all our authors to ensure that their books have broad and lasting impact. With each of our books we aim to constructively affect and amplify cultural and political discourse and to engender positive social change.

Nation Books is a project of The Nation Institute, a nonprofit media center established to extend the reach of democratic ideals and strengthen the independent press. The Nation Institute is home to a dynamic range of programs: the award-winning Investigative Fund, which supports groundbreaking investigative journalism; the widely read and syndicated website TomDispatch; journalism fellowships that support and cultivate over twenty-five emerging and high-profile reporters each year; and the Victor S. Navasky Internship Program.

For more information on Nation Books and The Nation Institute, please visit:

www.nationbooks.org
www.nationinstitute.org
www.facebook.com/nationbooks.ny
Twitter: @nationbooks